# Wearing the Baggy Green

# Wearing the Baggy Green

## Australian Cricket Encyclopedia

Ian Ferguson

Published by Brolga Publishing Pty Ltd
ABN 46 063 962 443
PO Box 12544
A'Beckett St, VIC, 8006
Australia
email: markzocchi@brolgapublishing.com.au

National Library of Australia
Cataloguing-in-Publication data

Fergusion, Ian, 1941–.
Wearing the baggy green : an encyclopedia of Australian cricket.

Bibliography.
Includes index.
ISBN 1 920785 93 0 (pbk)
ISBN 9781920785932 (pbk)

1. Cricket – Australia.
2. Cricket players – Australia.
I. Title.

796.3580994

Printed in Singapore
Cover design by David Khan
Cover photo of Ricky Ponting by nellistc @ Flickr
Designed and typeset by Diana Evans

---

# CONTENTS

# DEDICATION

*This book is dedicated to
the 397 Australian Test cricketers
who have proudly worn
"the baggy green", and to
the future players who will follow
in their footsteps.*

# ACKNOWLEDGEMENTS

My main vote of thanks goes to my wife Ann who deserves a place in heaven for her continued support of my writing projects.

I also express special thanks to my son Simon Ferguson for his astute editorial and proof reading skills, and I am grateful to my publisher Mark Zocchi for encouraging me to write this book.

I am also indebted to my friend Ian Wisken for the conscientious statistical research that he provided for "Wearing The Baggy Green."

The Sydney "Daily Telegraph" provided many of the photographs for this book, and I thank them for their quality prints.

Every effort has been made to contact the owners of copyright material used in these pages. If any person believes that they have not been acknowledged they are invited to contact the publisher.

Finally I am grateful to all the past and present Australian Test cricketers. They became very real personalities to me during my research, and it has been a fascinating experience to learn about their achievements, their characters, and the highs and lows of their lives.

Ian Ferguson
Pakenham, 2006

# AUTHOR'S NOTES
## THE BAGGY GREEN

The Australian Test cricketers' baggy green cap, along with the diggers' slouch hat and the bushmans' hat with attached corks, is the nation's most celebrated headgear.

The origins of the baggy green cap are lost in history, but hats worn in the first few decades of Test history had no uniformity. After 1906, when the Australian coat of arms was made official, it was included on all Test caps.

It was not until the 1980s that new captain Mark Taylor introduced ritual procedures that embraced the significance of the "baggy green". Now players were presented with their first Australian cap at a brief ceremony prior to play beginning on the first day of a Test, and this commendable practice has been enthusiastically continued by Steve Waugh and the current skipper, Ricky Ponting.

The players wear the Australian cap with much pride, and Steve Waugh (168 Test matches between 1985–2004) made these passionate observations about the personal significance of his own much worn and tattered baggy green cap after his outstanding 19 year old Test match career ended.

"My love of what it stands for makes it my prized possession. I saw the stains, (and) tears, fading and fraying as badges of honour. To trade it in would have been a betrayal."[1]

1. "Inside Cricket", p32

# OFFICIAL TEST NUMBERS

This practice was instituted by the Australian Cricket Board (ACB) and the Australian Cricketers' Association (ACA) in 2003 at a celebratory dinner where all living Test players were recognised with a commemorative cap.

The players are listed in numerical order according to when they were first chosen in the national team, starting from those who first represented Australia in the 1877 Test at the Melbourne Cricket Ground (MCG).

Ian Ferguson
Pakenham, 2006

# IN THE BEGINNING

The exact origins of cricket are shrouded in mystery, but in England an embryonic form of the game was played around the open country and forest areas of Kent and Sussex more than seven hundred years ago. The game was certainly well established by the early years of the Tudor monarchy, when Sir Francis Drake abandoned his preferred sport to deal with the Spanish Armada problem that threatened the security of the island kingdom.

In Australia cricket became the national game long before there was a nation, with details of an 1804 match being recorded in the "Sydney Gazette and New South Wales Advertiser". In 1821 Governor Lachlan Macquarie commissioned a carpenter to fashion a cricket bat from local timber for his son, and by the 1830s matches were frequently being played at Sydney's Hyde Park. In 1851, five years after Port Phillip separated from New South Wales (NSW), the new identity of Victoria defeated the founding colony. This match was organised by the legendary sporting identity, Tom Wills, who later planned the 1868 aboriginal cricket tour of England.

In 1851 Edward Hargreaves discovered gold in a creek near Bathurst in NSW, and this event became a defining moment in the history of the continent. Thousands of people from all over the world rushed to the new El Dorado after significant new discoveries of the coveted metal were made in Victoria and Western Australia, and within a decade the populations of the colonies had risen by over

73,000. By 1858 the new arrivals were seeking the right to vote in Victoria, a quest that soon became prominent in the other colonies.

In the summer of 1861–62 H. H. Stephenson brought the first English touring cricket team to the southern continent, and their arrival was greeted with great enthusiasm in the major colonies. 15,000–20,000 people watched the first match between England and a team from Australia on New Year's Day at the Melbourne Cricket Ground (MCG). The visitors were victorious by 213 runs, and it was England's Billy Caffyn who bowled the first ball in an England–Australia match to Melbourne's Jerry Bryant.

Overall the tourists won six matches, drew two, and lost one match in the first ever tour, and the attitude of the hardened English professionals towards the irreverent and boisterous newcomers, was summed up by one of their players before he returned home.

"I don't think much of their play," commented Yorkshire's Roger Iddison, "but they're a fine lot of drinking men!"[2]

George Parr captained the second English team to visit our shores in 1864, and on this more extensive tour, the visitors won ten matches and drew one. Tom Carpenter entered the history books when he became the first English player to register a century on Australian soil, after he scored 121 at Ballarat.

In 1873–74 the legendary Dr. W. G. Grace led the third English tour to our colonies, and a memorable defeat was suffered in the Victorian town of Stawell. After arriving at the venue, the unimpressed English captain grumpily asked about the location of the wicket.

"You're standing on it!" retorted a local,

2. Piesse and Ferguson, 1986, pp37-9

before the English team suffered defeat from Stawell by ten wickets. Their complaints about ground conditions were acknowledged, but "The Australian" writer offered further insights about why "the might of England was beaten by a country town".

"The reasons for defeat were the bad ground and good liquor. Some of the professionals were unable to perform their tasks because of the hospitality offered to them."

Overall the visiting team coped well with the long distances between venues and the excessive heat that they often endured. Of their 13 matches, Grace's team won ten and lost three. However Sam Costick, one of Victoria's leading players, provided the following prophetic comment about future contests.

"Bar W. G., we're as good as they are, and some day we'll lick 'em."[3]

Since 1861 more land had been opened up to free settlers, and within the decade over 30,000 new farmers were cultivating land in the slowly developing outback areas. This era was dubbed "the golden age of the bourgeoisie," when the building and manufacturing industries began to boom in the developing cities. By 1887 the number of native born was beginning to outnumber the immigrants.

In that year J J.Lillywhite captained an English touring team to the colonies, and the first ever Test match was played at the MCG. Nat Thompson, Charles Bannerman, Dave Gregory and Ned Gregory were the Sydney players selected for that historic contest, while Tom Kendall, Jack Hodges, Tom Garrett, Tom Horan, Bransbury Cooper, William Midwinter and Jack Blackham were chosen from Victoria. The Australian X1 was seven years younger on average than their English

**"Bar W. G., we're as good as they are, and some day we'll lick 'em."**

3. Ibid.

counterparts, whose average age was ballooned by the selection of 45 year old James Shaw and 49 year old James Southerton.

The first Test began on March 15th, 1877, but only 3–4 hours of play were possible on the opening day because of rain interruptions. From the early stages of the game Australia gained the upper hand, and they finally won by the margin of 45 runs. Opener Charles Bannerman scored a fine 165 before retiring hurt, while Billy Midwinter distinguished himself with the ball, capturing 5/78 in England's first innings. Another bowler to shine was Tom Kendall, who made his first class debut in this game. Kendall became a match winner after he claimed 7/55, when England was dismissed for a meagre 108 in its second innings.

England gained revenge at the same ground on April 4th, when it won by four wickets in the deciding Test of the summer.

Cricket's most famous rivalry had begun.

# AUSTRALIA'S FIRST TEST PLAYERS

## 1. BANNERMAN, C. (Charles) :
### 1851–1930.
Tests: (3)
239 runs at 59.75

It is fitting that Charles Bannerman was allocated the status of number one in Cricket Australia's numerical list of Test players, as he was very much a premier performer.

He not only played in Australia's first Test team at the MCG – he also received the first ever Test delivery from England's Alfred Shaw, he scored the first five in Test cricket, and his undefeated innings of 165 was the first century recorded in Test cricket history.

This English born opening batsman was also the first Australian batsman to score a century in Canada (125 in Montreal in 1878), and the first Aussie to register three figures in New Zealand (125 at Invercargill in 1878).

On Australia's first official tour of England he headed the Australian aggregates and averages, and his century against Leicestershire was the first recorded by an Australian on English soil.

In later years Bannerman coached extensively in Melbourne, Sydney and New Zealand, and shortly before he died he saw Don Bradman score 452 not out at the SCG.

It was fitting that Charles Bannerman, Australia's first batsman of world class, met the player who became the greatest batsman of all time.

## 2. BLACKHAM, J.M. (Jack)
## 1854–1932.

Tests (35)
800 runs at 15.68
Dismissals: 60 (36 caught, 24 stumped)

Described by South Australia's great all-rounder George Giffen as being "the prince of wicketkeepers", Blackham kept wickets with distinction for 20 years, standing mostly up on the stumps, (which was a revolutionary practice for his era), and his safe hands eliminated the need for a long stop.

Blackham was Australia's keeper in the very first Test match, and he played in all the important early Tests that shaped the future course of international cricket. He was a member of the first eight Australian teams which toured England, and he captained the side on his last tour in 1893.

## 3. COOPER, B. B (Bransbury)
## 1844–1914.

Tests (1)
18 runs at 9.00

Born in India, and educated at Rugby, Cooper played successfully in England before immigrating to Geelong in Victoria. This hard hitting batsman scored 15 and 3 in his only Test match, which was the inaugural 1877 game at the MCG.

## 4. GARRETT, T. W. (Tom) : 1858–1943.

Tests(19)
339 runs at 12.55
36 wickets at 26.94

Born in Wollongong, Garrett became a highly successful captain of NSW teams, and an experienced and capable Test all-rounder. He made his debut in the very first Test at the tender age of 18 years and 232 days, which made him the youngest player to represent Australia against England.

He toured England in 1878, 1882 and 1886, and on his first two trips he was an outstanding success, capturing over 100 wickets. His best performance was in the 1881–82 home series when he collected 9/163 at Sydney and finished with 18 Test wickets for the summer.

## 5. GREGORY, D. W. (Dave) : 1845–1919.

Tests (3)

60 runs at 20.00

Australia's first ever Test captain at the age of 31, and he was elected unanimously to this position by his teammates .His astute captaincy and business management was a crucial factor in the 1878 world tour to New Zealand and America being such a playing and a financial success, and touring players became financially secure for life.

The thrice married Gregory fathered 16 children, and he played in his third and last Test in 1879.

## 6. GREGORY, E.J (Edward "Ned") : 1839–1899.

Tests (1)

11 runs at 5.50

"Ned" Gregory, Dave's brother and the father of Syd, is burdened with the dubious distinction of scoring the first duck in Test cricket.

He "achieved" this feat in the 1877 MCG Test, and later became a curator at the Sydney Cricket Ground (SCG), a respected designer of scoreboards, and a popular fishing companion when English touring teams visited Sydney.

## 7. HODGES, J. R. (John) : 1856–1933.
Tests (2)
10 runs at 3.30
6 wickets at 14.00

The man who replaced Frank Allan in Australia's first Test team, when his fellow Victorian controversially made himself unavailable to play. At that stage Hodges had never represented his colony, but he performed well, returning match figures of 3/34 from 16 overs.

In his second Test the fast medium left-arm bowler performed poorly, and he disappeared from international cricket. However some believe that the J. Hodges who began officiating as an umpire in the Fifth Test in 1888, before withdrawing his services after his umpiring was criticised, was the same man who represented Australia in the very first Test.

## 8. HORAN, T.P. (Tom "Felix") : 1854–1916.
Tests (15)
471 runs at 18.84
11 wickets at 13.00

The English born all-rounder went on to

captain his adopted country twice against England when the Australians were thrashed on both occasions.

He performed well on Gregory's 1878 tour, after representing Australia in the first Test in 1877, but his finest performance was reserved for his home Test in Melbourne in 1881–82 when he scored 124 and partnered George Giffen in Australia's first ever century stand. Horan then transferred that fine batting form to England, where he scored 1175 runs on the 1882 tour and played in the first Ashes Test.

He wore black pads while batting 100 years before coloured pads were adopted by WSC players, and after he retired as a player Horan gained fame as a cricket writer in "The Australasian" under the pen name of "Felix".

## 9. KENDALL, T.K. (Tom) : 1851–1924.
Tests (2)
39 runs at 13.00
14 wickets at 15.35

Born in England, but became an Australian hero in the first ever Test, and was rated as the best bowler never to tour England. His 7/55 in England's second innings of the 1877 MCG Test was second only to Bannerman's century in match winning terms, and he also performed well in the other Test match of the series.

The slow left arm bowler did accompany the Australian touring team to England as far as Perth, but was mysteriously sent back for "reasons other than cricket." He later relocated to Tasmania, where he is still regarded as one of the best coaches that the island state has seen.

## 10. MIDWINTER, W. E. (William "Billy") : 1851–1890.

Tests (8 for Australia and 4 for England)
174 runs at 23.78 for Australia
95 runs at 13.57 for England
14 wickets at 23.78 for Australia
10 wickets at 27.20 for England

A Gloucestershire born all-rounder, who remains the only player to ever play for Australia, England, and then Australia again.

"The Bendigo Giant" was one of Australia's stars in the 1877 Test match win, after which he played with Gloucestershire, before linking up that same season with the 1878 Australian touring team.

After playing ten matches with the tourists, Dr. W.G. Grace persuaded him to resume his career with Gloucestershire. This action produced tension between the Australian team and Grace, which was finally resolved after the famous doctor apologised to the management of the Australian team.

Midwinter toured Australia with Shaw's team in 1881–82, and represented England in four Tests. However when Ivor Bligh's MCC team toured down under during the 1882–83 summer, Midwinter was in the Australian team for one Test. He continued to represent his adopted country at this level until 1887.

Following the tragic death of his wife and two children from illnesses, Midwinter became so depressed that he was committed to the Kew Asylum for the Insane, where he died at the age of 39.

# 11. THOMPSON, N. F. G. (Nathaniel, "Nat") : 1838–1916.

Tests (2)
67 runs at 16.75
1 wicket at 31.00

Thompson was the first player to be dismissed in Test cricket, being bowled for one after he opened the batting with Charles Bannerman in the 1877 Test match.

The Birmingham born Sydneysider played first class cricket for 23 years, and after he retired he became an umpire and a successful coach.

# BIRTH OF THE ASHES

The following players were selected to tour England in 1878.

Dave Gregory (c), Tom Horan, Tom Kendall, Charles Bannerman, George Bailey, John Blackham, Fred Spofforth, Frank Allan, Billy Murdoch, Harry Boyle, Billy Midwinter and Tom Garrett. Bailey was a late replacement for Tasmania's John Arthur, who died two days after receiving his invitation to tour.

Despite the success of the previous series, no official Test matches were offered in England, but the Australians dominated most of their scheduled fixtures on their short tour.

On May 2nd Fred Spofforth's match figures of 11/20, which included a hat trick, decimated a strong MCC team, and a correspondent from "Punch" magazine was obviously impressed by the form of the touring colonials. *"The Australians came down like a wolf on the fold,*
*The Marylebone cracks for a trifle were bowled.*
*Our Grace before dinner was very well done,*
*But our Grace after dinner did not get a run."*

Charles Bannerman became part of cricket history when he scored 133 at Leicester, as his century was the first recorded by an Australian player in an English first class fixture.

Spofforth "the Demon" decisively bowled an Australian side to a Melbourne victory, claiming the first hat trick in Test cricket, and gaining the superb match figures of 13/110 from 70 overs when Lord Harris' MCC team toured Australia in the 1878–79 season.

Bailey was a late replacement for Tasmania's John Arthur, who died two days after receiving his invitation to tour.

George Coulthard officiated as an umpire in this game, and three years later he debuted as an Australian player when he scored six against Albert Shaw's English team.

During that decade major economic and social changes impacted greatly on life in the colonies. Free, compulsory and secular education had begun in the 1870s, and the advent of telephone exchanges throughout the vast continent significantly improved communication. By the 1880s the number of native born Australians outnumbered the immigrant population, and in that same decade colonial industries were exporting products back to the "mother country".

In 1892 a depression abruptly ended the economic boom times, and when the working classes began to endure hard times, a succession of militant strikes broke out in major cities across the continent. Writers such as Henry Lawson began to eulogise the virtues of "mateship" among the battlers in Australian society, and an aggressively new spirit of nationalism began to emerge. By 1897–98 five of the colonial premiers had agreed to work towards establishing a federation of states within the Commonwealth of Australia.

Perhaps it was this growing independent spirit that erupted into militant action at the SCG on February 15th 1879. On that day a large and angry crowd invaded the playing area when local hero Billy Murdoch was controversially ruled to be run out after scoring 82 in the match between NSW and the English X1. Lord Harris, his English teammates and the umpires were jostled by "larrikin" elements at the game following Murdoch's dismissal. After the match the NSW Cricket Association (NSWCA) issued an apology to the English team.

The apology was accepted, but Lord Harris' additional comments that "the events would not easily be forgotten", appeared to resonate throughout much of the 1880 tour of England that followed soon after. Perhaps it was Harris' influence which caused the Australian team to be frequently snubbed by their English hosts, who conveniently found it easier to arrange fixtures for the more popular Canadian team.

Luckily, however, the touring captain, Murdoch, and England's skipper W.G. Grace, struck up a friendship which helped make the Australians more acceptable as the tour progressed. An Oval Test was agreed on, and England won by five wickets, in this first such encounter played in their country. Overall the colonial team performed well, but significantly lost the last four matches of their tour after Spofforth became sidelined with a broken finger.

Australia won all four Test Matches when Albert Shaw captained the 1881–82 team which toured Australia, and the resurgent colonials also enjoyed outstanding success when they toured England in the following northern summer. They were victorious in 23 matches, with four of the touring team scoring over 1,000 runs while another four took more than 100 wickets.

On 27th August, 1882, the Australians achieved a comprehensive Test victory against a full strength English team after trailing by 38 runs on the first innings. Spofforth was carried in triumph from the Oval after capturing a match winning 7/46 from 36.3 overs. This was the first occasion that England had suffered a Test defeat on home soil, and the shock waves reverberated strongly among English cricket lovers. George Spendlove, aged 48,

**George Spendlove, aged 48, actually died at the game after suffering a heart attack, and another fan reportedly bit through the handle of his umbrella when England was dismissed for a humiliating 77 in its second innings.**

actually died at the game after suffering a heart attack, and another fan reportedly bit through the handle of his umbrella when England was dismissed for a humiliating 77 in its second innings.

Six days after this unexpected defeat the young journalist Raymond Brooks penned this now historic mock obituary in the "Sporting Times".

*"In Affectionate*
*Remembrance*
*of*
*ENGLISH CRICKET*
*which died at the Oval*
*on*
*29th August, 1882.*
*Deeply lamented by a large*
*circle of Sorrowing Friends*
*and Acquaintances*
*R.I.P.*
*N.B. The body will be cremated and the ashes*
*Taken to Australia.*[4]

Despite rumours to the contrary, it seems that no stumps, bats, balls or indeed any cricket equipment used in that game were set on fire. However, the Ashes image grew so strongly in the public imagination that England's new captain, Ivor Bligh, referred to this mythical "corpse" of English cricket before he sailed with his team on the "Pershawar" for the 1882 series in Australia. "We will bring back the Ashes," he vowed.

These prophetic words heralded the start of an international contest that still has no rival in the world of sport.

4. Haigh, 2004, p56

# THE ROMANCE AND MYSTERY OF THE ASHES

There is conflicting anecdotal evidence about the actual origin of the Ashes, and the following version places a Sydney woman and Bligh's Australian true love Florence Morphy strongly in the frame.

After Bligh's team gained a series' clinching win in the 1882 Sydney Test, the victorious captain returned to the suburban residence in Woollahra where he was being billeted. Before Bligh departed for Melbourne it is alleged that his hostess, Mrs. Annie Fletcher, presented him with a velvet bag in which he could store the future ashes of English cricket.

In Melbourne he reunited with Miss Florence Morphy, a young woman from the Victorian town of Beechworth, to whom he had become romantically attached during the long voyage from England to Australia. Miss Murphy and her friends decided that the bag was not grand enough for such a celebrated trophy, so they purchased a small urn into which ashes were poured.

Another rumour on the tour added further to the intrigue. On the voyage to Australia Bligh became friendly with William Clarke, a wealthy Victorian pastoralist who had been recommended to Queen Victoria as a candidate for baronetcy. Clarke was president of the Melbourne Cricket Club, and he extended an invitation to the English team to spend the Christmas and New Year holiday period at his "Rupertswood" property in Sunbury.

On Christmas Eve 1882 a very enjoyable social cricket game was played at "Rupertswood" between the English players and a local team, and at dinner that evening Lady Clarke, who employed Florence Morphy both as her companion and her children's music teacher, presented Ivor Bligh with a pottery urn. The contents supposedly contained the charred remains of a burnt bail that had been used in the game played earlier that day, and Lady Clarke declared that Australia and England now had a real trophy for which to play.

Speculation about the true origin of the Ashes, however, still continued. It is believed by some, that in that same summer, the bail ashes were accidentally spilt by a maid in a residence where Bligh was staying, and that she replaced the revered contents with humble ashes from a fireplace.

At the end of the tour the remains in the urn of a burned stump, bail, ball, stick or perhaps Miss Morphy's hat, were taken back to England by the besotted future Lord Darnley, who later returned to Australia and married Florence Morphy in February 1884. "Rupertswood" was the venue for a lavish reception for the newly weds. The young couple made their first home in Melbourne, before relocating to Cotham Hall in Kent in 1900 after Bligh inherited the Earldom and became the eighth Lord Darnley, while Florence became his Countess. Years later Australians of the World War I era carried fond memories of the couple, as many of their recuperating soldiers were made welcome in the Darnley's English home while they recovered from the horrors of battle.

Eight years after her husband died, Lady Darnley donated the precious Ashes urn to the Marylebone Cricket Club (MCC), who placed it in the cricket museum at Lords. There "the Holy Grail" of cricket has remained since the 1930s, though in recent years replicas of the revered urn have been awarded to winning Ashes teams. The only time this precious trophy left its display cabinet was in 1988 for the Australian Bicentennial celebrations. Police escorts ensured that its journey to and from its destination was safely guarded at all times.

Andrew Lloyd Webber reminds us in one of his famous compositions that "Love Changes Everything." In regard to the various legends about the Ashes, the romance between England's captain and his young Australian sweetheart, changed a myth into a reality that still remains strong after more than 120 years of engrossing contests.

# AUSTRALIAN PRE-ASHES AND ASHES PLAYERS:

## 12. KELLY, T.J.D. (Tom) : 1844–93.
Tests (2)
64 runs at 21.33

An Irish born free-hitting batsman who immigrated to Australia at the age of 19 where he played 16 first class matches for Victoria. He is best remembered for smiting eight successive fours in his score of 35 during the second Test of the 1876–77 Test series.

## 13. MURDOCH, W. L. (William "Billy") : 1854–1911.
Tests (18 for Australia and 1 for England)
For Australia: 896 runs at 32.00, 13 catches and 1 stumping
For England: 12 runs at 12.00, 1 stumping

Murdoch, who was renowned for his quick footwork and handsome off driving, has been described as the first great Australian batsman, with only W.G. Grace being ranked ahead of him during the prime years of his career. Murdoch scored the first double century in Test cricket (a stylish 211 at the Oval in 1884), and on his five tours of England he topped the batting averages on four occasions.

He was the team captain on four of his English tours, and after he finished playing in Australia he captained Sussex for seven years. In the early years of his career Murdoch was an accomplished wicket keeper, and he returned to that role for England in a 1891–92 Test against South Africa in Cape Town.

Murdoch's tact and charm were vital on the tense 1880 tour of England when Lord Harris made life difficult for much of the summer. After captaining Australia in 16 Tests, the 36 year old was dropped from the team because he was considered too old. Murdoch made a mockery of this decision by going on to captain Sussex with great success, and the ever popular Australian was still scoring first class centuries in his late 40s.

## 14. SPOFFORTH, F.R. (Fred "The Demon") : 1853–1926.

Tests (18)
217 runs at 9.43
94 wickets at 18.41

Australia's original "demon" fast bowler, who intimidated many batsmen of his era with his satanic appearance and fast-medium leg and off breaks. The greater the challenge, the better "the Demon" bowled, and he enjoyed legendary success with New South Wales, Victoria, Australia and Derbyshire.

The swarthy, black-haired lady killer with a droopy moustache and long sideburns always seemed to be in the spotlight. One of his legendary performances occurred in a 1881–82 country match in Victoria, when Spofforth reportedly rode a horse over 400 miles for the round trip, and twice bowled out all ten batsmen!

Spofforth was named in Australia's first Test team in 1877, but he refused to play because Billy Murdoch was overlooked, as he regarded his combination with the NSW keeper as being a vital ingredient in his bowling success. However he soon returned to the team, and went on to tour England five times

**Spofforth reportedly rode a horse over 400 miles for the round trip, and twice bowled out all ten batsmen.**

with remarkable success.

On his first tour in 1878 Spofforth captured 107 wickets at 11.71, while in 1880 he achieved the amazing tour figures of 763 wickets at an average of 5.49. His record at home was not as brilliant as on the soft pitches of England, though he still registered many excellent performances. In 1878–79 he captured 13/110 including a hat trick against Lord Harris' team, and he also bowled admirably in the 1882–83 and 1884–85 home tours.

Spofforth's most memorable performance, however, remains the famous 1882 Ashes Test at the Oval, where he was carried shoulder-high from the ground after capturing the match winning figures of 14/90.

After he retired from the game, Fred Spofforth became a director of the Star Tea Company in England, and he was a wealthy man when he died in Surrey at the age of 73.[5]

## 15. ALLAN, F. E. (Frank) : 1849–1917.
Tests (1) 5 runs at 5.00
4 wickets at 20.00

**He marred his career by withdrawing from Australia's first Test team, because he had arranged to meet some friends at the Warrnambool Show.**

Allan was once described as being the "bowler of the century", but he marred his career by withdrawing from Australia's first Test team, because he had arranged to meet some friends at the Warrnambool Show.

In his first and only Test in 1879 he performed with modest success, and he also had a disappointing tour of England in 1878.

The fast medium bowler, who is credited with pioneering fast swing bowling, was probably at his best before international tours began.

5. Pollard, 1982, p947

## 16. BANNERMAN, A.C. (Alexander "Alick") : 1854–1924.
### Tests (28)
### 1,018 runs at 23.08
### 4 wickets at 40.75.

It was once said about "Barndoor" Bannerman's batting that "snails could have sneaked past him with sneers on their faces", but this noted stonewaller of Australian cricket. won many matches for Australia with his stubborn defence.

"Alick", the brother of Charles Bannerman, had not played inter-colonial cricket when he was first chosen to tour England in 1878, but he soon established himself in the team, and made six tours of the "old country" during his long career.

His highest score in Test cricket was achieved in the 1891–92 Sydney Test, when he reached 91 during his seven and a half hours stay at the crease. On his retirement as a player, Alex Bannerman became coach of the New South Wales Cricket Association (NSWCA).

**...snails could have sneaked past him with sneers on their faces...**

## 17. BOYLE, H.F. (Henry "Harry").
### Tests (12)
### 153 runs at 12.75
### 32 wickets at 20.03

Boyle first came to notice after he bowled Dr. W.G. Grace in a 1873 match in Australia, but both he and Fred Spofforth were not highly rated when they arrived in England for the 1878 tour.

However Spofforth ("The Demon") and Boyle ("The Devil") soon changed that largely anonymous perception, after they cut a

**They cut a swathe through the cream of England's batsmen that summer.**

swathe through the cream of England's batsmen that summer. Boyle, whose accurate bowling was a perfect foil for the flamboyance and pace of Spofforth, captured 51 wickets in 19 tour matches.

Boyle toured England on six occasions, and in 1880 he was replaced as captain by Murdoch, after a team shipboard meeting voted for a change of leadership. The self effacing Bendigo bowler apparently bore no ill will about his demotion, and he continued to perform well both in England and Australia.

On his final tour of England in 1888 the 41 year old Boyle served as player-manager, and shortly after his return he retired to open a sporting goods emporium in Melbourne.

## 18. ALEXANDER, G. (George) : 1851–1930.

Tests (2)
52 runs at 13.00
2 wickets at 46.50

This hard hitting batsman and handy change bowler from Melbourne played in the 1880 Test at the Oval, and the Adelaide Test of 1884, but he is best remembered for his player management skills.

Alexander managed both the 1880 and 1884 Australian teams which toured England, and he also managed Ivor Bligh's MCC team that visited Australia in 1882–83.

## 19. BONNOR, G.J. (George) : 1855–1912.

Tests (17)
512 runs at 17.06
2 wickets at 46.00

Nicknames "Bonnor The Basher" and the "Colonial Hercules", this  giant of a man, (6' 6" and 16 stone), was one of the biggest hitters of all time. At Mitcham Green near London in 1880 he hit a ball over 140 metres on the full, and he could also throw a cricket ball distances of more than 100 metres.

The Bathurst born player yearned to be regarded as a polished batsman, but he was a born hitter who often pulled Australia out of a tight spot. His only Test century was a match winning 128 out of a total of 169 at the SCG in 1884–85.

Bonnor also has the dubious honour of being the third victim in Test cricket's first hat trick, which was obtained by England's Billy Bates in the second Test at Melbourne in 1882–83. Bonnor toured with Australian teams on five occasions, and when he died in Orange New South Wales he was a country cricket legend.

### 20. GROUBE, T.U. (Thomas) : 1857–1927.
#### Tests (1)
#### 11 runs at 5.50

A New Zealand born all rounder who represented Australia in the first Test on English soil in 1880, after he replaced an ill Charles Bannerman in the touring side.

He scored 11 and 0 in that Oval Test, and disappeared from international cricket at the completion of the tour.

### 21 McDONNELL, P.S. (Percy "Greatheart") : 1858–96.
#### Tests (19)
#### 950 runs at 28.78

**At Mitcham Green near London in 1880 he hit a ball over 140 metres on the full, and he could also throw a cricket ball distances of more than 100 metres.**

**He was at his best when things were worst.**

His admiring teammate George Giffen bestowed the nick name of "Greatheart" on McDonnell, because "he was at his best when things were worst".

McDonnell was born in London, and debuted with Victoria at the age of 20. Medical studies often made him unavailable for games, but this elegant and effective batsman represented Victoria, New South Wales, Queensland and Australia with distinction, before he unexpectedly died of a heart attack at the age of 36.

McDonnell scored three Test centuries, and he also captained Australia on six occasions between1886–88.

## 22. MOULE, W.H. (William) : 1858–1939.

Tests (1)
40 runs at 20.00
3 wickets at 7.66

A useful batsman and medium pace bowler, who replaced an ill Spofforth in his first and only Test at the Oval in 1880.

Moule had a distinguished legal career, being a principal partner in one of Melbourne's leading law firms, and later serving as a judge.

## 23. PALMER, G.E. (George "Joey") : 1860–1910.

Tests (17)
296 runs at 14.09
78 wickets at 21.51

A notable all-rounder for Victoria, Tasmania and Australia during the early days of international cricket. He debuted in Test matches at the age of 18 against Lord Harris' MCC team in 1878–79 and he returned the impressive match figures of 9/94.

This performance gained Palmer selection for the 1880 tour of England, and he also represented Australia in the "home country" in 1882 and 1886. On his final tour Palmer became the first Australian to achieve the double in England of taking over 100 wickets and scoring more than 1000 runs.

During the early 1880s Palmer was regarded as the finest bowler in Australia, but his international career was cut short by a knee injury in 1886. The last decade of his playing career was spent in Tasmania.

## 24. SLIGHT, J. (James) : 1855–1930.

Tests (1)

11 runs at 5.50

Slight's one tour of England in 1880 was unfortunately ruined by poor health, and in his only Test match at the Oval the Victorian born batsman scored 11 and 0.

## 25. COOPER, W.H (William) : 1859–1939.

Tests (2)

13 runs at 6.50

9 wickets at 25.11

The Kent-born slow bowler did not play cricket until he was 27, but three years later was chosen in Victoria's team. He obtained prodigious turn with his leg breaks, and though he was frequently inaccurate, he obtained many vital opposition wickets.

After gaining match figures of 9/200 in the 1881–82 Melbourne Test against Ivor

Bligh's team, high hopes were held for his prospects on the 1884 English tour. However a serious hand injury ruined his chances, and on his return to Australia Cooper retired from the game.

## 26. EVANS, E. (Edwin) : 1849–1921.

Tests (6)
83 runs at 10.25
7 wickets at 47.42

Evans was rated as the best all-rounder in the country in the 1870s, and his first English opponents commented that the NSW slow-medium bowler "could pitch the ball on a six-pence"[6].

In Tests at home in the late 1870s he performed well, but his best years were past him when he toured England in 1886. In later years he was an inspector of farm selections, and his skill as a marksman around rural areas was much admired by the famous poet, A.B. "Banjo" Patterson.

## 27. GIFFEN, G. (George) : 1859–1927.

Tests (31)
1,238 runs at 23.35
103 wickets at 27.09

One of the best all-rounders Australia has produced, and the first to score over 1,000 runs and take more than 100 wickets at Test match level.

Giffen was a star performer for South Australia, and after he scored 271 and captured match figures of 16 for 166 runs against Victoria in 1891–92, a respected English historian described his performance as "surely the

6. Pollard, 1982, p34

greatest all-round performance in recorded cricket history of any class". Giffen represented his state until the age of 44, and today a grandstand at the Adelaide Oval is named after him.[7]

Between 1882–96 Giffen toured England on five occasions. He obtained more turn with the ball in England with his off-breaks and cutters, but he was also a match winner in home Tests. Giffen captained Australia in four Tests, but he was not a success as he tended to over bowl himself.

His only Test century, (a fine innings of 161), was scored in 1891–92 in Sydney, but he passed half-century scores in six Tests, and on seven occasions he obtained five wickets or better. In 1898 Giffen wrote a highly respected cricket book, and in later years he became an esteemed coach.

## 28. MASSIE, H. H. (Hugh) :
## 1854–1938.
### Tests (9)
### 249 runs at 15.56

A hard hitting batsman who rescued Australia with his valiant innings of 55 on a rain affected Oval wicket in the famous Ashes Test. His banking career previously caused him to withdraw from the 1880 team which toured England, but he was second only to Murdoch in the run aggregates on the 1882 tour.

This genial and popular man also captained Australia in a Sydney Test in 1884 85. His son, Robert John Allright Massie, performed promisingly in 16 matches for NSW, before his career was tragically shortened after

**Today a grandstand at the Adelaide Oval is named after him.**

7. Pollard, 1982, p431

he was wounded at Gallipoli in 1915.

## 29. COULTHARD, G. (George) : 1856–83.

Tests (1)
6 runs, n.a.

After umpiring the first Test on the 1881–82 tour, Coulthard played in the 1882 Melbourne Test, but made little impact.

By then an umpiring decision in the 1879 NSW–England fixture had made Coulthard a controversial figure, as one of the game's worst riots broke out after he ruled that the local hero Murdoch had been run out.

International cricket almost ended before it properly began that day, and the 27 year old Coulthard himself died soon after from tuberculosis.

## 30. JONES, S. P. (Samuel) : 1861–1951.

Tests (12)
432 runs at 21 60
6 wickets at 18.66.

A cautious batsman who played a long innings for Australia in the victorious Ashes Test. Jones also toured England on three other occasions, but his 1886 English tour was the most successful, when he finished only behind Giffen in the batting averages. He also commenced promisingly on the 1888 tour before falling seriously ill with smallpox.

The Sydney reared player relocated to Queensland in 1890, and the last 47 years of his life were spent in New Zealand, where he settled after becoming a master at Auckland Grammar School in 1904.

# TROUBLED TIMES

Rumblings of discontent were evident among members of the Australian team when they returned to the colonies after their narrow defeat in the 1884 Test series in England. Their arch rivals were receiving greater financial rewards from the game, and when the colonial authorities rejected their demands for a more generous return from gate receipts for the 1884–85 home series against England, their anger flared into open rebellion.

Their arch rivals were receiving greater financial rewards from the game

Most NSW based members of the team refused to represent their colony against the English X1, and they then withdrew their services for the Second Test in Melbourne. The Victorian Cricket Association (VCA) responded by selecting nine debutant players, and appointing Tom Horan as the new Australian captain. Blackham, Boyle, Bonner, McDonnell, Palmer and Scott were all disqualified from playing, and England predictably achieved an easy series victory.

The dispute continued at the end of the summer, when Murdoch, McDonnell and "Alick" Bannerman were not selected for the 1886 tour of England because they had "breached their amateur status". The Australian team was further weakened when Horan, Boyle and Massie withdrew, and the new captain, Scott, faced the unenviable task of welding this untried group into a competitive team.

It proved to be virtually an impossible task. The team did not assemble together as a unit on the trip until Naples, team spirit appeared to be poor throughout the tour, England won the series 3:0, and Scott retired from first class cricket at the end of that unsuccessful summer.

There was little improvement in morale over the next two Australian seasons. In 1886–87 fights were reported within the Australian team ranks, and on one occasion members of the English team were said to be physically harassed. Five new players were added to the Australian team for the Second Test after another pay dispute, and the public showed little interest in the two Tests which were easily won by England.

George Giffen, Horan, Bruce and Jarvis all refused to play during the following Australian summer as the pay disputes continued, and it was not until the 1891–92 home series that Australia wrested back the Ashes.

Money wrangles helped produce eight years in the wilderness for Australia during the 1880s Ashes campaign. This disruptive scenario resurfaced again in 1977.

# PLAYERS OF THIS TROUBLED ERA

## 31. SCOTT, H. J. H. (Dr. Henry "Tup") : 1858–1910.
### Tests (5)
### 359 runs at 27.61

A player who enjoyed a fruitful first tour of England in 1884, scoring 973 runs at 22.62, the highlight of which was a magnificent 102 in his second Test at the Oval.

Scott later became the first Victorian to lead an Australian Test team in England. However his captaincy of the 1886 team was marred by quarrels within the team group, as well as by injuries to key players, and all three Test matches were lost.

At the end of that disastrous tour, Scott completed his medical studies in England, and after he returned to Australia he dropped out of first class cricket. Scott ended his days as a much respected doctor in the NSW country towns of Bathurst and Scone, where the local hospital was named in his honour. When he died from typhoid fever at the age of 51, his close friend "Banjo" Patterson was among the mourners.

**When he died from typhoid fever at the age of 51, his close friend "Banjo" Patterson was among the mourners.**

## 32. BRUCE, W. (William) : 1864–1925.
### Tests (14)
### 702 runs at 23.97
### 12 wickets at 36.66

The first of many notable left handed batsmen to tour England, and this graceful player participated in both the 1886 and 1893 tours. He once scored a triple century in Melbourne club ranks, and in first class cricket he totalled four centuries.

Bruce, who also bowled useful left arm spin deliveries, later became a keen coach of left-handed batsmen, and a well known Melbourne solicitor.

## 33. JARVIS, A. H. (Arthur "Affie") : 1860–1933.

Tests (11)
303 runs at 16.83
18 dismissals (9 catches, 9 stumpings)

Jarvis was a fine wicketkeeper, who was unfortunately overshadowed by the superior prowess of Jack Blackham during his first class career. However this Adelaide coach builder still toured England on four occasions between 1880 and 1893, and his ability to stand up to the stumps to fast bowlers was unrivalled.

Jarvis' most memorable keeping performance occurred in 1884–85 when regulars such as Blackham refused to play. Jarvis took five catches and a stumping in the first Test, which contributed greatly to Australia's surprise victory. "Affie" Jarvis was also an accomplished batsman who scored 82 in his debut Test match in 1882, but he never registered a century in first class cricket.

## 34. MARR, A. P (Alfred) : 1862–1940.

Tests (1)
5 runs at 2.50.

A useful all-rounder who was selected on three occasions in Australian touring teams to England, but was unavailable each time. This NSW player was selected in his only Test match for the Melbourne fixture of 1884–85, when 11 changes were made to the team because of a financial dispute.

Marr disappeared from the international arena after Australia suffered a ten wicket defeat in this match. He continued to play for decades in Sydney club cricket, where he scored a century at the age of 67.

**He scored a century at the age of 67.**

## 35. MORRIS, S. (Samuel) : 1855–1931.

The first coloured man to represent Australia. This Tasmanian born all-rounder, whose West Indian parents were lured to Australia by the gold rush, scored 4 and 10 not out and captured two wickets for 75 runs in his first and only Test match at Melbourne in 1885.

Morris became a noted player and grounds curator at Melbourne clubs for many years. He still attended games decades after blindness forced him to relinquish his employment as a curator.

**He still attended games decades after blindness forced him to relinquish his employment as a curator.**

## 36. MUSGROVE, H.A. (Henry) : 1860–1931.
### Tests (1)
### 13 runs at 6.50

Another player who gained Test selection when key players in the 1884–85 season declared themselves unavailable over match payments disputes. Twelve years later he won respect from his player group when he managed the 1896 Australian team on their tour of England.

Musgrove later became a board member of the famous J.C. Williamson Theatres Limited.

**37. POPE, R. J. (Dr. Roland) :
1864–1952.**
Tests (1)
3 runs at 1.50

Performed poorly in his only Test of the ill fated 1884–85 series, but went on to become Australia's most famous "camp follower", travelling at his own expense with up to 40 pieces of luggage that contained every conceivable item that a touring cricketer would ever need.

In 1926 he produced a button hook from one of his many bags for a player in need. The only known time that he failed to deliver was on tour in 1921, when Edgar Mayne unexpectedly requested a bicycle pump.

**38. ROBERTSON, W. J. (William "Digger") : 1861–1938.**
Tests (1)
2 runs at 1.00

After capturing eight wickets for Victoria against Alfred Shaw's 1884–85 team, this leg break bowler was selected to play in the Melbourne Test match soon afterwards, but failed to perform well.

Robertson only played seven first class matches, but performed with credit for many years in Melbourne club cricket.

**39. TRUMBLE, J. W. (John) :
1863–1944.**
Tests (7)
243 runs at 20.25
10 wickets at 22.20

John Trumble, the elder brother of the

**Australia's most famous "camp follower", travelling at his own expense with up to 40 pieces of luggage that contained every conceivable item that a touring cricketer would ever need.**

more famous Hugh, was selected for the 1886 tour of England, but failed to justify high expectations about his prowess.

His first class experiences were restricted by his legal studies, and he later became a successful Melbourne solicitor.

### 40. WORRALL, J. (John), : 1863–1937.
Tests (11)
475 runs at 25.15
1 wicket at 127

An accomplished all-round sportsman who toured England in 1888 and 1899. His aggressive batting was seen at its best when he scored a rapid 76 not out in 75 minutes at the 1899 Leeds Test, which remained his highest score at this level.

In later years he was Victoria's state coach, and he is also credited with inventing the term "Bodyline" after he became a highly respected sportswriter for Melbourne newspapers.

### 41. MCSHANE, P.G. (Patrick) : 1857–1903.
Tests (3)
26 runs at 5.20
1 wicket at 48.00

McShane, a left hander with bat and ball, achieved a rare distinction when he umpired the 1884–85 Fourth Test match in Sydney before playing in the Fifth Test in Melbourne.

The St Kilda curator's Test career was interrupted when he required attention in a mental home.

**The St Kilda curator's Test career was interrupted when herequired attention in a mental home.**

## 42. WALTERS, F.H. (Francis) : 1860–1922.

Tests (1)

12 runs at 6

Walters played in one Test in the 1884–85 series, and he toured England with the 1890 Australian team, but the fine array of strokes that characterised his state performances with both Victoria and NSW seemed to disappear on the international stage.

This one time ironmonger later became a hotel owner, before he died at sea near Bombay.

## 43. MCILLWRAITH, J. (John) : 1857–1938.

Tests (1)

9 runs at 4.50

A hard hitting Victorian batsman who had a disappointing tour of England in 1886, after being a prolific scorer at club and colonial level.

## 44. FERRIS, J.J. (John) : 1867–1900.

Tests for Australia (5)

98 runs at 8.16

48 wickets at 14.25

Tests for England (1)

16 runs at 16.00

13 wickets at 7.00

Along with C.T.B. Turner, Ferris formed one of the game's greatest fast bowling partnerships. In his prime years Ferris, a left arm new ball bowler, maintained an immaculate length and swung the new ball both ways, as he cut a swathe through England's finest batsmen.

Ferris made an auspicious international debut in the 1887 Australian summer, capturing the respective match figures of 9/103 and 9/140 in his first two Tests., and his impressive form continued on the 1888 tour of England. The 21 year old returned the amazing tour figures of 220 wickets at 14.10. Ferris became more highly rated than "Terror Turner" on his other tour of England two years later when he captured 215 wickets at 13.20.

After capturing 9/74 in his last Test for Australia at the Oval in 1890, Ferris qualified to play English county cricket with Gloucestershire. On an English tour of South Africa he captured 13/91in his only Test appearance for his adopted country, but soon after his revered skills inexplicably deserted him.

He played briefly again in Australian colonial matches between1895–98, and he later enlisted for service in the Boer War in South Africa. It was there in 1900 that the 33 year old Ferris died from enteric fever in the port city of Durban.

## 45. MOSES, H. (Henry, "Harry") : 1858–1938.
### Tests (6)
### 198 runs at 19.80

Moses, one of the best left handed bats men seen in Australia, sadly declined many opportunities to tour England because of his work commitments with a Sydney wine merchant. At his best he challenged Murdoch as being Australia's premier batsman, and he plundered many runs from English bowlers when they toured Australia.

In his Sydney Test debut match in

1886–87, his innings of 31 and 34 on a bowler friendly wicket was the best Australian batting performance for the match. Moses, however, faded out of Test cricket after injuring a tendon in his left leg when Lord Sheffield's English team was touring Australia in 1891–92.

## 46. TURNER, C.T.B. (Charles "The Terror").
Tests (17)
323 runs at 11.53
101 wickets at 16.53

**Turner "The Terror" bowled an amazing 2,589.3 overs, with 1,222 maidens, and captured 314 tour wickets at 11.12 each.**

Turner, a medium pace bowler of deadly accuracy, who obtained vicious turn from the off, followed Spofforth as the second great Australian bowler. On the 1888 English tour Turner "The Terror" bowled an amazing 2,589.3 overs, with 1,222 maidens, and captured 314 tour wickets at 11.12 each.

He first came to notice in the 1881–82 season after capturing the superb figures of 10/36 against England in his home town of Bathurst. Despite this incredible performance he did not make his debut with NSW until the following season, but by the 1888 tour of England Turner and Ferris were an almost unplayable bowling combination for the hapless English batsmen.

On this and his other two tours he made of "the old country", Turner amazed astute judges such as W.G. Grace with the speed and spin he generated from English wickets, and he was equally effective on home surfaces.

Previously, in 1887–88, he became the first bowler to capture 100 wickets in an Australian season, and in all first class matches Turner collected five wickets in an innings 102 times, and ten wickets in a match 35 times. "The Terror's" Test bowling average of 16.53 in his tally of 101 wickets is a long standing record.

## 47. ALLEN, R.C. (Reginald) : 1858–1952.
### Tests (1)
### 44 runs at 22.00

A gritty NSW batsman who played in the final Test against Shrewsbury's touring England team in 1886–87. Allen only played 17 first class matches.

## 48. BURTON, F.J. (Frederick) : 1866–1929.
### Tests (2)
### 4 runs at 2.00
### dismissals 2 (1 catch, 1 stumping)

A wicket keeper for NSW, Victoria, and in two Tests for Australia. He was originally selected because of his batting reputation, but failed to impress.

Burton settled in New Zealand, after first touring there with a NSW team in 1895.

## 49. COTTAM, J.C. (John) : 1867–1897.
### Tests (1)
### 4 runs at 2.00

Chosen at the age of 19 to represent Australia in the 1886–87 Sydney Test, but failed to make an impact. Cottam drifted out of first class cricket four years later, and he died at the age of 29 after contacting typhoid fever in the Western Australian town of Coolgardie.

## 50. GIFFEN, W.F. (Walter) : 1863–1949.
Tests (3)
11 runs at 1.83

**He only gained selection in the 1893 touring team to England because his famous older brother George insisted that he be included.**

It was rumoured that he only gained selection in the 1893 touring team to England because his famous older brother George insisted that he be included. Walter's modest batting contribution for the tour was 245 runs at an average of 15.31.

His career was badly affected by the loss of two fingers on his left hand from an Adelaide gasworks accident.

## 51. LYONS, J.J. (John) : 1863–1927.
Tests (14)
731 runs at 27.07
6 wickets at 24.83

A South Australian who became one of the most exciting big hitters in the game. Lyons struck the ball with exceptional power all around the wicket, and his prowess was shown at its best on his three tours to England in 1888, 1890 and 1893.

At the Lords Test on his last tour, Lyons thrashed a rapid century in an hour, and when he was dismissed for 149 he had clouted 22 boundaries. In Australia he played in all the Tests between 1887 and 1897, and in the 1891–92 Sydney fixture against England, he smashed 134 runs of the 174 stand that he shared with "Alick" Bannerman.

After his retirement from the game, John Lyons became a stockbroker.

## 52. EDWARDS, J.G. (John) : 1862–1911.
### Tests (3)
### 48 runs at 9.60

Toured England in 1888 with the Australian team, but performed disappointingly scoring a meagre 527 runs at 12.85, and missing many games through injury.

Edwards was regarded as being an unrealised talent, after being highly sought after by Melbourne clubs following his fine record in school cricket with Wesley College.

## 53. TROTT, G. H. S. (George "Harry") : 1866–1917.
### Tests (24)
### 921 runs at 21.92
### 29 wickets at 35.13

George Trott, the elder brother of Albert Trott, who also represented Australia in Tests, was a gifted cricketer but experienced problems away from the game.

The great George Giffen described him as "the best all round player that Victoria ever sent to England", and Trott scored more than 1,000 runs on each of his four tours between 1888–96, and also captured a total of 175 wickets. Trott led the 1896 team, and his overall Australian Test captaincy record was five wins and three losses from eight Tests. Clem Hill regarded him as being Australia's best captain in his era.

Soon after he returned from that tour, Trott's health broke down and he was admitted into a psychiatric institution. Fortunately he recovered and played with Victoria until the 1907–08 season.

**"The best all round player that Victoria ever sent to England"**

## 54. WOODS, S. M. J. (SAMUEL) : 1867–1931.

Tests (6) for Australia (3)
32 runs at 5.33
5 wickets at 24.20
Tests for England (3)
122 runs at 30.50
5 wickets at 25.80

A dual international sportsman, playing for both Australia and England in cricket, and representing England in rugby.

Woods grew up in Sydney, but spent much of his senior secondary and tertiary education years at Brighton College in England. At Cambridge he caught the attention of Sir Pelham Warner, who described Woods as being "the most artistic and subtle fast bowler that he had seen."

In cricket he went on to play and captain at Somerset for 25 years. During those years he joined the 1888 Australian touring team, and he also represented England. From 1893 Woods pace as a bowler deserted him, but his batting skills improved greatly. He also represented England in 13 international rugby internationals.

## 55. BARRETT, J.E. (Dr. John) : 1866–1916.

Tests (2)
80 runs at 26.66

A stubborn opening batsman and medium pace bowler, who first represented Victoria at the age of 18.

Barrett toured England in 1890 and finished second in the batting averages behind

Murdoch. In the Lords Test that summer he scored 67 not out on his way to becoming the first Australian to carry his bat through a Test innings.

His work as a doctor shortened his Test career.

## 56. BURN, E. J. K. (Edwin) : 1862–1956.
### Tests (2)
### 41 runs at 10.25

Burn topped the Tasmanian Cricket Association's batting average 11 times, but he is better remembered as the player who was Australia's worst selection blunder in the game's history.

When a group of leading players from Victoria and NSW selected the 1890 team to tour England, they disagreed over who should be Jack Blackham's reserve wicket keeper. Blackham himself finally decided that Burn should be chosen. Two days later Burn met his new teammates at the Adelaide wharf and said, "Here I am – but I have never kept wickets in my life."[8]

Burn refused to don the gloves, and he endured a miserable tour scoring 41 runs in four Test innings, and totalling 355 runs at 10.14 in that English summer. On his return he played the game only in Tasmania, where he enjoyed outstanding success as a batsman.

**He is better remembered as the player who was Australia's worst selection blunder in the game's history.**

## 57. CHARLTON, P.C. (Dr. Percy) : 1867–1954.
### Tests (2)
### 29 runs at 7.25
### 3 wickets at 8.00

8. Pollard, 1982, p217

An accomplished all-rounder who gave fine service to the game in NSW as a player and administrator.

He represented Australia in two Tests during the 1890 tour of England, where his excellent slip fielding drew much praise. His career in medicine ended his playing career, but in 1927 he was made a Life Member of the NSWCA.

## 58. GREGORY, S.E. (Sydney "Little Titch") : 1870–1929.
Tests (58)
2,282 runs at 24.53

Syd was the son of "Ned' Gregory who scored Australia's first duck in Test cricket. "Ned's" son was a technically correct and fast scoring batsman, who toured England on eight occasions. During his 22 years of international cricket Syd Gregory played in 58 Tests, which was a record that stood for 40 years, until it was bettered by Ray Lindwall. At the age of 43 this diminutive batsman, (he was only 5'4" in height), was recalled to the team to captain the depleted 1912 Australian team which toured England. It proved to be a disappointing end to a fine career.

The highlight of his many Test innings was the 201 he scored in Sydney in 1894, which was the first Test double century scored in Australia. In total, Syd Gregory scored 25 first class centuries, with ten of them being recorded in England.

Along with his reliable batting in a crisis, Syd Gregory's daring running between wickets, and his brilliant fielding at cover point, made him a crowd favourite and an inspiration to his teammates.

## 59. TRUMBLE, H. (Hugh) : 1867–1935.

Tests (32)
851 runs at 19.79
141 wickets at 21.78

An all-rounder of the highest class, who scored three first class centuries, and he was ranked as the finest and most astute bowler of his time. "A perfect master of the whole art of placing fieldsmen and changing bowlers", was how English star C.B. Fry described him.

The cagey Victorian captained winning Australian teams twice in the 1901–02 Tests, and he also claimed two Test hat tricks at the MCG with his deadly accurate medium pace off spinners. In all first class matches he claimed five wickets in an innings on 69 occasions, and 10 wickets in a match 25 times.

Hugh Trumble was secretary of the Melbourne Cricket Club for 27 years, and he administered major improvements to the ground. He also became a well respected cricket writer after his playing days ended.

**"A perfect master of the whole art of placing fieldsmen and changing bowlers", was how English star C.B. Fry described him.**

## 60. CALLAWAY, S.T. (Sydney) : 1868–1923.

Tests (30)
87 runs at 17.40
6 wickets at 23.66

His short Test career was highlighted by his share of an 81 run partnership for the last wicket with A.E. Trott at Adelaide in the 1894–95 Test match.

After touring New Zealand with a NSW team, Callaway eventually settled there, and represented both Canterbury and New Zealand teams.

### 61. DONNAN, H. (Henry "Harry") : 1864–1956.
Tests (5)
75 runs at 8.33

Donnan was the last round-arm bowler of quality, and a stubborn batsman. The Sydneysider toured England with moderate success in 1896, but his poor fielding hampered his progress at Test level.

Donnan, the brother-in-law of Syd Gregory, was employed at the Colonial Sugar's head office for 42 years.

### 62. MCLEOD, R.W. (Robert) : 1868–1907.
Tests (6)
146 runs at 13.27
12 wickets at 32.00

Robert McLeod was part of a remarkable family of seven brothers, all of whom played for the Melbourne Cricket Club. Three McLeods went on to represent Victoria, while Robert and his brother Charles were both Australian players.

Robert, a stylish left handed batsman, and handy medium pace bowler, was chosen in the 1890 Australian team which toured England, but declined because "he could not spare the time". After continuing to perform well for Victoria, McLeod did tour England in 1893, and captured 5/29 from 19 overs in an exciting Test match at Lords.

Robert McLeod became an unusual part of the game's history in an 1896 Melbourne club match, after he was run out in both innings without facing a ball.

**He was run out in both innings without facing a ball.**

## 63. GRAHAM, H. (Henry "The Little Dasher") : 1870–1911.
### Tests (6)
### 301 runs at 30.1

Graham became one of the few Australians to score a Test century on debut, a feat he achieved at Lords in 1893. The attacking stroke player was selected for this tour at the age of 22 after making a fine impression with the Victorian team. He also scored 105 against the Englishmen at Sydney in 1894–95, which resulted in him scoring a century in his first two Tests in both countries.

Poor health resulted in Graham having a disappointing tour of England in 1896. In 1903 he relocated to New Zealand where he played representative cricket for both Otago and the South Island.

# THE GOLDEN AGE (1894–1914)

A growing optimism was evident in Australian society during these two decades. By the end of the century the rapid development in production, transport and communication across most of the continent had invigorated the Federation movement, and in 1901 the colonists narrowly voted to establish the Commonwealth of Australia.

The growing nationalism was reflected in the promotion of international cricket, for it was "Australia" playing "England" when A.E. Stoddart's team visited our shores in the 1894–95 season, whereas in previous seasons it had been an "Australian X1" opposing an "English X1". The public appeared to embrace this change enthusiastically, and Stoddart's victorious team were treated like national heroes when they returned to England at the end of the tour.

There appeared to be great confidence in the leadership of Australia's teams of during these optimistic times. The captaincy of "Harry" Trott and Joe Darling received much praise, while Monty Noble gained the following lavish compliment from a writer in the prestigious "Wisden" magazine.

"The method of placing a field became in Noble's hand almost an exact science … that I have never seen equalled."

Truly great players make their mark in all eras, but the period between 1894 and 1914 yielded so many champions.

Australia boasted players of the calibre of Noble, Clem Hill, Hugh Trumble, Victor

**Truly great players make their mark in all eras, but the period between 1894 and 1914 yielded so many champions.**

Trumper, Syd Gregory, Warren Bardsley, Vernon Ransford, Warwick Armstrong and Charlie Macartney during those cherished 20 years, and England was similarly blessed with sublime talent.

Dr. W.G. Grace was still a formidable presence, while K.S.Ranjitsinhji, Tom Richardson, C. B. Fry, Wilfred Rhodes, S.F Barnes, George Hirst and Jack Hobbs also graced the playing fields of England and Australia during "Cricket's Golden Age."

# PLAYERS OF
# THE GOLDEN AGE

### 64. DARLING, J. (Joseph "Joe", "Paddy") : 1870–1946.
Tests (34)
1,657 runs at 28.56

Joe Darling is regarded as being one of Australia's finest left handed batsmen ever, and he was also one of the most respected captains.

Darling was selected in the South Australian XV shortly after he scored a double century as a 14 year old, but his father ruled him out of competitive sport for two years so that he could devote himself to more important priorities in life. He returned to cricket two years later, and after performing well against Stoddart's English team in 1894–95, Joe Darling was chosen for the first of his four English tours in 1896. On the 1889, 1902 and 1905 tours he captained the touring Australian teams. The most successful period of his Test career occurred in the 1897–98 home season, when he scored three centuries against England.

As the team leader he initiated some far reaching changes to the rules of the game. He persuaded the MCC to award a six rather than a five for hits over the boundary rope, he made it mandatory for captains to exchange team lists before the start of the match, and he had the law on declarations altered.

In 1908 Darling relocated to Tasmania, where he became a pioneer agriculturist and served as a state parliamentarian for 25 years.

### 65. IREDALE, F.A. (Francis) : 1867–1926.

Tests (14)
807 runs at 36.86

A resourceful NSW batsman who constantly battled the problem of making nervous starts to his innings. He scored 81 in his first Test against Stoddart's 1894–95 English team, and then registered an impressive total of 140 in the Third Test in Adelaide

Iredale headed the Test averages on the 1896 tour of England, and he also performed well on the 1899 tour. He retired from first class cricket in 1902 to pursue a career as a journalist, and he also wrote a book entitled "Thirty-Three Years Of Cricket." In 1922 he became secretary of the NSWCA.

### 66. JONES, E. (Ernest "Jonah") : 1869–1943.

Tests (19)
126 runs at 5.04
64 wickets at 29.01

Jones was sometimes dubbed "the Broken hill catapult", and the larger than life character from that NSW mining town was a fine fast bowler for both South Australia and Australia.

After leaving Broken Hill "Jonah" Jones was employed in Adelaide as a city sanitary cart driver. During that time he met the Prince of Wales, (who later became King Edward V11), at a state cricket team reception.

The royal guest asked "Jonah" if he ever attended St. Peter's College, a prestigious Adelaide school.

"Yes," replied "Jonah", "I often collect the

night soil from there."[9]

Between 1894–1903 Jones played in 19 Tests, with a best performance of 7/88 against England in 1897–98, and during his career he captured five wickets or more a staggering 46 times. He was also a noted big hitter who once clouted 70 in 35 minutes in an Adelaide district cricket match.

"Jonah" Jones toured England on three occasions, and took 121 wickets in 1896, 135 in 1899, and 71 in 1902.

## 67. McLEOD, C. E. (Charles) : 1869–1918.
### Tests (17)
### 573 runs at 23.87
### 33 wickets at 32.00

A cautious batsman and useful medium pace bowler who followed his older brother Robert into Test cricket when he gained selection in all five internationals against Stoddart's 1894–95 English team. The highlight of his debut season was his Second Test innings of 112 in his home city of Melbourne.

Charles McLeod toured England with only moderate success in 1899 and 1905, as the harder pitches in Australia were better suited to his batting technique. He is one of the few batsmen who have both opened and batted number 11 for Australia.

## 68. REEDMAN. J.C. (John "Dinny") : 1867–1924.
### Tests (1)
### 21 runs at 10.50
### 1 wicket at 24.00

9. Pollard, 1982, p559

A determined batsman with little style, but who scored over 3000 runs for South Australia, whom he captained on several occasions.

In his only Test against England in 1894–95 Reedman captured 1/24 and took one catch.

Reedman, an Adelaide postman, was also an accomplished Australian Rules footballer.

## 69. CONINGHAM, A. (Arthur) : 1863–1939.

Tests (1)
13 runs at 6.50
2 wickets at 38.00

An outstanding sportsman whose Test cricket career was thwarted by his off-field problems.

The Victorian born Conningham was the first player to score a century for his adopted state of Queensland, and in 1891–92 he also became the first Australian player to take a wicket with his first delivery in Test cricket.

Conningham toured England with the 1893 Australian team, but he was often mysteriously absent from the team. On one occasion in a match at Lords, he reportedly gathered twigs and branches and lit a fire to keep himself warm. He scored 249 runs at 13.10 and captured 31 wickets at 18.00 on the tour.

At various time in his life Conningham was a bookmaker, a tobacconist, a professional gambler and a book salesman. He was involved in a protracted and sensational divorce case, (where a loaded revolver was removed from him in court and furniture was broken in a scuffle). He died in a Sydney mental home in 1937.

On one occasion in a match at Lords he reportedly gathered twigs and branches and lit a fire to keep himself warm.

## 70. HARRY, J. (John) : 1857–1919.
Tests (1)
8 runs at 4.00

A valuable wicket keeper-batsman and ambidextrous bowler for Victoria, who was unlucky to miss two tours of England.

In 1890 Harry was the victim of the worst of all selection blunders when Burn, who had never kept wickets, replaced him. Then, when his second opportunity arose in 1896, Harry was forced to withdraw from the team with a knee injury.

## 71. TROTT, A.E. (Albert "Alberto") : 1873–1914.
Tests for Australia (3)
205 runs at 102.05
9 wickets at 21.33
Tests for England (2)
23 runs at 5.75
17 wickets at 11.64

An outstanding and colourful all-rounder who had match winning capabilities with both bat and ball.

After performing well against Stoddart's 1892–93 English team, he performed disappointingly in the following domestic season and he was not chosen for the 1896 tour of England. Trott did however join Middlesex in the same season, and he performed brilliantly with them in county cricket for the next 12 seasons.

In five Tests, three for Australia and two for England, Albert Trott took 15 wickets at 15 runs apiece. During his career he collected five wickets in an innings 132 times and ten wickets in a innings 41 times.

In 1914 a series of illnesses seriously depressed the 41 year old Trott. He shot himself in his London lodgings, leaving his wardrobe and approximately $10.00 in cash to his landlady.

## 72. MCKIBBIN, T.R. (Thomas) : 1870–1939.

Tests (5)
88 runs at 14.66
17 wickets at 29.17

A popular cricketer at the end of the 19th century, but also one whose bowling action was much discussed.

He moved from Bathurst to Sydney to further his cricket career, and in 1896 he toured England, America and New Zealand with the Australian team.

Shortly after that that tour McKibbin was labelled a "chucker', a slur which virtually ended his international career.

## 73. EADY, C. J. (Charles) : 1870–1945.

Tests (2)
20 runs at 6.66
7 wickets at 16.00

An impressive Tasmanian batsman who scored 566 in 473 minutes over four Saturdays in a 1902 Hobart club game, which arguably remains the highest club score anywhere in the world. Eady also headed the Tasmanian bowling averages on 12 occasions.

He toured England with the Australian team in 1896, but ill health resulted in him enduring a disappointing tour.

In his island state, Eady enjoyed a fine reputation in legal circles, and he served in state parliament for many years.

## 74. HILL, C. (Clem) : 1877–1945.
### Tests (49)
### 3,412 runs at 39.21

One of Australia's most distinguished batsmen in the years before Bradman and Ponsford. He was a quality left hander who scored 45 first class centuries, 13 of them in England on the four tours he made there between 1896 and 1905. The South Australian was also a man with very definite ideas, who declined two other opportunities to play in the "old country" because of financial and administrative quarrels with Australian cricket authorities.

Hill topped the South Australian batting averages at the age of 18 in the 1895–96 season, and a year later he was added as an after thought to the 1896 Australian team to tour England. In his seventh Test he scored 188, which was the highest score by a batsman under the age of 21.

He retired from the game prematurely, because of his employment in the horse racing industry. He was a handicapper with the Geelong Racing Club before he died after falling out of a Melbourne tram in a 1945 traffic accident. His body was taken back to his home city of Adelaide for burial.

## 75. KELLY, J.J. (James) : 1867–1938.
### Tests (36)
### 664 runs at 17.02
### dismissals 63 (43 caught, 20 stumped)

One of many distinguished Australian Test wicketkeepers, who only gained recognition once he transferred from Victoria to NSW.

Kelly's opportunities were blocked by the presence of Blackham in his home state, but, while he lacked the flair of his famous rival, Kelly matched up statistically with him by the end of his career.

He was adept at keeping up to the stumps, and will always command a place in Test records because of the eight catches he took in the 1901–02 Test against England at the SCG. Kelly is also well remembered for conceding no byes when England scored 551 at Sydney in 1897–98.

Kelly toured England on four occasions between 1896–1905, and top scored with eight runs when Australia was bundled out for 18 against the MCC at Lords in 1896. Badly damaged fingers, and a blow over the heart when he was batting at Old Trafford, forced Kelly's retirement from the game.

## 76. NOBLE, M.A. (Montague "Monty", "Mary Ann") : 1873–1940.

Tests (42)
1997 runs at 30.25
121 wickets at 25.00

A master cricketer, one of our great captains, and a player who strongly respected good sportsmanship.

Noble played much of his cricket with Paddington in Sydney, and when he retired from the game in 1924 he had scored more than 10,000 runs and taken over 600 wickets for the club at first grade level.

In first class cricket Noble scored 37 centuries, with 14 of them being recorded in

England where he toured four times between 1899–1909, and captained Australia on his final trip. Noble also toured South Africa in 1902–03, and New Zealand on two occasions. On damp wickets his medium pace swing bowling was devastating. He was also an accomplished batsman who played several match saving innings and scored a Test century.

Noble qualified in dentistry during his playing days, he wrote a number of well regarded cricket books, and he commentated in the early broadcasts of Tests from England. The M.A. Noble stand at the Sydney Cricket Ground is a lasting testimony to Monty Noble's distinguished career.

## 77. HOWELL, W.P. (William "Farmer Bill") : 1869–1940.

Tests (18)
158 runs at 7.52
49 wickets at 28.71

A Penrith bee keeper, whose cricket talent in the first class arena was unknown until he was 25 years of age, when he performed well for a country team in Sydney. Soon after Howell was chosen for NSW as a batsman against Stoddart's 1894 English team, but he gained more recognition as a bowler after he captured 5/44.

In 1897–98 he made his Test debut in Adelaide against England, and captured 4/70 in their first innings. On his first of three tours of England in 1899, he captured all ten Surrey wickets in the opening game, and his bowling performances there were consistently impressive. At his best there were few batsmen who countered Howell's clever flight and his ability to turn the ball both ways at a brisk pace.

### 78. LAVER, F.J. (Frank) : 1869–1919.
Tests (15)
196 runs at 11.52
37 wickets at 26.05

**Much respected by his Australian teammates, but became unpopular with the game's authorities.**

An ungainly right handed batsman and a highly skilled seam bowler on the soft pitches of England, who was much respected by his Australian teammates, but became unpopular with the game's authorities.

As a gangling 18 year old Laver joined the East Melbourne club where he and Peter McAlister became the backbone of the first X1, and later of Victorian cricket. Laver scored 104 against South Australian 1892–93, but he was not selected to tour England on either the 1893 or the 1896 tours. When Laver finally received the selectors' nod in 1899, he was a match winning bowler in the crucial Lords Test which Australia won by ten wickets.

Frank Laver's battle with the national selectors continued, despite his bowling success in England. He retained his place in the 1901–02 home Tests, missed out on the 1902 side which toured England, and regained his place again in the 1903–04 Australian team. Laver's close friendship with Peter McAlister ended when he was chosen ahead of him in the 1905 English touring team.

In 1909 Laver was the player-manager of the Australian touring team in England, and McAlister was chosen as vice-captain and team treasurer. Laver again bowled well on tour, but the 40 year old McAlister was a failure with the bat and a disaster as a treasurer as he had kept no financial records.

Before the 1913 English touring team was chosen, the Australian Board of Control (with Board member McAlister a key figure in the decision), appointed another manager, where-upon Hill, Trumper, Cotter, Ransford and Armstrong announced that they would not tour unless Laver was re-instated. This dispute caused a 20 minute fist fight between Hill and McAlister. However Laver was not re-instated as team manager, and at the end of that acri-monious 1912–13 summer he dropped out of international cricket.



## 79. TRUMPER, V.T. (Victor) : 1877–1915.
### Tests (48)
### 3,163 runs at 39.04
### 8 wickets at 37.62

Others have scored more runs, but the fans of Victor Trumper believe that he was the most brilliant of all Australian batsmen. Neville Cardus commented that when Trumper was out, the lights seemed to go out for a time in an Australian innings, and the English cricket historian, Harry Altham, described him in these glowing terms.



"The measure of Trumper's genius is not to be found in any figures: it was essentially qualitative rather than quantitative..There was no limit to the range (of his strokes), or flaw in their fluency or timing…; the better the bowl-ing, the more difficult the wicket, the more likely was his genius to rise to the challenge."

His NSW and Australian teammates also revered him, both for his exquisite batting skills and his noble character. Trumper was Arthur Mailey's special hero, and after he bowled him in a Sydney grade match he wrote "I felt like a boy who had killed a dove."[10]

At first the 18 year old Trumper failed to

10. Pollard, 1982, p1009

score runs with the NSW side after he debuted in the 1894–95 season. However, after some impressive late season performances he was added to the original Australian team which toured England in 1899. There, after a shaky start to the northern summer, the 21 year old champion scored a brilliant 135 not out in the Second Test at Lords.

After achieving this milestone, Trumper then amassed 300 against Sussex, which was the first triple century scored by an Australian in England. He finished his first tour in 'the mother country' with an aggregate of 1556 runs. Then after a lean patch of form back in Australia, Trumper's form blossomed again when he toured England again in 1902. He scored 11 centuries in a very wet English summer, including another Test 100, and totalled 2750 runs for the tour at an average of 48.49. Trumper also toured England in 1905 and 1909, but not with the same success as his golden summer of 1902.

By then the unassuming Sydneysider was a national hero, a man who was renowned for his generous spirit as well as his exceptional cricket ability. In 1913 he was awarded a Testimonial match at the SCG, and he featured in Guy Eden's "Bush Ballads and Other Verse".

Trumper was in poor health when he toured New Zealand in 1914, and a year later the popular legend of the game endured much pain from Blight's disease before he died at the age of 37.

## 80. ARMSTRONG, W.W. (Warwick "The Big Ship") : 1879–1947.

Tests (50)
2,863 runs at 38.68
87 wickets at 33.59

A huge, irascible and talented all-rounder, who was much admired by fellow cricketers and the public, but despised by many cricket officials with whom he clashed often.

Armstrong, from the Victorian town of Kyneton, captained Australia in ten occasions for ten victories, and he led the 1921 Australian touring team which won all of the first three Ashes Tests within three days. The star studded group, which only lost two of its 39 tour fixtures during that English summer, has been compared in quality to Bradman's famous "Invincibles" team.

Armstrong visited England on four occasions between1902–1921, and he was one of the rebels who refused to tour in 1912 under the Board of Control's terms. His most successful trip was in 1905, when he scored 2002 runs and captured 130 wickets. In total he scored six centuries for Australia, and he also obtained valuable wickets with his accurate leg breaks and top spinners.

An English writer dubbed him a "monolithic obelisk", and Armstrong's fondness for whisky was partly responsible for him ballooning to 22 stone before he retired from the game at the age of 42. He became an agent for a whisky distillery, and was a wealthy man when he died in Sydney at the age of 68.

### 81. DUFF, R.A. (Reginald) : 1878–1911.

Tests (22)
1,377 runs at 35.59
4 wickets at 21.25

Victor Trumper's opening partner, and at times his performances matched his famous fellow Sydneysider. Duff joined an elite group after he scored a century in his first Test match at the MCG in 1901–02, when he scored 104 batting at number ten.

Duff's innings of 146 against England at The Oval in 1905 is still rated as one of the best centuries in Test match history. He also toured England in 1902, and amassed over 1000 runs on both tours.

The SCG was Duff's favourite ground, with only one of his Sheffield Shield centuries being scored away from his spiritual home. Reggie Duff retired in 1908 after scoring ten centuries in his career of 121 first class matches.

## 82. HOPKINS, H.J.Y (Albert "Bert") : 1876–1931.
Tests (20)
509 runs at 16.42
26 wickets at 26.76

A fine all-rounder who remains relatively unrecognised because of the depth of player talent that prevailed during "cricket's golden years."

"Bert" Hopkins debuted for NSW at the age of 20, and he made five overseas trips with Australian teams and appeared in two Test series at home. He toured England with reasonable success in 1902 and 1905, but his last tour in 1909 was disappointing.

The big hitter and useful swing bowler continued to play Shield cricket in Australia until 1915, when he retired from first class cricket.

## 83. SAUNDERS, J. V (John) : 1876–1927.

Tests (14)
39 runs at 2.29
79 wickets at 22.73

A tall Victorian bowler who was the best left arm spinner of his time, especially on sticky wickets.

In his first international match Saunders captured the match figures of 11/130 in the Fourth Test match of the 1901–02 series against England. His good form continued in England in 1902 when he captured 127 wickets at 17.07 for the tour. In 14 Tests he six times took five wickets or more in an innings, with his best effort being 7/34 against South Africa at Johannesburg.

At the end of the 1909–10 Australian season, Saunders settled on the North Island of New Zealand where he played for Wellington and the national team until 1914.

## 84. TRAVERS, J.P.F. (Joseph) : 1871–1942.

Tests (1)
10 runs at 5.00
1 wicket at 14.00

A South Australian slow left-arm bowler who captured more wickets than any other state bowler in three seasons between 1900 and 1906, even though Ernie Jones and George Giffen were two of his bowling teammates. He was also a useful late order batsman.

Travers represented Australia against England in the Fifth Test match of the 1901–02 season, but was given limited opportunities and had little impact.

## 85. COTTER, A. (Albert "Tibby") : 1883–1917.

Tests (21)
457 runs at 13.05
89 wickets at 28.64

**Six long stops were required to stop his thunderbolt deliveries in Sydney school playground matches.**

The strongly built Cotter was the Jeff Thomson of his era, spraying his deliveries frequently but bowling with enormous pace. "Tibby" Cotter was a menacing performer from his earliest years, and six long stops were required to stop his thunderbolt deliveries in Sydney school playground matches.

The NSW fast bowler toured England in 1905 and 1909, and captured 121 wickets at 20.19 on his first visit. His best Test performance came in the 1903–04 season when he captured 8/65 in the Fifth Test in Melbourne.

Cotter was on of six players who withdrew over a pay dispute from the 1912 team which toured England. He later died at the age of 24 in World War I action near Beersheba.

## 86. McAlister, P.A. (Peter) : 1869–1938.

Tests (8)
252 runs at 16.80

A Victorian opening batsman who scored prolifically at state level, but was a poor performer in his eight Test appearances.

Though seemingly mild mannered, McAlister became the centre of dispute between the Board of Control and Frank Laver, the manager of the 1909 Australian team. Then in the 1911–12 season McAlister was involved in a fist fight with fellow selector Clem Hill.

His highest Test score was 41, and when he toured England in 1909 as vice-captain and treasurer, he was criticised in both roles. He retired from first class cricket in 1910, and his contributions as a selector and administrator were more impressive legacies to the game than his achievements as a player.

## 87. GEHRS, D.R.A. (Donald "Algie") : 1880–1953.
### Tests (6)
### 221 runs at 20.09

A dashing batsman who scored 13 stylish centuries for South Australia between 1902 and 1921, but failed to reproduce that form in the Test match arena.

Gehrs scored a modest 612 runs at 20.10 on his only tour of England in 1905.

## 88. CARTER, H. (Hanson "Sammy") : 1878–1948.
### Tests (28)
### 873 runs at 22.97
### dismissals 65 (44 catches, 21 stumpings)

One of Australia's most successful wicket-keepers, who was born in the English town of Halifax. When Australia played at Headingley in 1921 Carter was the only Yorkshireman on the ground, even though he was playing in the Australian side.

Carter was raised in Sydney and took some remarkable catches standing up to the wicket in his open-slatted pads. He was also a useful batsman, who toured England in 1902, 1909 and 1921. Carter would probably have also gained selection in 1912 had he not joined the other player rebels in their stand against the Board of Control.

The small, lean gloveman was an under-

**The small, lean gloveman was an undertaker by trade, which often resulted in him travelling from the cemetery to the cricket in a hearse.**

taker by trade, which often resulted in him travelling from the cemetery to the cricket in a hearse. Carter played first class cricket for 27 years, and came out of retirement at the age of 54 to join Arthur Mailey's 1932 team which toured America and Canada.

## 89. HAZLITT, G. R. (Gervys "Gerry") : 1888–1915.

Tests (9)
89 runs at 11.12
23 wickets at 27.08

An almost forgotten potential star of the game, who died prematurely at the age of 27 from a heart attack.

Hazlitt debuted for Victoria as a 17 year old schoolboy, and he became a Test player two years later. He was a talented batsman, but it was his ability to bowl medium pace cutters and off breaks that was his main forte.

Hazlitt was one of the few successes in the Australian team which toured England in 1912, capturing 7/25 in the Third Test at Lords. Overall he captured an impressive 101 wickets at 18.96 in that English summer.

When his heart failed him four months after Trumper's death, Hazlitt was a master at King's school in the Sydney suburb of Parramatta.

## 90. MACARTNEY, C.G. (Charles "The Governor General") : 1886–1958.

Tests (35)
2,131 runs at 41.78
45 wickets at 27.55

A self-taught and gifted all-rounder,

whose batting capabilities flourished in his later years in the game. In fact when Macartney first toured England in 1909 his impressive left arm spinners gained him third spot in the Australian averages, but he batted number 11 in most matches.

However by the end of World War I Macartney's batting overshadowed his bowling, and his aggressive performances at the top of the order yielded him seven Test centuries and nine scores in excess of 50. Some of his performances, including the century before lunch in the 1926 Leeds Test, are rated as being among the best innings ever played.

"Length could not curb him," wrote the great English cricket writer R.C. Robertson-Glasgow, "and his defence was lost and included in his attack. No Australian batsman, not even Bradman, has approached him for insolence of attack. He made slaves of bowlers."[11]

The Maitland born Macartney was dubbed "the Governor General" because of his imperious manner at the crease. He toured England four times, and he also played in South Africa, New Zealand, North America and India during his long career in big cricket.

After retiring from the first class scene, Charlie Macartney continued to plunder huge totals with the Sydney club Gordon. He scored 7638 runs at 48.34 and captured 547 wickets in his 29 year association with the Gordon club.

**No Australian batsman, not even Bradman, has approached him for insolence of attack. He made slaves of bowlers.**

## 91. RANSFORD, V.S. (Vernon) :
## 1885–1958.
### Tests (20)
### 1,211 runs at 37.84
### 1 wicket at 28.00

11. Pollard, 1982, p650

A capable left handed batsman and a brilliant fieldsman, whose blossoming international career came to an abrupt halt after he and other influential players confronted the Board of Control over management issues relating to the 1912 tour of England.

Ransford was at his peak during the 1909 English tour when he scored 1783 runs in one of the wettest northern summers on record. This aggregate included a patient 143 not out at Lords, which was his sole Test century. Between 1907 and 1912 Ransford scored over 50 on seven other occasions, and he also amassed 13 centuries for Victoria during his 20 year career in state cricket.

In his retirement Ransford became secretary of the Melbourne Cricket Club in 1938, and he held this position with distinction until he stood down from the post in 1957.

## 92. HARTIGAN, R.J. (Roger) : 1879–1958.

Tests (2)
170 runs at 42.50

Hartigan became the fourth Australian to score a century on debut in Test cricket, but his late order innings of 116 in 1907–08 against England, failed to gain him regular national selection. In cricket's golden era the competition for team spots from the greats of the game proved to be too big a hurdle. Hartigan managed to score 603 runs from limited opportunities on the 1909 tour of England, but failed to make a Test appearance.

His cause was not helped by playing for his adopted state of Queensland, which was not highly rated during the former Sydneysider's state career. Hartigan pressed hard for Queensland to be awarded a Test match venue during his 35 years on the Board of Control, and his perseverance was  finally rewarded in 1928, when Brisbane was awarded a spot in the Test  fixtures calendar.

### 93. O'CONNOR, J.D.A. (John) : 1875–1941.
#### Tests (4)
#### 86 runs at 12.28
#### 13 wickets at 26.15

A tall fast medium bowler who collected the fine match figures of 8/150 on debut against England in 1907–08, but failed to win national selection on a regular basis.

O'Connor played for his native state of NSW until he was 29, but he enjoyed more cricket success when he moved with his family to South Australia. There he headed the state bowling averages in consecutive seasons between1907–09, and he toured England with modest success with the 1909 Australian team.

### 94. BARDSLEY, W. (Warren) : 1882–1954.
#### Tests (41)
#### 2,469 runs at 40.47

A distinguished left handed batsman who was unrivalled in his ability to combat spin bowling on turning pitches. By the end of his marathon stay of 24 years in first class cricket, Bardsley was considered to be more masterful on English wickets than at home, an opinion that was strongly supported by statistics.

Bardsley scored more than 2,000 runs on three of his four English tours between 1909–1926. In 1909 he became the first batsman to score a century in each innings of a

Test match. At the age of 43 he amassed an undefeated 193, when he batted at Lords for over six hours against an English Test attack that included quality new ball bowlers such as Tate and Larwood.

Neat footwork and a copybook defence were the hallmarks of Bardsley's batting, and his technique only failed him in the 1911–12 home season, when England pace bowlers S.F. Barnes and Frank Foster dominated the Test series. Bardsley was dropped for the Fifth Test, but countless hours of practice remedied his problems, and he scored prolifically again when he revisited England in1912.

In his impressive long first career Bardsley was never called upon to bowl, but he scored 53 centuries, with six of them being achieved at Test match level. He also served as a club and NSW selector. Bardsley was a clerk for most of his working years, and he died at the age of 69 after being married to Gertrude Cope for only seven years.

## 95: WHITTY, W.J. (William) : 1886–1974.
Tests (14)
161 runs at 13.41
65 wickets at 21.12

A left arm opening bowler from NSW who matured into a fine bowler after he moved to South Australia. Whitty was able to swing the new ball appreciatively, and later bowl useful left arm orthodox deliveries when the shine was off the ball.

Bill Whitty toured England with success in 1909 and 1912, but World War I drew a curtain on his Test career. After hostilities ceased he continued to play both in Adelaide the Mt

Gambier area where he relocated in 1938.

## 96. KELLEWAY, C. (Charles) : 1899–1944.

Tests (26)
1,422 runs at 37.42
52 wickets at 32.36

A reliable all-rounder who was capable of bowling long accurate spells with his medium pace deliveries, and he was more famously one of the noted stonewallers of all time. "One Kelleway in a side is enough. Two or three would be intolerable," commented "Wisden" in 1913.[12]

The Lismore born Kelleway first appeared for NSW at the age of 18, and debuted for Australia against South Africa in 1910–11. Though he succumbed often, like many other Australians, to the brilliant bowling of Barnes and Foster a season later, he was still selected for the 1912 triangular tournament in England. He performed well, being second to Bardsley in the batting averages.

After serving as an Army captain in World War I Kelleway briefly led the AIF team in England, before he returned home after being replaced by Collins. A year later he scored his only Test century against England when he occupied the crease for nearly seven hours to score 147 at the Adelaide Oval.

Kelleway was unavailable through business reasons to tour England in 1921, and he was overlooked for the 1926 tour. He did, however, represent Australia both in the 1924–25 season and the First Test of the 1928–29 season, but that was his final international appearance.

12. Pollard, 1982, p563

## 97. HORDEN, Dr. H.G. (Herbert "Ranji") : 1884–1938.
Tests (7)
254 runs at 23.09
46 wickets at 23.36

Considered by English players C.B Fry and Pelman Warner to be the best googly bowler they ever encountered, after Horden's superb season in the 1911–12 series. Horden captured 32 Test wickets against the dominant English team, and he dismissed five batsmen in an innings on four occasions.

Horden was a dentist, and his profession curtailed his international career. He was unavailable for selection on the 1912 tour of England, and never toured overseas in an Australian team.

Although he played only 33 first class matches, the genial Horden was ranked by some experts to be a superior spin bowler to either Mailey or Grimmett. "I'm inclined to place Horden ahead of the others," wrote the famous commentator Johnny Moyes.[13]

## 98. MINNETT, R.B. (Roy) : 1888–1955.

Roy Minnett, along with his two brothers, Leslie and Rupert, all represented NSW, but Roy was the only family member who also played for Australia.

Roy Minnett, a right hand batsman and fast-medium bowler, scored a fine 90 in his 1911–12 Test debut, and he also performed well in the triangular series in England during that northern summer.

13. Pollard, 1982, p503

## 99. MATTHEWS, T.J. (Thomas) :
## 1884–1943.
### Tests (80)
### 153 runs at 17.00
### 16 wickets at 26.18

A tiny leg spin bowler and stubborn batsman who was mostly a fringe Test player. However Matthews achieved international glory when he captured a hat trick in both innings of the First Test of the triangular tournament against South Africa in1912.

Matthews scored 53 in his Test debut against England during the previous Australian summer, but he only gained selection in the 1912 touring team when leading players became unavailable because of squabbles with the Board of Control.

After his historic achievement Matthews continued to bowl well in England on hard pitches, but was less hostile on rain affected surfaces. He gained a total of four hat tricks during his first class career, which ended with the advent of World War I.

After peace was declared, Matthews resumed his duties as a curator in the Melbourne suburb of Williamstown, where he first began his cricket career.

## 100. McLAREN, J.W. (John) :
## 1887–1921.
### Tests (1)
### 0 runs
### 1 wicket at 70.00

McLaren became the first native born Queenslander to play Test cricket, when he played his first and only Test against England at Sydney in 1912. He toured England with the 1912 Australian team, but failed to gain Test selection.

## 101. CARKEEK, W. (William) : 1878–1937.
Tests (6)
16 runs at 5.33
dismissals 6 catches

A blacksmith from the Victorian gold mining town of Walhalla, who was a competent wicketkeeper, but fell well short of the class of Blackham, Jarvis, Kelly and Carter who preceded him in Australian Test teams.

Carkeek toured England in 1909 and 1912, and he would also have toured South Africa in 1914–15, if war had not temporarily ended international cricket.

## 102. EMERY, S.H. (Sidney) : 1886–1967.
Tests (4)
6 runs at 4.00
5 wickets at 49.80

A right arm spin bowler who was unplayable at times, but found it difficult to maintain accuracy. Monty Noble told him that he would be a great bowler if he could learn to control his googly. Emery, dubbed "Mad Mick" by a teammate, prophetically replied," I'd be a great man if I learnt to control myself."[14]

Sid Emery played in two Tests against South Africa and two against England. The strongly built NSW bowler toured England and North America in the 1912 Australian team.

14. Pollard, 1982, p34

**"I'd be a great man if I learnt to control myself."**

## 103. JENNINGS, C. B.(Claude) :
## 1884–1950.
### Tests (6)
### 107 runs at 17.83

Jennings, a tidy opening batsman for South Australia, Queensland and Australia, appeared in all six Tests on the 1912 tour of England, but proved to be short of international standard.

Claude Jennings scored one century in his ten year first class career. He became a prominent Adelaide businessman and South Australia's representative on the Australian Board of Control after he retired.

## 104. SMITH, D. B. M. (David) :
## 1884–1963.
### Tests (2)
### 30 runs at 15.00

A fast scoring Victorian batsman, who toured England in 1912 as a replacement player when six others withdrew from the original team.

Smith scored a modest 316 runs at 13.73 in England, and a leg injury prematurely forced his retirement from the first class scene after the tour ended.

## 105. MAYNE, E.R. (Edgar "Ernie") :
## 1884–1961.
### Tests (4)
### 64 runs at 21.33.

A sound opening batsman who scored 14 centuries for South Australia and Victoria, but had the misfortune to be in his prime when the Australian batting line-up was extremely strong.

Mayne played in all four Tests in England in 1912, but he enjoyed little success when he toured England in 1921 with Armstrong's Australian team.

His major triumph was to score 209 in his 40th year for Victoria against Queensland at the MCG in 1923–24. Mayne captained both South Australia and Victoria during his long career, and he helped provide one of the first radio commentaries of Test cricket.

# ARMSTRONG'S ASCENDANCY

Australia suffered heavy casualties in the 1914–18 Great War, with nearly 60,000 young men and women being killed, while over 150,000 were injured on the battlefields of Europe.

As many serving cricketers were close to England when hostilities ceased, it was decided to organise a series of matches for the 1919 northern summer. The First AIF team consisted of 15 players, with only Collins and Kelleway being established first class players at that stage.

However the tour was a huge success. The matches attracted large crowds, and the AIF team won 15 matches, drew 15, and only suffered losses in four fixtures.

All-rounder Jack Gregory showed that he would be a future Australian star, and the general public in both England and Australia were hungry for more Ashes clashes once peace was restored.

Warwick Armstrong was the dominant figure in Australian cricket in this era. Australia gained a clean sweep in 1920–21 winning 5:0. Then in England during the northern summer of 1921 Armstrong's Australians were again undefeated in the four-Test series, and the star-studded team only lost two of their 38 tour matches.

# PLAYERS OF THE ERA

## 106. COLLINS, H.L. (Herbert "Horseshoe", "Squirrel") : 1889–1959.
Tests (19)
1,352 runs at 45.06
4 wickets at 63.00

An enigma of a man who was a compulsive gambler off the field, but one of Australia's most methodical and astute on-field captains in the history of Test cricket. Collins captained the 1919 AIF team before he went on to lead Australia to 11 wins and only two defeats in Test match contests.

Collins was an opening batsman of unlimited patience who scored 32 first class centuries. His most noteworthy batting performance came in the Fourth Test of the 1921 series at Manchester, when his patient innings of 40 in 289 minutes salvaged a draw for Australia. Between 1913 and 1926 Collins toured New Zealand, North America, South Africa and England in 1921 and 1926. His highest Test score was 203 against South Africa, and in total he notched four Test centuries after making his debut at the age of 32.

Collins became a licensed bookmaker in retirement, and his addiction to late night card games continued until he died at the age of 70 in his home city of Sydney.

## 107. GREGORY, J.M. (John "Jack") : 1856–1933.
Tests (24)
1,146 runs at 36.96
85 wickets at 31.15

Jack Gregory was one of Australia's greatest all-rounders, and, along with Keith Miller, probably the most eye-catching. His bowling was very quick, and he used his formidable height to gain sharp lift from the wicket. His adventurous batting once gained him a Test century in 70 minutes against South Africa, and he was a brilliant slips fieldsman.

Gregory was arguably the finest of a fine cricket family dynasty. His father Charles played for NSW, his uncle Dave was Australia's first Test captain, and his cousin Syd played 58 Tests for Australia.

Jack Gregory made a spectacular first class debut with the 1919 AIF team in England, becoming the first Australian to take over 100 first class wickets in his first season. His all-round ability was even more obvious when he faced the Englishmen at home in 1920–21. In the Test series Gregory scored a century, he was third in both the batting and bowling averages, and he also took 15 catches in Australia's winning Ashes team.

Along with Tasmanian speedster Ted McDonald, he formed a fearsome fast bowling duo when Australia convincingly retained the Ashes on the 1921 tour of England. The host team tried 30 players in that series, but most failed to cope with the pace and fire of Gregory and McDonald.

By the 1924–25 Australian season, however, Gregory's blistering pace began to diminish, and when he returned to England in 1926 he was a spent force taking only 36 wickets on the tour. His career ended sadly when knee ligament problems forced the 32 year old ailing legend out of the game in the Fifth Test against England of the 1928–29 season.

During his impressive first class career, Jack Gregory scored 13 centuries, accepted 195 catches and took five wickets in an innings on 33 occasions. His retirement years were spent quietly in Bega on the NSW south coast.

## 108. MAILEY, A.A. (Arthur) : 1886–1967.
Tests (21)
222 runs at 11.10
99 wickets at 33.91

A sometimes brilliant spin bowler with an impish sense of humour who bowled his leg breaks and googlies in Moose Jaw, Canada, in Piccadilly Circus after midnight immaculately clad in a dinner jacket, and on the SCG in his Testimonial match wearing an overcoat.

He grew up in humble circumstances in Sydney's Botany Bay area, and his boyhood hero was Victor Trumper. A picture of the great batsman was pinned to the hessian curtain in his bedroom, and when the wind billowed the curtain towards his bed, the boy imagined that Trumper was advancing down the wicket to his bowling.

Some years later Mailey opposed Trumper in a Sydney club match, and he bowled his hero when he missed the ball after advancing down the wicket to drive. His triumph was a complete anti-climax to the remorseful Mailey. "I felt like a small boy who had killed a dove," he later lamented.

**"I felt like a small boy who had killed a dove," he later lamented.**

Mailey was 32 after he returned from World War I service, and three years later when he began his Test career, he was regarded as the best googly bowler in international cricket. Against Johnny Douglas' 1920–21 English team he established an Australian record which lasted for 58 years when he snared 36 wickets in the Four Test series, including a bag of 9/121 at Melbourne in the final Test of the summer.

He toured England in 1921 and 1926, collecting 146 wickets on his first trip at 19.78, and 141 wickets at 18.70 on his second tour. Mailey made his 10/66 in 1921 against Gloucestershire even more memorable, because it became the inspiration for his whimsical cricket book entitled "Ten for 66 — and All That". His favourite match, however, was the 1926 Sheffield Shield match at Melbourne when Victoria scored a world record 1,107 runs and Mailey returned the figures of 4/362.

"A chap in the crowd kept dropping his catches," explained an ever cheerful Mailey, "(and) I was just finding a length when the innings finished."

Mailey retired from first class cricket after the 1926 English tour when the Board of Control objected to him writing and commentating on the game while he was still a player. He continued working as a journalist and cartoonist for many years, and he also derived great pleasure from organising fun-filled trips to cricket outposts of the world.

## 109. OLDFIELD, W.A. ( William "Bert", "Cracker") : 1894 –1976.

Tests (54)
1,427 runs at 22.65
dismissals 130 (78 catches, 52 stumpings)

One of Australia's great wicket-keepers who stood behind the stumps for Australia for 17 years. The stylish and reliable Oldfield toured England four times between 1921 and 1934, and he also participated in two Test tours to South Africa.

After playing only two matches of Sydney grade cricket with Glebe, Oldfield enlisted in the Field Ambulance Corps for World War I duties, and he was lucky to survive a 1917 bombing attack in France.

After the war ended, Oldfield was in London when he was unexpectedly drafted into the 1919 AIF team because the first choice keeper, Ted Long, was sidelined with a facial injury. Oldfield protested that he was promoted out of his depth, but after he gave a flawless exhibition of glove work in his first AIF game, Long informed his captain Collins that he now expected to become the new reserve keeper.

England's Les Ames was the only contemporary keeper who approached Oldfield in class, and after the completion of the 1926 tour of England Australia's captain, Herb Collins, commented that he could not recall Oldfield making a mistake behind the stumps. The champion gloveman was also a handy batsman who passed half-century totals in Tests on four occasions.

In the infamous 1932–33 Bodyline series a short delivery from Harold Larwood during the Third Test deflected from Oldfield's bat onto his temple. Oldfield always insisted that it was not Larwood's fault, but this did not placate the angry Adelaide crowd who had witnessed Bill Woodfull's terrible blow above the heart from another short ball the day before. After Larwood relocated to Australia with his family in 1950, he resumed his strong friendship with Oldfield.

Oldfield was a religious man who was scrupulously fair in his on-field performances. In later years he managed several Australian schoolboy teams on overseas tours. After he died in 1976 Harold Larwood was one of the pall bearers at Bert Oldfield's funeral.

**After he died in 1976 Harold Larwood was one of the pall bearers at Bert Oldfield's funeral.**

## 110. PELLEW, C.E. (Clarence "Nip") :
## 1893–1981.
Tests (10)
484 runs at 37.23

"Nip" Pellew was one of four brothers to represent South Australia, but he was the only member of the family who played for Australia.

Pellew was an attacking batsman and a superb fieldsman who first attracted internationala when he played with the 1919 AIF team in England. He scored four centuries on tour, and on his return home he scored a chanceless 271 for South Australia, which was his only century in state cricket.

Pellew debuted at international level against England in 1920–21, and in his second Test at Melbourne he scored 116, which was the first of two Test hundreds. He then toured England in 1921, but retired to life on the farm two year later.

His life away from the game was short lived, as he returned to state ranks five years later and between1930–39 he served his first term as South Australia's coach. Nineteen years later Pellew returned to that post for a further 12 years until he stood down at the age of 77. The durable veteran had previously participated in club games until he was 63, and when he passed away in 1981 at the age of 87, he was briefly Australia's oldest Test cricketer.

## 111. RYDER, J. (John "Jack") :
## 1889–1977.
Tests (20)
1,394 runs at 51.62
17 wickets at 43.70

A hard hitting batsman and competent medium pace bowler, who found it difficult to gain a permanent spot in national teams because of the abundance of great players of his time.

Ryder scored three centuries for Victoria before the start of World War I, and after peace was declared he made his Test debut against England in the 1920–21 season. Although he finished fourth in the batting averages during the following English northern summer, Ryder failed to gain selection for any of the 1921 Tests. He did, however, score 142 against South Africa on the return trip to Australia.

He returned to the Australian team for the Third Test of the 1924–25 series against England, and scored a determined 201. Ryder later toured England with little success in 1926, and he became a surprise choice as captain of Australia after Collins retired. He performed well with the bat during his captaincy stint, but his leadership record was an unflattering four losses from five Tests.

Soon afterwards Ryder became a selector, and there was much angst in his home suburb of Collingwood and elsewhere when his fellow selectors dropped the 43 year old Ryder from the 1930 team which toured England. Five years later he retired as a player after scoring three centuries and nine 50s in his 20 Test matches.

Incredibly Jack Ryder was 84 before he retired from his national selection duties, and shortly before he died "the king of Collingwood" led the parade of old Australian Test cricketers at Melbourne's Centenary Test in March, 1977.

**Shortly before he died "the king of Collingwood" led the parade of old Australian Test cricketers at Melbourne's Centenary Test in March, 1977.**

## 112.TAYLOR, J.M. (John) :
## 1895–1971.
Tests (20)
997 runs at 35.60
1 wicket at 45.00

A dashing batsman who was plucked out of schoolboy cricket to represent NSW, but enlisted as a gunner in World War I soon after.

Following some brilliant performances with the 1919 AIF team in England, Taylor gained Test selection for the home series in 1920–21, and he later toured England both in 1921 and 1926. The 1925–26 series at home was Taylor's most successful season. He was Australia's leading run scorer, and scored 108 (his only Test century) in the Sydney fixture.

John Taylor retired from first class cricket in 1927 to concentrate on his dentistry career.

## 113. PARK, Dr. R.L. (Roy) :
## 1892–1947.
Tests (1)
0 runs

An outstanding batsman with a sure defence who scored nine centuries for Victoria just before and soon after World War I.

The Great War and medical studies, drastically curtailed Park's cricket career, and in his only Test in the 1920–21 series against England, he was bowled first ball.

Park was also an excellent Australian rules footballer with the Footscray club.

**In his only Test in the 1920–21 series against England, he was bowled first ball.**

## 114. McDONALD, E.A. (Edgar "Ted") : 1891–1937.

Tests (11)
116 runs at 16.57
43 wickets at 33.27

Ted McDonald only appeared in 11 Test matches, but he made a huge impact in his short international career. He is rated by some as one of the best fast bowlers of all time. The respected English critic Ian Peebles recalls that the superbly built Tasmanian was a grand sight when he cruised athletically to the crease from his 15 pace run up and released his thunderbolt deliveries.[15]

After representing his island state at the age of 17, McDonald moved to Victoria, and he gained selection in the final three Tests of the 1920–21 series. He was then chosen in the 1921 team to tour England, where Ted he and Jack Gregory formed a fast bowling combination which was as famous then as the future duos of Lindwall and Miller, and Lillee and Thomson. In the five Test series of 1921 McDonald captured 27 wickets at 29.74, while Gregory collected 19 wickets at 29.05.

In 1922 McDonald moved into English League ranks before signing with Lancashire two seasons later. He performed superbly capturing 1,053 county cricket wickets in the seven seasons between 1924–1931. Overall Ted McDonald captured 10 wickets in an innings 31 times, and five wickets in an innings on 119 occasions.

The great fast bowler died tragically in a road accident in Bolton, England in 1937.

15. Pollard, 1982, p662

## 115. ANDREWS, T.J.E. (Thomas "Tommy") : 1890–1970.
### Tests (16)
### 592 runs at 26.90
### 1 wicket for 116 runs

A dashing batsman who scored 90s at Test level but never reached the coveted century. He was revered for his superb fielding, and often anchored fleet-footed batsmen to the crease with his famous throwing arm.

Tommy Andrews played first class cricket from 1913 to 1931, he toured England in 1921 and 1926, and he scored 12 centuries and two double centuries during his career.

Andrews was a stonemason by trade, and he made the headstones for Archie Jackson and Victor Trumper for their final resting places in Sydney.

## 116. HENDRY, H.S.T.L. (Hunter "Stork") : 1895–1988.
### Tests (11)
### 335 runs at 20.93
### 16 wickets at 40.00

A long-legged all-rounder who represented NSW, Victoria and Australia during his 17 years in first class cricket.

Hendry toured England in 1921 and 1926, and in the Second Test of the 1928–29 series (when Bradman was 12th man), "Stork" Hendry scored 112 against England.

He retired from the game after amassing 10 centuries for Victoria, three for NSW and one for Australia. Hendry was always a strong advocate for fair play, and a forthright opponent of World Series Cricket (WSC).

### 117. PONSFORD, W.H. (William "Bill", "Pudding") : 1900–1991.
Tests (29)
2,122 runs at 48.22

**"He was the only one who could play in Bradman's company and make it a duet."**

A shy and taciturn man, who was the most prolific run scorer of all time until Bradman burst onto the scene.

Ponsford was the first batsman to score 400 in a first class match outside England, and the first to score six centuries in an Australian season. He went on to register another score in excess of 400, he scored 110 in his Test debut, and he scored 110 again in his first Test match at Lords. His precise footwork made him an even better player of spin bowling than Bradman. The noted English cricket writer R.C. Robertson-Glascow summed up Ponsford's prowess succinctly when he said, "He was the only one who could play in Bradman's company and make it a duet." [16]

He was born eight years before Bradman, and he gained a permanent spot in Victoria's team after scoring 429 against Tasmania in 1923. Ponsford toured England in 1926, 1930 and 1934, and on those three tours he totalled an amazing 4,273 runs at an average of 55.49. His overall total of centuries in first class cricket was 47, with seven of them being recorded in Test matches.

Ponsford retired from the game at the age of 34, (after averaging an impressive 94.83 against England in the 1934 Test series), to become a journalist and the Assistant Secretary of the MCG, where a grandstand was named in his honour.

16. Pollard, 1982, p804

## 118. RICHARDSON, A.J. (Arthur) :
## 1888–1973.
Tests (9)
403 runs at 31.00
12 wickets at 43.41

A fine South Australian all-rounder who was not related to his famous namesake, Victor Richardson.

Arthur Richardson scored 11 centuries for South Australia during eight years of state cricket, and he also enjoyed success in two seasons of Test cricket. He was noted for his fierce driving, but could also play a cautious innings when required

At the age of 37 years and 351 days Richardson became the oldest player to score a Test century on debut when he made 100 at Leeds in 1926. His sound batting and handy off-spinners proved successful with Bacup in Lancashire League ranks. Richardson also coached and umpired with success in the West Indies during the 1930s.

## 119. RICHARDSON, V.Y. (Victor) :
## 1894–1969.
Tests (19)
706 runs at 23.53

A handsome larger than life character who excelled in many sports and proved to be an inspirational captain. Victor Richardson scored 27 centuries in first class cricket and he represented Australia in baseball and South Australia in golf and tennis. He also starred as a centre-man in three Sturt premiership teams in Australian Football, and tied for the prestigious Magarey Medal in 1920.

Victor Richardson scored 138 in his second Test match against England in 1924–25. As a batsman he was a at his best when forcing the pace with fierce driving and hooking, and soon after he clouted Harold Larwood into the pavilion of the Adelaide Oval to register a century with a six, the "Victor York Richardson Gates" at the Adelaide Oval came into being. Richardson also had no equal as a fieldsman, and once held five catches in a Test innings.

Richardson captained South Australia from 1921 until Bradman took over the reins in 1935, and he was vice-captain of the Australian team which toured England in 1930. When Bradman was unavailable because of ill health, Richardson became a highly successful skipper of the Australian team which toured South Africa in 1935–36. He is credited with introducing the leg-trap as a field placement tactic, which made Bill "Tiger" O'Reilly an even more formidable bowler.

After one of his daughters married Martin Chappell, Victor Richardson later became the grandfather of Ian, Greg and Trevor Chappell. In retirement Richardson became an internationally known broadcaster, especially when he co-commentated with the former English captain Arthur Gilligan.

## 120. HARTKOPF, Dr.A.E.V. (Albert) : 1889–1968.

Tests (1)
80 runs at 40.00
1 wicket at 134.00

A hard hitting batsman and a handy leg spin bowler who scored 80 in his only Test match appearance against England in 1924–25.

Hartkopf, who became a medical practitioner, scored two centuries and captured five wickets or better in an innings on seven occasions for Victoria.

### 121. GRIMMETT, C.V. (Clarrie "Scarlet") : 1891–1980.
Tests (37)
557 runs at 13.92
216 wickets at 24.21

A leg spinner of great skill who had no peer in his craft, until the advent of Shane Warne.

The New Zealand born Grimmett served a long apprenticeship in club and state cricket before he gained national selection in 1924–25 at the age of 34. Prior to then he had played Sydney grade cricket after emigrating from Wellington. He briefly gained selection with Victoria, before he decided that a career with South Australia was his best passport to international ranks.

After returning the impressive match figures of 11/82 in his first Test match against England, Grimmett gained selection for the 1926 English tour where he took 27 of the 41 opposition wickets that fell in the series. The gnome like figure, who wore a cap when he bowled to protect his premature baldness from the sun, continued to plague English batsmen both at home at abroad when he toured England again in 1930 and 1934.

Grimmett constantly experimented with subtle changes to his deliveries. However, he never revealed his new variations in matches until he had perfected them at practice sessions with his fox terrier dog, which was trained to retrieve balls that he bowled on his backyard pitch. Even when he was in his 80s, Grimmett still participated in home practice sessions

After enjoying great success against South African and West Indian teams, Grimmett was bitterly disappointed to miss selection in the 1936–37 and 1938 Australian teams that opposed England. Clarrie Grimmett ended his Test cricket  impressively, however, capturing 216 wickets at 24.21, and his overall figures in first class cricket were remarkable, as he took five wickets in an innings 127 times and 10 wickets in a match 33 times.

## 122. KIPPAX, A.F. (Alan "Kipper") : 1897–1972.
Tests (22)
1,192 runs at 36.12

**Kippax's batting should have been weighed in carats, not runs.**

The esteemed cricket writer Ray Robinson once commented that Alan Kippax's batting should have been weighed in carats, not runs, which aptly described the graceful style of this fine NSW and Australian player. Kippax tended to caress the ball through the field rather than bludgeon it, and  Robinson enthused that his delicate leg glances and cuts "had a kind of moonbeam beauty".

Kippax began playing first grade cricket with Waverly at the age of 16, but he waited a further five years before he represented his state in 1918–19, and it was not until the 1924–25 season that he made his Test debut. Kippax was in superb touch then, averaging 112 in Shield matches, but he was inexplicably left out of the 1926 team which toured England. Monty Noble described his omission as "a crime against the cricketing youth of Australia."[17]

17. Pollard, 1982, p571-3

A triple century for NSW against Queensland after the defeated Australian team returned home revived his prospects, and over the next two summers Kippax averaged 83.91 in first class games. In 1928–29 he returned to the national team, and scored 100 in the Melbourne Test against a quality English attack that was spearheaded by Harold Larwood.

At the age of 33 Kippax finally gained selection in the 1930 Australian team which toured England, and the elegant right hander was a dominant player. He became the first Australian batsman since Warren Bardsley to score a century in both innings of a match on his first English tour, and only Bradman had a higher batting average when that wet English summer ended.

Kippax also performed well when he toured England in 1934, but by then his golden years were behind him. He had suffered two nasty head injuries in Australia while batting in the 1931–32 season, and he never played in Tests with quite the same aplomb after those mishaps, though he still performed impressively at state level. His 8005 runs for NSW at 67.26 was a record achievement, and Kippax notched 43 centuries during his first class career

He was involved in a successful Sydney sporting goods business for many years, and in retirement Alan Kippax became an excellent lawn bowler.

## 123. WOODFULL, W.M. (William "Bill") : 1897–1965.
### Tests (35)
### 2300 runs at 46.00

A reserved Victorian schoolmaster who

served Australia admirably from 1926 until 1934, both as an opening batsman and as a captain during some years of turmoil in international cricket.

Woodfull was raised in the Victorian country town of Maldon, and he did not play regular club cricket until the age of 22. He began a famous state and national opening partnership with Bill Ponsford when he gained Victorian selection in 1921–22, and four years on Woodford was Ponsford's fellow opener in the Australian team. He then played in the next seven international seasons, which incorporated three highly successful tours of England between 1926 and 1934, as well as the notorious 'Bodyline' Tests in Australia.

Woodfull generated enormous respect as Australia's captain from his teammates and the general public because of the dignified way in which he conducted himself during that tense series. His remark to the English manager Pelham "Plum" Warner, after he was struck a fearful blow to the chest from a dangerous delivery, that "there are two teams out there, but only one is playing cricket," still remains a part of cricket folk lore.[18]

Bill Woodfull is regarded as being one of Australia's best captains, and he led national teams in 25 of the 35 Tests in which he played. In his prime he was dubbed "the unbowlable", and scored an impressive 49 first class centuries, with seven of them being recorded in Test matches. Woodfull enjoyed a distinguished career in education before he died at the age of 68.

> "there are two teams out there, but only one is playing cricket"

18. Pollard, 1982, p1132

# THE BRADMAN ERA

## AN INSPIRATION IN TIMES OF TUMULT

Australia was still recovering from the carnage and devastation of World War I when the global Great Depression impacted strongly on our economy, and many lives were adversely affected from 1929 until the early 1930s. Wheat and wool exports halved, the national income fell by 80,000,000 pounds, and by 1933 nearly one third of workers were unemployed.

Many turned to sport as a diversion from their problems, so when a diminutive 20 year old batsman from the NSW town of Bowral scored a century against England in only his second Test match, the 1928–29 New Year Melbourne crowd recognised his feat with special warmth. The English fieldsmen rested on the grass while the sustained applause reverberated around the vast ground, and in the city people danced in the streets, car horns were blown, and tram drivers clanged their bells to celebrate the popular achievement.

The Bradman legend had begun.

# PLAYERS OF THE ERA

## 124. BRADMAN, SIR D.G. (Donald "the Don") : 1908–2001.

Tests (52)
6996 runs at 99.94
2 wickets at 36.00

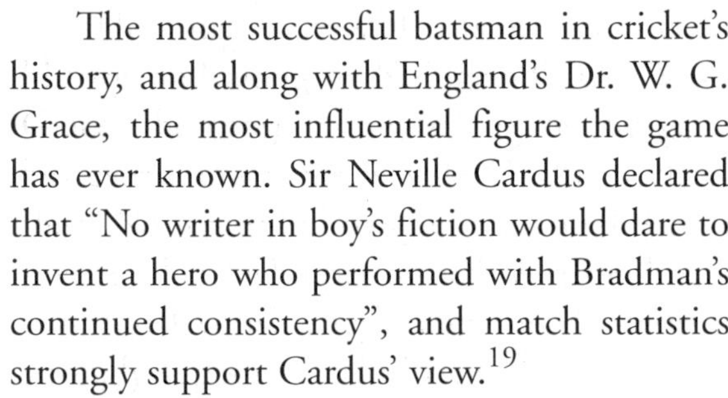

"No writer in boy's fiction would dare to invent a hero who performed with Bradman's continued consistency"

The most successful batsman in cricket's history, and along with England's Dr. W. G. Grace, the most influential figure the game has ever known. Sir Neville Cardus declared that "No writer in boy's fiction would dare to invent a hero who performed with Bradman's continued consistency", and match statistics strongly support Cardus' view.[19]

No other first class player has challenged Bradman's achievement of scoring a century in one third of his innings, and his three figure totals included one innings of over 400, six triple centuries, and 37 double centuries. In Bradman's 52 Test matches he was top scorer 24 times, in 1949 he became the only Australian to receive a knighthood for his services to cricket, and in 1979 he received the Companion of the Order of Australia award.

Donald George Bradman was born in the NSW town of Cootamundra, but lived in the nearby hamlet of Yeo Yeo until the family moved to Bowral when Don was two years old. As a small boy he would throw a golf ball against the family water tank, and attempt to hit it with a cricket stump which sharpened his already strong co-ordination skills.

At the age of 12 Bradman scored his first century, and five years later he compiled 234 for Bowral against Wingello. The bowler who

19. Ferguson, 1996, p88

finally dismissed Bradman in that country game was a young Bill "Tiger" O'Reilly, and 52 years later O'Reilly again bowled to Bradman when Bowral's Sir Donald Bradman Memorial Oval was opened. "The Don" consistently rated "Tiger" as being the best bowler of his era.

After the Bowral boy scored a triple century against Moss Vale, his big scoring feats were noticed in higher cricket circles. Bradman was recruited by the Sydney grade club St.George, and scored 112 in his turf match debut. Another triple century ended the season against the hapless Moss Vale team, and Bradman's cricket career was poised on the brink of greatness.

In the 1928–29 season the 19 year old Bowral recruit scored 118 on debut for NSW against South Australia, but in his first Test match against Percy Chapman's English team at Brisbane that season, he only managed totals of 18 and one. Relegation to 12th man followed for the next Test in Sydney, but by the series' end he had compiled two Test centuries.

After scoring a mammoth 452 for NSW against Queensland the following season, Bradman gained selection in Bill Woodfull's team which toured England . In an enthralling Test series Bradman was the hero of the visitor's narrow series' win, with impressive scores of 131, 254, 232 and 334, (an innings which is still regarded by many as being the best ever played in England). His superb Test average of 139.14 made a mockery of pre-tour predictions from Surrey captain Percy Fender, that Bradman's technique was too flawed for English conditions.

Bradman did have an unorthodox batting grip, and he was not a stylist at the

**Bradman's technique was too flawed for English conditions.**

crease. However his concentration ability was amazing, his appetite for runs seemingly insatiable, and no-one dominated opposition attacks as successfully as the ever assertive Bradman. He scored off the first delivery he received more than any other player, and he was such a superb judge of chances to score between wickets, that he was only run out once in his 52 Tests.

Following the 1930 tour Bradman became the sporting legend the Australian public craved. After he relocated to Adelaide for increased business opportunities, large crowds gathered to watch him play for Kensington in club matches. Most would quickly depart if there was no prospect of seeing the great man bat that day.

Bruce Bowley, a former club teammate of Bradman's, recalls a crowd of about 5,000 in attendance at the Glenelg Oval one afternoon when he ventured to the batting crease ahead of Bradman. "Get off the ground ya mug," yelled a good-natured barracker, "we didn't come to see you!"

Former Australian opener Bill Brown was exposed to similar experiences. In 2002 the then ninety-two year old Brown still vividly remembered that if he and fellow opener Jack Fingleton occupied the batting crease after the lunch break, then the growing crowd would become restless – the two notable players were eating up "Bradman time."

During the height of his career Bradman would receive 600 letters a week from his fans. He replied to every one. Noted entertainer Jack O'Hagan penned his famous "Our Don Bradman" tune which attracted wide popularity.

"Our Don Bradman, every Aussie dips his lid to you!

Our Don Bradman, now I ask you is he any
good?
Our Don Bradman, as a batsman he is cer-
tainly plum pud!
Tate and Larwood would meet their fate
For it is always shut the gate!
When the boy from Bowral hits four after
four.
Our Don Bradman, what a welcome waits
for you back home."[20]

The appeal of the Bradman legend still remained strong in 1984, when the television series "Bodyline" broke viewing records.

English fast bowler Harold Larwood candidly admitted the motivations behind bodyline after he migrated to Australia years later. "Let me confirm what so many people have always believed. Bodyline was devised to stifle Bradman's genius."[21]

The plan was devised by England's aloof captain Douglas Jardine, but it was Larwood and fellow pace bowler Bill Voce who mostly implemented this controversial form of attack in the 1932–33 series in Australia, when England regained the Ashes. Though Bradman scored 396 Test runs (including three centuries), and his average of 56.57 was still the best performance by an Australian batsman, his effectiveness was diminished by the constant barrage of fast, short-pitched bowling aimed at his rib and chest area

By the end of this divisive tour, the experiment of bodyline threatened the future of the Ashes series, and laws were hastily drafted which effectively outlawed the practice. The trauma of the experience, and the ever increasing intrusions on the Bradman family's priva-

20. Piesse and Ferguson, 1986, p23
21. Pollard, 1982, p193

cy, appeared to result in "the Don" becoming a more reserved personality. He still however attended admirably to his guest speaking engagements, and his form on the field remained brilliant.

After scoring heavily in home Test fixtures against West Indian and South African teams, Bradman was named vice-captain of Woodfull's successful 1934 English touring team, and he headed the Test aggregates with 758 runs. Near the end of that northern summer he almost died from acute appendicitis, and continuing health problems resulted in him being unavailable for the 1935–36 tour of South Africa.

At the age of 28 Bradman was appointed as Australia's captain when "Gubby" Allen's English team toured our shores in 1936–37, and he led the host team to an exciting series' victory that was watched by record crowds. Bradman scored 270, 212 and 169 in the final three Tests, and all were chanceless innings. When he again led Australia to victory on the 1938 tour of England, he averaged 155.66, the best-ever average for an English season.

By then Bradman was seriously contemplating retirement, but six years of war in Europe and the Pacific altered that decision.

# THE CARNAGE OF WORLD WAR II

Between 1939 and 1945 Australia lost over 27,000 young lives in World War II, and some of the country's best cricketers were among those killed or seriously wounded.

Promising batsman Ross Gregory, who impressed all in his two Test appearances, lost his life at the age of 26 while serving with the RAAF in the Middle East. Reserve Australian wicket-keeper Charles "Chilla" Walker also never returned, and another Test player in Alan Fairfax recuperated for seven years from war time injuries. Don Tallon, one of Australia's great wicket-keepers, was also troubled for much of his career by a medical condition that developed during World War II.

Hard hitting Queensland and Victorian batsman Frank Sides perished in action near New Guinea, while Ernest Parker from Western Australia (WA) and South Australia's Ken Ridings were other state players who paid the ultimate sacrifice. NSW and WA Test hopeful Keith Carmody's health was badly affected by his experiences in German POW camps, and Stan Sismey, the NSW wicket-keeper in the pre-war period, suffered serious shrapnel wounds when his plane was shot down over the Mediterranean Sea.

Bradman, with the support of his wife Lady Jessie, decided that he had an obligation to promote cricket in the post-war recovery years, and he led Australia to home series' wins over a depleted English team in 1946–47 and India in 1947–48. He then embarked on the last and most memorable tour of his presti-

**The all-conquering Australians became known as "The Invincibles".**

**He only needed to score four runs in his final international match to finish with the landmark Test average of 100.**

gious career – the 1948 tour of England.

The all-conquering Australians became known as "The Invincibles" as they steam-rolled their way through county teams and the English Test side in a landscape that was still scarred by war time bombing raids.. A record 72% of games were won, which easily eclipsed the 1921 record of Warwick Armstrong's side that gained victory in 58% of their tour fix-tures. The 40 year old Bradman revealed vin-tage form scoring eight successive centuries, with two of his 11 tour hundreds being recorded in Tests. He only needed to score four runs in his final international match to finish with the landmark Test average of 100.

The English crowd erupted into applause when cricket's hero strode to the wicket for his last Test and the English team formed a respectful guard of honour near the Oval wicket to give him three cheers before his innings began, but for once the cricket gods deserted Bradman. English spinner Eric Hollies bowled cricket's greatest batsman for a duck, which resulted in Sir Donald Bradman ending his Test career with a batting average of 99.94, a record achievement which will surely last forever.

Sir Donald became a highly accomplished cricket administrator, selector and business-man, before he passed away in Adelaide in his 93rd year.

The legend of the Don, however, still lives on. His birth place of Cootamundra, where he spent so little of his long life, remains a shrine to his memory. Visitors can stay at the Bradman Motor Inn, visit the Bradman Cottage in 89 Adams Street where he was born, and gaze across the road from that small, neat home to the Bradman Oval. In Bowral the Bradman Museum  regularly attracts large

crowds of interested cricket fans from all over
he world.

Sir Donald Bradman will be revered for as
long as the game of cricket is played.

# PLAYERS OF THE ERA

## 125. IRONMONGER, H. (Herbert "Dainty") : 1882–1971.
Tests (14)
42 runs at 2.62
74 wickets at 17.97

One of the characters of the game, who overcame the disability of having half of two fingers missing from his bowling hand to make his Test debut against Chapman's 1928–29 English team at the age of 46, though he claimed he was only 41.

His nickname came from his ungainliness in the field, and he only clung onto three catches in his 14 Test career. As a batsman he was so inept that when Ironmonger's wife rang him one day at the MCG just after he had gone out to bat, she reportedly said "Oh. Then I'd better hold on."[22]

However as a left arm spinner he bowled with incredible accuracy and posed a real threat if the pitch was worn or wet. He was born in the rural area of Pine Mountain near Ipswich, and represented Queensland with distinction before his cricket ambitions lured him south first to Melbourne, then Sydney, and back to Melbourne again.

Ironmonger worked as a gardener and as a groundsman. His best performances in Tests against England were achieved in the 1932–33 home season when he captured 15 wickets in four international matches. He travelled to New Zealand in 1920–21 with an Australian team, but was never selected for an English tour.

22. Pollard, 1982, p538

# 126. BLACKIE, D.D. (Donald "Rock") : 1882–1955.
## Tests (3)
## 24 runs at 8.00
## 14 wickets at 31.71

Another persistent veteran, who debuted for Australia when he was 46 years and 235 days against Percy Chapman's 1928–29 English team. Blackie had actually retired from the game before he was enticed back to share spin bowling duties with "Dainty" Ironmonger at the St Kilda club in Melbourne, and from there he gained both state and national selection.

Blackie was a clever off-spinner who spun the ball sharply and flighted the ball well. His accurate bowling was underrated by authorities of his time, and many believe that his opportunities in big cricket should have come at a younger age.

# 127. NOTHLING, O.E. (Dr. Otto) : 1900–65.
## Tests (1)
## 52 runs at 26.00
## 0 wickets for 72 runs

An impressive Queensland player who became an important administrator in the game. He scored 52 runs in his only Test appearance against Chapman's English side, and he also represented Australia in Rugby Union.

Nothling was president of the Queensland Cricket Association (QCA) when he died.

# 128. A'BECKETT, E.L. (Edward "Ted") : 1907–89.

Tests (40
143 runs at 20.42
3 wickets at 105.06

Ted a'Beckett debuted with Victoria at the age of 20 and retired four years later at the peak of his prowess to pursue a legal career.

A'Beckett replaced an injured Jack Gregory in the 1928–29 Australian Test team after playing in only six first class matches, and the fast medium swing bowler later gained selection in Australia's touring team to England where he played in one Test match. A' Beckett also represented Australia in one Test against South Africa.

## 129. OXENHAM, R.K. (Ronald) : 1891–39.

Tests (7)
151 runs at 15.10
14 wickets at 37.28

One of Queensland's best all-rounders, who bowled accurate medium-pace cutters, was a useful batsman, and a brilliant fieldsman

Oxenham debuted for his state in 1911–12 but did not break into the Australian team until the age of 37. He played in three Tests that season against Chapman's English team, and he also represented Australia against South Africa and the West Indies.

The lean dark complexioned Oxenham was considered a certain selection for the 1930 English tour after taking 4/67 in one of the 1928–29 Tests, but the Victorian all-rounder a'Beckett was preferred. During his career he did, however, tour both New Zealand and India with success.

Ron Oxenham suffered serious injuries in

a 1937 car accident, and he died two years later at the age of 48.

## 130. JACKSON, A. (Archibald "Archie") : 1909–33.
### Tests (8)
### 474 runs at 47.40

An elegant batsman who emerged from the slums of Sydney to become Australia's youngest Test century maker, before he tragically died from tuberculosis at the age of 23.

Jackson's shot making inventiveness was comparable to Victor Trumper's, and there was also a similarity to Kippax in his graceful style. At the age of 17 he scored two centuries in his first season for NSW, and two year later he debuted as an opener for Australia against Chapman's 1928–29 English team.

It was certainly a baptism of fire in the early overs when Australia lurched to 3/19 against the fiery pace attack of Larwood, Tate and "Farmer" White, but the 19 year old Jackson scored a superb 164 to become Australia's youngest century maker on debut. The 1930 tour to England followed where Jackson, despite suffering health problems, totalled 1097 runs, and his graceful innings of 73 in the Fifth Test at The Oval helped secure victory for Australia.

Jackson's continued poor health required a recuperation period in a sanatorium after he returned to Sydney, and he hoped that a move to Brisbane would improve his health. However he collapsed after a club game with Northern Suburbs, and at a nearby hospital he was diagnosed with tuberculosis in both lungs. Soon after announcing his engagement to his 21 year old sweetheart Phyllis Thomas, his

An elegant batsman who emerged from the slums of Sydney to become Australia's youngest Test century maker.

condition worsened. On February 16th during the 1933 Test match between Australia and England, Jackson died not long before England regained the Ashes.

At his Sydney funeral was the leading Labor politician, Dr. H.V. Evatt, who financially supported Jackson throughout his cricket career. Bill Woodfull, Vic Richardson, Don Bradman, Bert Oldfield, Stan McCabe, Bill Ponsford and Alan Kippax were pall bearers. A vast crowd filled the Field of Mars cemetery and the surrounding streets to pay their last respects.

**A vast crowd filled the Field of Mars cemetery and the surrounding streets to pay their last respects.**

## 131. FAIRFAX, A. G. (Alan) : 1906–55.

Tests (10)
410 runs at 51.25
21 wickets at 30.71

Fairfax and Bradman were both first selected to play for Australia in the 1928–29 season, and they were also the first players to gain national selection from Sydney's St. George club. Fairfax did not match the deeds of his famous club-mate, but the valuable all-rounder scored four 50s in his Test career.

He toured England with the 1930's team, scoring 49 and 53 not out in the Fourth and Fifth Tests, and his medium pace deliveries removed Jack Hobbs for nine in the great English batsman's last Test match.

Fairfax returned to England in 1932 to play in the Lancashire League and manage an indoor coaching centre. War injuries later hospitalised Fairfax for seven years, and after he recovered he became a cricket writer for "The People", a popular London Sunday newspaper. Fairfax died from a heart attack shortly after covering an English tour of Australia.

## 132. HORNIBROOK, P.M. (Percival) : 1899–1976.

Tests (6)
60 runs at 10.00
17 wickets at 39.05

A left arm spinner who bowled splendidly for Queensland over many seasons, and was unlucky not to have been given the opportunity to play Test cricket earlier in his career.

Hornibrook was born in the small country town of Obi Obi. He tended to bowl in a fast medium mode early in an innings, before reverting to quickish orthodox spinners later in the innings. He toured New Zealand with an Australian XI in 1920–21, and many experts believed hat he was unlucky to miss selection for both the 1921 and 1926 English tours.

Hornibrook gained a place on the 1930 tour, and bowled more overs in that English summer than any other bowler apart from Grimmett. In the Oval Test match he captured the excellent figures of 7/92 , with Sutcliffe, Duleepsinhji, Hammond and Leyland being included in his bag of wickets.

Percy Hornibrook retired from the first class scene shortly afterwards. He continued playing Brisbane grade cricket with Toombul, for whom he snared 833 wickets at 12.70 over 20 highly successful seasons.

## 133. WALL, T.W. (Thomas "Tim") : 1904–81.

Tests (18)
121 runs at 6.36
56 wickets at 35.89

A fast-medium opening bowler who performed with great accuracy for both South Australia and Australia. Along with Peter Allen and Ian Brayshaw, he is the only bowler who has taken all ten wickets in a Sheffield Shield innings, a feat he accomplished with the figures of 10/36 against NSW in the 1932–33 season.

Wall collected the match figures of 8/189 in his debut Test for Australia against Chapman's 1928–29 English team, and he went on to play in four home series. In the infamous 1931–32 Bodyline series Wall headed Australia's bowling with 16 wickets at 25.56. He also toured England in 1930 and 1934.

## 134. McCABE, S.J. (Stanley "Napper") : 1910–68.

Tests (39)
2748 runs at 48.21
36 wickets at 42.86

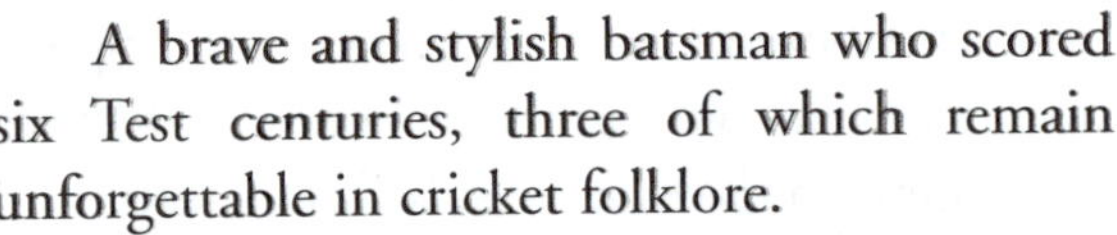

A brave and stylish batsman who scored six Test centuries, three of which remain unforgettable in cricket folklore.

McCabe was raised in the NSW country town of Grenfell, and the fluent stroke-player with an excellent technique was named in his state team at the age of 18. He was included as a developmental player in Woodfull's 1930 team which toured England after recording only one first class century, and justified the selector's faith by scoring 1012 runs in that northern summer.

After performing well against South Africa in five home Tests, the 21 year old McCabe decided to invite his parents to Sydney to watch him play in the 1931–32 season, as they had never seen their son perform at Test match level. The visiting English team had received much media criticism for their bodyline tactics, and McCabe was worried that his excitable mother might jump the fence and remonstrate with any offender, if her son was hit by the short pitched bowling.

There was no cause for alarm as it was McCabe who did the hitting, hooking boundary after boundary off his chest and eyebrows as he thrashed an unbeaten 187 from the feared English pace attack. It is still regarded as one of the great innings of Test cricket, and partly overshadows the fact that England won the match by ten wickets.

Two other McCabe centuries remain legendary Test match achievements. Against South Africa in the 1935–36 Durban Test, the game was abandoned after the fielding host captain Herbie Wade complained that McCabe's powerful hitting was endangering his players in the gloomy light conditions that prevailed! When the umpires upheld Wade's appeal, Australia required 125 runs for victory in 180 minutes, and McCabe remained unconquered on 189.

His third classic innings was the 232 he scored while 300 runs were added when he was at the crease in the 1938 Test match at Trent Bridge in England. McCabe thrashed 44 runs from three Doug Wright overs that day, and collected 72 runs in 28 minutes when 77 runs were added for the last wicket with Fleetwood-Smith. His captain Bradman insisted that all his teammates watch McCabe's epic performance, and commented later that "I would give a great deal to be able to play an innings like that."[23]

Stan McCabe was also a capable medium pace bowler, whose dismissal of Hammond in the 1930 Oval Test probably decided the

23. Pollard, 1982, p653

series. After his third tour of England in 1938, McCabe struggled to perform as well again because of a lingering foot injury. He ran a Sydney sports store for many years, and died in 1968 after falling from a cliff near his Mosman home.

## 135. HURWOOD, A. (Alexander) : 1902–82.

Tests (2)
5 runs at 2.50
11 wickets at 15.45

**Hurwood hit Bradman's stumps after "The Don" had scored 80. To the Queenslander's dismay, the bails were not dislodged and the great man went on to score a mammoth 452 not out.**

The tall Queenslander was one of the unlucky bowlers of Australian cricket. Against NSW in the Sydney Shield game of 1930–31, a typically accurate medium pace delivery from Hurwood hit Bradman's stumps after "The Don" had scored 80. To the Queenslander's dismay, the bails were not dislodged and the great man went on to score a mammoth 452 not out.

Hurwood, who toured England in 1930 without appearing in Tests, did gain selection in two internationals against the West Indies in 1930–31. However after capturing 4/22 when the Windies capitulated for the meagre total of 90, Hurwood was dropped from the Australian team!

## 136. RIGG, K.E. (Keith) : 1906–55.

Tests (8)
401 runs at 33.41

A tall batsman who captained Victoria and scored 14 first class centuries, but still struggled to cement a spot in the star studded Australian team of that time.

Rigg played his first Test against the West

Indies in 1930–31, and in the following season he scored 127 against South Africa in the Second Test match of the summer.

He was considered unlucky to miss selection in the 1930 Australian team that toured England, but did play two Ashes Tests in the 1936–37 home series.

Keith Rigg saw war-time action with the RAAF in New Guinea after he retired from first class cricket, he served as a Victorian selector for 12 years, and he was also awarded Life Membership of the Melbourne Cricket Club.

## 137. NITSCHKE, H.C. (Homesdale "Slinger") : 1905–82.
### Tests (2)
### 53 runs at 26.50

A hard hitting left-handed South Australian who scored nine first class centuries and represented Australia in two Tests against South Africa during the 1931–32 season.

During the winter months over many years Nitschke managed an outback property, and after he retired from cricket he became a successful race horse breeder. One of his horses, Dayana, won four Derbies in four states in 1972, and the following year it won the $100,000 Perth Cup.

## 138. LEE, P.K. (Phillip) : 1904–80.
### Tests (2)
### 57 runs at 19.00
### 5 wickets at 42.40

An aggressive batsman and handy off-spin bowler, who achieved the double of 1,000 runs and 100 wickets for South Australia.

Lee played in two Tests, one against South

Africa and the other against England.

## 139. HUNT, W.A. (William) : 1908–83.
Tests (1)
0 runs
0 wickets for 39 runs

A medium pace bowler who quit Australian cricket for Lancashire League ranks after playing one Test against South Africa, because he believed that he had no future in international cricket while Bill Woodfull was Test captain.

Hunt grew up in the Sydney suburb of Balmain, and early in his career, along with Archie Jackson, he received generous sponsorship from Dr. H. V. Evatt.

In the 1933 season Hunt snared an astonishing five hat tricks, a feat he achieved 11 times at various levels during his long career.

## 140. O'REILLY, W.J. (Bill "Tiger") : 1905–92.
Tests (27)
410 runs at 12.81
144 wickets at 22.59

**A great character and one of the greatest bowlers Australia has ever known.**

A great character and one of the greatest bowlers Australia has ever known. At first glance his bowling action was clumsy, but he performed with good rhythm and had outstanding stamina. O'Reilly was a medium pace spinner rather than a traditional slow bowler, and the big man bowled his leg spinners, googlies and top spinners with special venom when he was annoyed by some incident.

O'Reilly at one stage lived in a town close to Bowral, and as youngsters he and Bradman had many stirring on-field duels. His advancement to big time cricket was slower than the Don's however, because  of his outback teaching appointments to remote areas.  It wasn't till the 1931–32 season that he clinched his place in the NSW side and also gained Australian selection.

In that Bodyline series O'Reilly was the most dominant bowler, collecting 27 wickets at 26.81, which included match figures of 10/128 in the Melbourne Test, the only match that Australia won. In England in 1934 he captured 28 Test wickets at 24.92 to edge out Grimmett in the bowling averages. O'Reilly remained the nemesis of English batsmen for the remainder of his career. He produced a match and series winning burst on the 1938 tour of the "Old Dart", and in that same summer "Tiger" joined a select band of five previous Australian bowlers when he snared his 100th wicket in Anglo–Australian Tests. Little wonder that Bradman later rated O'Reilly as the greatest bowler he ever faced.

O'Reilly retired from first class cricket shortly after the war, after taking five wickets in an innings 63 times, and ten wickets in a match 17 times. He also won the Sydney grade bowling averages on 12 occasions.

In later years "Tiger" became a much loved and respected cricket writer, and to the end he scorned the use of modern computers, choosing instead to compile his entertaining and provocative articles on an antiquated old typewriter.

**Little wonder that Bradman later rated O'Reilly as the greatest bowler he ever faced.**

## 141. THURLOW, H.M. (Hugh "Pud") : 1903–75.
### Tests (1)
### 0 runs
### 0 wickets for 86 runs

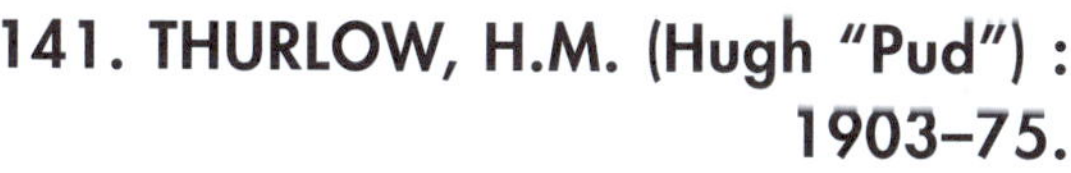

**When he was run out for a duck, Bradman was left stranded on 299 not out!**

A lively fast bowler from Queensland whose only Test against South Africa in the 1931–32 season is well remembered because when he was run out for a duck, Bradman was left stranded on 299 not out!

Thurlow also became unpopular with Bill Woodfull and Alan Kippax when deliveries from him caused serious injuries, but he was liked in Queensland, for whom he captured five wickets in an innings on five occasions.

## 142. FINGLETON, J.H.W. (John "Jack") : 1908–91.
Tests (18)
1189 runs at 42.46

A batsman who possessed a rich array of strokes, but who often chose a stodgy approach in Test matches against England. His great friend, Bill O'Reilly, believes that his approach to batting altered after he was left out of the 1934 touring team to England, despite the fact that he had performed well against Jardine's 1931–32 Bodyline attack.

Fingleton made his debut for NSW in 1930–31, and during the following season he gained Test selection against South Africa. Fingleton appeared to especially enjoy batting against the Springboks. He dispensed with his cautious batting when he toured South Africa in Victor Richardson's team during the 1935–36 season, and scored three successive Test centuries in cavalier style. Fingleton then entered cricket record books when he added a fourth hundred in his next Test innings against England in Brisbane.

Fingleton trained as a journalist, and English team manager Sir Pelham Warner was convinced that it was he who leaked details of the dressing room row between Warner and the Australian captain Bill Woodfull to media outlets of the day. Fingleton denied this charge, and in turn blamed Bradman for the release of the unseemly details. The feud between the two Australians lasted many years, partly because Fingleton frequently made jibes about Bradman in his many newspaper reports.

He ended his career after scoring five Test centuries, and later persuaded his old Bodyline foe, Harold Larwood, to immigrate to Australia. Fingleton also became a highly respected political writer and cricket author. His most influential books on the game, such as "Cricket Crisis', "Brightly Fades The Don" and "The Immortal Victor Trumper" remain much sought after by cricket buffs around the world.

## 143. NASH, L.J. (Laurie) : 1910–86.

Tests (2)
30 runs at 15.00
10 wickets at 12.60

A brilliant Australian Rules footballer, who had the unusual distinction of representing his country in Test cricket before he played in an official Sheffield Shield game.

The Tasmanian based tearaway fast bowler blitzed South Africa in his first Test, capturing 4/18 when the visitors were bundled out for the embarrassing total of 36. However Nash's football career intervened, and the South Melbourne centre half-forward became one of the greats of Australian Football.

Nash returned briefly to Test cricket to oppose the English touring team in the 1936–37 season after he had delivered a barrage of bumpers to the unimpressed visitors in the Victoria/ MCC fixture. He returned the notable figures of 4/70, accepted six catches, scored 29, and soon afterwards disappeared from first class cricket.

## 144. NAGLE, L.E. (Lisle) : 1905–71.
Tests (1)
21 runs no average
2 wickets at 55.00

A medium pace swing bowler whose career was shortened by a bizarre incident when he turned his head to speak to a team-mate while fielding in the 1933–34 Blackie-Ironmonger Testimonial match in Melbourne, and badly ricked his neck.

The Bendigo born giant and his twin brother Vernon both represented Victoria, and figures of 8/32 from ten overs against England for his state gained Lyle Nagle selection in his only Test match in the 1931–32 Bodyline series. He failed to consolidate his place, but Lyle Nagle later toured India with Frank Tarrant's Commonwealth team in 1934–35

## 145. O'BRIEN, L.P.J. (Leo) : 1907–97.
Tests (5)
211 runs at 26.37

A competent Victorian left hand opening batsman who struggled against the class and fire of England's Bodyline bowlers during the 1931–32 series in Australia. He did, however, score a fine 61 in the Adelaide Test of that troubled summer after Richardson, Woodfull and Bradman had all fallen cheaply.

O'Brien toured South Africa in 1935–36 where he appeared in two Test matches to complement the three he played against England between 1932 and 1937.

## 146. BROMLEY, E. H. (Ernest "Slogger") : 1912–67.

Tests (2)
38 runs at 9.50

A tall all-rounder who was born in Western Australia but who made a bigger impression in cricket after he relocated to Victoria. Bromley possessed a renowned throwing arm, and he staggered onlookers when he hurled a cricket ball 130 yards in a 1933 throwing contest at the MCG.[24]

Bromley gained selection in the Adelaide Bodyline Test, and he clinched selection for the 1934 English tour after he scored two excellent centuries before the team was chosen. In England, however, he had a disappointing tour scoring only 312 runs at an average of 16.42.

He staggered onlookers when he hurled a cricket ball 130 yards in a 1933 throwing contest at the MCG.

## 147. DARLING, L.S (Leonard) : 1909–92.

Tests (12)
474 runs at 27.88

Rated by some to be the most promising left handed batsman in the country during his youth, but he became a player who failed to live up to early expectations.

The 1931–32 Bodyline series was a turning point in the Victorian's career, as both he and McCabe handled the fiery English pace attack competently during the Test series. Darling then gained selection in the 1934 Australian team which toured England, where

24. Pollard, 1982, p135

the accomplished stroke player scored 1,022 runs for the season at an average of 34.06. By then Darling's increasing weight forced his captain Woodfull to field him close to the wicket, where he snapped up some brilliant catches.

During the 1936–37 season Len Darling toured South Africa where he played in all five Tests. In his 18 appearances at this level Darling scored half-centuries on three occasions. He dropped out of first class cricket shortly after he married and settled in Adelaide.

## 148. LOVE, H.S.B. (Hampden "Hammy") : 1895–1969.
Tests (1)
8 runs at 4.00
dismissals 3 catches

"Hammy" Love had the misfortune to play in the era when Bert Oldfield was entrenched as Australia's wicket keeper. He did replace Oldfield for his only Test appearance after Oldfield was hit on the head from a Larwood lifter during the Third Test of the 1931–32 Ashes series, and accepted the three catches that came his way.

The accomplished wicket-keeper batsman toured India with Jack Ryder's 1935–36 team. When he retired to Sydney grade ranks, after representing both NSW and Victoria, Love totalled seven centuries in his 54 match first class career.

## 149. ALEXANDER, H.H. (Harry "Bull") : 1905–93.
Tests (1)
17 runs at 17.00
1 wicket at 154.00

A strongly built Victorian speedster who troubled the English captain Douglas Jardine in the early overs of his sole Test appearance during the 1931–32 Bodyline series, before finishing with the unflattering match figures of 1/154.

Alexander opened Victoria's bowling for seven seasons, and toured India with Frank Tarrant's Commonwealth team in 1935–36. He served overseas in the AIF during World War II, and settled finally in the country town of Euroa. There he became a councillor, and had the "H.H. Alexander Pavilion" named in his honour at the local sportsground.

## 150. BROWN, W.A. (Bill) : 1912—.
### Tests (22)
### 1,592 runs at 46.82

A fine opening batsman who represented Australia with distinction between 1934 and 1948, and scored over 1000 runs on each of his three English tours. This impressive tally included both a century and a double century in separate Lords' Tests, and Brown's imposing Test career aggregate contained four centuries and nine scores over 50.

Brown, born in Toowoomba but raised in Sydney, debuted for NSW at the age of 20. A year later he made his 1934 Test debut in England at Trent Bridge, where he scored 73. The amiable 21 year old opener showed that he could handle the English swing bowling attacks well, and he possessed excellent onside shots.

Prior to World War II Brown opened a sports store in Brisbane. He became an astute captain of Queensland in Sheffield Shield ranks, but his relocation back north resulted in Brown moving away from the national selectors' focus, and he was supplanted in the

Test side by the NSW pair, Morris and Barnes. By 1948, on his final tour of England, Brown only played in two Tests, despite scoring eight centuries during that northern summer.

Brown is now in his 90s, and the friendly Queenslander remains ever ready to co-operate with both the media and cricket authorities. As recently as 2005 he was at the Gabba before Australia played the West Indies, to present promising newcomer Mike Hussey with his first baggy green cap.

## 151. CHIPPERFIELD, A.G. (Arthur "Chipper") : 1905–87.
Tests (14)
552 runs at 32.47
5 wickets at 87.40

A superb slips fieldsman and a dashing but unpredictable batsman who scored 99 in the first session of his debut Test match at Trent Bridge in 1934, but was dismissed on the third ball after the interval without adding to his tally. Fortunately, two seasons later in South Africa, Chipperfield did record his first and only Test century.

Chipperfield was also a useful slow bowler, and his all-round potential probably influenced the national selectors when they selected him for that 1934 tour after he had played only three matches for NSW. A tour tally of 899 runs at an average of 40.86 vindicated his selection.

Chipperfield again toured the "Old Dart" in 1938, but he was often sidelined with appendicitis problems, and only managed the overall tally of 424 runs. He retired in 1940 after scoring nine first class centuries, and became an enthusiastic fisherman.

## 152. EBELING, H.I. (Hans) : 1905–80.

Tests (1)

43 runs at 21.50

3 wickets at 29.66

Ebeling was handy all-rounder, who gave great service to Victoria as a player and captain, despite the fact that his cricket career was often overshadowed by his business interests. He toured with the 1934 Australian team to England, where his accurate swing bowling skills won praise from an esteemed opponent in Jack Hobbs.

In retirement Ebeling devoted much time to developing the MCG cricket museum, and he was the driving force behind the organisation of the 1977 Centenary Test in Melbourne, which is still lauded as being an entrepreneurial showpiece of Australian cricket.

He was the driving force behind the organisation of the 1977 Centennary Test in Melbourne, which is still lauded as being an entrepreneurial showpiece of Australian cricket.

## 153. FLEETWOOD-SMITH, L.O. (Leslie, "Chuck") : 1908–71.

Tests (10)

54 runs at 9.00

42 wickets at 37.38.

"Tiger "O'Reilly believed that "Chuck" Fleetwood-Smith "would have been the greatest spinner of all time if his temperament (had matched) his magnificent talents". At net sessions the great all-rounder Keith Miller only knew which way "Chuck's" deliveries would turn, when the unpredictable spinner from the country town of Stawell called down the pitch what to expect before he delivered the ball! It was often said of Fleetwood-Smith that "he could spin the ball so much that you could hear it humming in the air."

"He could spin the ball so much that you could hear it humming in the air."

Fleetwood-Smith captured five wickets in an innings for Victoria an amazing 31 times, but on days when he mimicked bird calls as he skipped in to bowl, he also suffered some fearful hidings from opposing batsmen. Against opponents of real class, however, the bird calls were dispensed with, and Fleetwood-Smith bowled at his lethal best. In the 1936–37 Adelaide Test match against England "Chuck" captured match winning figures of 10/229, and on his 1934 and 1938 trips to England he finished second in the averages on both tours.[24]

After World War II, however, Fleetwood-Smith disappeared from the sports pages into the wine bars and parks frequented by Melbourne's derelict community. His shocked friends and many former teammates rallied around him after he was charged with vagrancy in April 1969, but the health of the destitute former star continued to decline, and he died two years later. "Too many friends, parties and social drinks" was his own tragic epitaph.

**"Too many friends, parties and social drinks" was his own tragic epitaph.**

### 154. McCORMICK, E.L. (Ernest "Goldie") : 1906–91.
Tests (12)
54 runs at 6.00
36 wickets at 29.97

In the decade before World War II, Ernie McCormick possessed the longest run up, and at times the most pace, of any fast bowler of his era. When he lost his rhythm he was plagued by no ball problems, and in the opening match tour of the 1938  tour of England McCormick was no-balled 35 times in 20

24. Piesse and Ferguson, 1986, pp418-9

overs. "I'll be right after lunch," the wisecracking McCormick said to his teammates after being called eight times in his opening over, "The umpire's getting hoarse."[25]

In his debut Test in 1937–38 Ernie McCormick captured the wicket of Worthington with the first delivery of the game. He also removed both Hammond and Fagg cheaply in that innings, and after four whirlwind overs McCormick had the impressive figures of 3/16. His best performance in first class cricket was when he captured 9/40 off 11 overs for Victoria at the Adelaide Oval in that same season.

McCormick debuted for Australia at the age of 29 on the 1935–36 South African tour. His career closed when he joined the RAAF in 1939, and in later years McCormick was a Melbourne jeweller.

## 155. BADCOCK, C.L. (Clayvell "Jack") : 1914–82.
### Tests (7)
### 160 runs at 14.54

Seen as a potential champion when he debuted for Tasmania at the age of 15, and in domestic cricket he was a prolific scorer. However in the international arena Jack Badcock failed to capitalise on his obvious talent.

Badcock moved to South Australia in 1934 to advance his claims, and first represented Australia in 1936. In that same year he scored 325 against Victoria, but his only century at Test level was the 118 he registered against England at Melbourne in 1937. He scored heavily against county teams in England on the 1938 tour but contributed

25. Pollard, 1982, p658

only 32 from his eight Test innings.

After registering two double centuries in the Sheffield Shield following the English tour, Jack Badcock was forced out of the game at the age of 27 by persistent attacks of lumbago.

## 156. ROBINSON, R.H. (Rayford) : 1914–65.
Tests (1)
5 runs at 2.50

A talented Newcastle batsman whose unpredictable off-field lifestyle thwarted his on-field progress. He debuted for Australia after scoring two Shield centuries for NSW in 1936–37, but failed in his only Test against England that summer.

After experiencing little cricket success following his move to South Australia, Robinson returned to Newcastle where he died at the age of 51.

## 157. SIEVERS, M.W. (Morris) : 1912–68.
Tests (3)
67 runs at 13.40
9 wickets at 17.88

A huge medium pace bowler and useful batsman who achieved great success on a wet wicket in one of his three Tests against England's 1936–37 team. On a Melbourne "glue pot" Sievers was almost unplayable with the lift he generated from the dodgy surface and he captured the fine figures of 5/21.

Sievers was a reliable performer for Victoria between 1934 and 1945, and he toured South Africa with the Australian team in 1935–36, but failed to gain Test selection.

## 158. WARD, F.A. (Francis) : 1909–74.

Tests (4)
36 runs at 6.00
11 wickets at 52.18.

A leg spin bowler who was overshadowed by O'Reilly, Grimmett and Fleetwood-Smith during his career.

Ward was an accomplished performer in Sydney grade ranks, but moved to South Australia to enhance his cricket prospects. There he formed a formidable spin bowling duo with Grimmett, and was preferred by Australian selectors to his aging but more esteemed teammate in 1936–37 Test matches, and the 1938 tour of England. He performed well against county teams on tour, but was only selected in one Test match.

World War II ended Ward's first class career, but not before he and Grimmett bowled South Australia to a Sheffield Shield title in 1938–39.

## 159. GREGORY, R.G. (Ross) : 1916–1942.

Tests (2)
153 runs at 51.00

A classy stroke player whose gallant batting helped Australia retain the Ashes in the 1936–37 season. "Heaven bless us," enthused Neville Cardus after Gregory scored a crucial 80 in the final Test match of the series, "We have witnessed strokes in a Test match, gay and handsome and cultured strokes."[26]

Unfortunately it was the first and last Test innings for the Victorian, as at the age of 26 he was killed in Assam in North Africa while serving with the RAAF. In his tragically short

**In his tragically short career Ross Gregory scored 1357 runs at 30.10 for Victoria in state cricket.**

career Ross Gregory scored 1357 runs at 30.10 for Victoria in state cricket.

## 160. BARNETT, B.A. (Benjamin) : 1908–79.
Tests (4)
195 runs at 27.85
Dismissals 5 (3 caught, 2 stumped)

A tidy wicketkeeper who was considered lucky to gain selection on two English tours, when he edged out Charlie Walker in 1934 and Don Tallon in 1938. He only performed moderately well in England, but returned to live there after World War II to captain Buckinghamshire.

The personable Victorian represented Australia for decades at many international cricket conferences, and returned to Australia shortly before he died.

## 161. HASSETT, A.L (Lindsay) : 1913–93.
Tests (43)
3073 runs at 46.56

**Cricket writer Jack Pollard believes that in the art of making friends for Australian cricket there has never been anything like him.**

A batsman of the highest calibre, a great team player, and an underrated and highly popular Australian captain. Cricket writer Jack Pollard believes that in the art of making friends for Australian cricket there has never been anything like him.

The Geelong born Hassett had scored only one century for Victoria when he was chosen to tour England in 1938, but he fully justified his selection finishing only behind Bradman and Brown in the tour averages. The small dapper stoke player was at his peak

26. Pollard, 1982, p450

before the onset of war, but after peace came he was more defensive in his batting.

Hassett was a cricket hero after World War II. His innovative captaincy of the AIF side which toured England and India greatly benefited charities and hospitals and revived cricket popularity. When Test cricket resumed Hassett was appointed as Australia's captain after Bradman retired, and he gained series wins against South Africa in 1949–50 and England in 1950–51 before narrowly losing the 1953 series in England. It was Australia's first Ashes loss since 1934, but the great post war sides had declined and a resurgent England was too strong.

Hassett scored two Test centuries in 1953, and when the tour ended his tally of first class centuries was 59 with ten of them being scored in Tests. In retirement his perceptive and witty comments on ABC radio during Test matches were appreciated by cricket lovers, before he retired to the NSW coastal town of Batehaven where he passed away in 1993.

## 162. WAITE, M.G. (Mervyn) : 1911–85.
### Tests (2)
11 runs at 3.66
1 wicket at 190.00

A determined South Australian all-rounder who performed well against county teams on the 1938 tour of England, but whose bowling was pulverised by English batsmen when they totalled 7/903 in the only Test match Waite played. His score of 339 in Adelaide club cricket during the 1935–36 season was a competition record that even Bradman did not surpass.

## 163. BARNES, S.G. (Sidney) : 1916–73.
Tests (13)
1072 runs at 63.05
4 wickets at 54.50

**A colourful, abrasive personality whose capable batting and fielding sometimes took second place to his controversial public comments and antics.**

A colourful, abrasive personality whose capable batting and fielding sometimes took second place to his controversial public comments and antics.

Barnes was selected for the 1938 tour of England after playing only eight matches for NSW, but missed many games after suffering a broken wrist. He was then an aggressive and brilliant stroke player, but after this initial tour Barnes became much more measured in his approach to batting in order to establish himself permanently in Australia's strong batting line-up. At club practices his focused approach made few friends, and Barnes was seen as being selfish and a poor team player.

Sid Barnes' first three figure score against England in 1946–47 occupied ten hours and 42 minutes, and spectators were irked by his incessant appeals against the light in his slow innings of 234. He scored a century at Lords in 1948, but at Manchester he suffered broken ribs after being struck fielding close to the wicket. This incident restricted his playing options for the rest of the tour.

Barnes declared himself unavailable for the 1949–50 tour of South Africa because of the Board's financial arrangements for the chosen players. From that point on he gradually drifted out of first class cricket after scoring three Test centuries and nine scores over 50. Barnes criticised his former teammates harshly in his newspaper reports on the 1953 tour of England, and 20 years later he died from an overdose of sleeping pills.

## 164. JOHNSON, I. B.G. (Ian) :
## 1918–98.
Tests (45)
1000 runs at 18.51
109 wickets at 29.19

One of Australia's few successful off-break bowlers who obtained good bounce and flighted the ball cleverly.

Johnson debuted for Australia against New Zealand in 1945–46, and in the following summer his figures of 6/42 off 30.1 overs against England clinched a spot in Bradman's "Invincibles" team which toured England in 1948 His opportunities were limited there because of the superb form of Australia's fast bowling attack, and, despite performing well on the 1949–50 tour of South Africa, Johnson missed selection in Hassett's 1953 team which toured England.

When Hassett retired it was Johnson who was preferred over Miller as Australia's next captain, and at first the diplomatic Victorian handled the role well. He led Australia to victory over the West Indies in the Caribbean tour of 1954, and series wins were also recorded against both Pakistan and India. However the 1956 tour of England was a disappointment. Many of the team veterans were past their best, and Johnson was not in the same class as English off-spinner Jim Laker, who captured 19 wickets in just one Test on a turning wicket at Manchester.

Johnson retired from first class cricket after capturing five wickets in an innings 27 times and ten wickets in a match on four occasions. He was appointed secretary of the

Melbourne Cricket Club in 1957, and played a leading role in the successful organisation of Melbourne's 1977 Centenary Test.

## 165. LINDWALL, R.R. (Raymond) : 1921–96.
Tests (61)
1502 runs at 21.15
228 wickets at 23.03

**A great fast bowler whose smooth approach to the bowling crease is still cherished by those who were privileged to see him in action.**

A great fast bowler whose smooth approach to the bowling crease is still cherished by those who were privileged to see him in action. Ray Lindwall varied his pace cleverly, he could swing the ball late both ways while maintaining deadly accuracy, and he possessed a lethal bouncer and a clever slower ball.

In his youth Lindwall had a choice between cricket and Rugby League as his main sporting pursuit. He was an exceptional fullback with St. George and played with NSW the age of 20. Many experts believe that he would have become a Test fullback if he had continued in the sport.

After returning from active service in World War II, Lindwall was in poor physical shape, and it took some time for him to bowl at full pace. However he scored an aggressive century against England in the Third Test of the 1946 series, and impressive bowling form against India during the following summer clinched Lindwall a spot in Bradman's famous 1948 English touring side.

Lindwall was enormously successful on tour, taking 18 Test wickets at 20.38, which was the best bowling average in either side. Together with Keith Miller he formed one of the most famous fast bowling attacks of all time. After bowling well with Hassett's side in

South Africa, Ray Lindwall returned to England both in 1953 and 1956, but by then he was a diminished force. He did, however, perform well with Ian Johnson's team on the Caribbean tour of 1954–55 where he scored his second Test century.

After moving to Queensland in 1954, where he captained the state team, Lindwall was able to prolong his Test career by becoming a medium pace swing bowler. In that role he was an effective force for Richie Benaud's team which won the 1958–59 home series against England. Overall in 61 Tests Ray Lindwall gained five wickets in an innings 12 times, he captured 228 wickets, and he scored two centuries. After retiring from the game, Lindwall opened a florist shop in Brisbane, where he died in 1996.

## 166. McCOOL, C.L. (Colin) : 1916–86.

Tests (14)
459 runs at 35.30
36 wickets at 26.61

One of the best all-rounders in NSW, Queensland and Australia during the immediate post-war period. The serious minded McCool was a superb slips fieldsman, a competent batsman who notched a Test century, and a leg spin bowler who gained considerable turn with his unusual round arm deliveries.

Colin McCool obtained a wicket with his second delivery in Test cricket when he claimed New Zealand's last batsman in a 1945–46 match, he captured eight wickets in the Second Test of the 1946–47 series against England, and in the Melbourne Test which followed he scored an undefeated 104.

This impressive form gained McCool a

place in Bradman's 1948 team which toured England, but the dominance of Lindwall and Miller kept him out of the Test side. He did however perform well in all five Tests of the 1949–50 series in South Africa, but shortly before the 1953 English touring team was chosen McCool committed himself to a professional career in county cricket. For five years he played with great success for Somerset. After finishing up there McCool returned to Australia where he became a market gardener at Umina near Gosford.

## 167. MEULMAN, K.D. (Kenneth) : 1923–2004.
Tests (1)
0 runs

A dour but accomplished batsman who failed in his only Test against New Zealand immediately after World War II, served as 12th man for the next three Test matches against Hammond's 1946–47 English team, and was never chosen again in Australian sides.

Meulman scored seven centuries for his native state Victoria. After moving then to Western Australia (WA) he hit a further 11 three figure scores in Sheffield Shield games for WA, whom he often captained between the 50s and early 60s. Ken Meulman's son Ron later played 18 matches for WA, and he notched an unbeaten century against NSW at Sydney in 1969–70.

## 168. MILLER, K.R. (Keith, "Nugget") : 1919–2004.
Tests (55)
2958 runs at 36.97
170 wickets at 22.97

A handsome and brilliant player who remains the best all-rounder Australia has produced. He mingled freely with royalty and millionaires, he was equally at ease with mug punters at racecourses, and he was the idol of the cricket public. Miller could completely alter the course of a game with some attacking batting, a vital wicket with an unplayable delivery, or a superb catch. John Arlott, the esteemed English cricket writer, once said of Miller: "If I had my choice of a player to win a match off the last ball, whether it required a catch, a six, or a wicket, I would pick only one player – Keith Ross Miller."[27]

During his memorable career Miller played for Victoria, the Australian Services, NSW, Australia, Nottinghamshire, the MCC, Manly and North Sydney. In many of these games the laconic champion would need to borrow items such as bats, pads and socks in order to play. He was also a star Australian Rules footballer, who represented St.Kilda Victoria and NSW, and during World War II he piloted aircrafts over battle zones of Germany with the same nonchalant daring that he displayed on the cricket field.

To Miller Test cricket was no more than an enjoyable game. When Michael Parkinson, the famous television interview host, once asked him about the pressures that international players faced, Miller laughingly responded with "Pressure? There's no pressure. Having a Messerschmitt flying up your arse – that's pressure !"

When Miller began his first class career with Victoria he played merely as a batsman, but included fast bowling in his cricket repertoire after the war. His Test debut in 1946–47 was predictably a spectacular success, as Miller

27. Pollard, 1982, p721

> "If I had my choice of a player to win a match off the last ball, whether it required a catch, a six, or a wicket, I would pick only one player – Keith Ross Miller."

scored 79 and then captured 7/60 in England's first innings. His fast bowling partnership with Lindwall became legendary, and he was a key member of Bradman's 1948 "Invincibles" which easily won the Ashes series. Miller also played in three losing Australian Ashes teams against England between 1953–1956 when his skills had slipped, and his motivation was possibly low after Ian Johnson was preferred to him as Australia's captain.

As captain of NSW Miller was a bold and sometimes brilliant leader during his 26 matches at the helm. Seven of his 41 first class centuries were doubles, and he captured five wickets in an innings on 26 occasions. After Miller retired from the game he became a journalist, sports commentator, advertising celebrity, public relations officer and the owner of some slow racehorses.

In 1959 at the age of 41, Miller was persuaded to end three years of retirement and play one match for Buckingham against Cambridge University. Predictably he was the hero of the match, scoring 62 and 102 not out. In his final years Miller lived in Melbourne where he died in 2004 after enduring many months of poor health.

## 169. TALLON, D. (Donald "Deafy") : 1916–84.
Tests (21)
394 runs at 17.13
Dismissals 58 (50 catches and 8 stumpings)

A fine wicket-keeper for Queensland and Australia, and one of the fastest and most skilled stumpers the game has seen. Don Tallon did not debut in Tests until he was 30, but in his short international career he displayed some stylish and masterful glove work. After the English tour of 1948, where he caught 29 players and stumped 14 in the 14 matches he played, Bradman declared that Tallon had performed better than any other Australian keeper in England. The catch he swooped on from a Len Hutton leg glance in the final Test of that series, is still regarded as a wicket keeping gem.

At the age of 19 in the 1935–36 season Tallon scored 193 for Queensland against Victoria, and he then assisted in the dismissal of five of the opposition team. Following this impressive display the tall, sun scarred Tallon was unexpectedly overlooked for the 1938 Australian team which toured England, but his consistent performances were rewarded after World War II ended.

Despite battling an illness brought on by his war service, Tallon gained national selection against New Zealand, and he then broke all Australian records when he dismissed 20 victims in his first Test series against England in the 1946–47 season. His fine performances that season established Don Tallon as Australia's Test keeper for the next seven years, before he retired after the 1953 English tour.

## 170. TOSHACK, E.R.H. (Ernest) : 1914–2003.
### Tests (12)
### 73 runs at 14.60
### 47 wickets at 21.04

An unusual left arm medium or slow bowler who was exceptionally accurate and could move the ball both ways off the pitch. These skills held Toshack in good stead when he emerged as a match winner in one of his 12 Tests.

Ernie Toshack was born in the small NSW mining town of Cobar, and remained in bush cricket competitions during the Great Depression years. Once he moved into higher standards of the game a ruptured appendix put him out of calculations for a 1938 tour of England, but figures of 6/18 off 20 overs against New Zealand in 1945–46 gained him a place in the opening Test at Brisbane against the 1946–47 English team.

On a pitch helpful to his bowling style, Toshack captured the fine match figures of 9/99, and his haul of 17 wickets for the series gained him a place in Bradman's 1948 team to tour England, despite mystery and misgivings about his age. "I stayed on 35 for a long time," reflected the easy going Toshack. Bradman predicted that the tall black-haired NSW player would be Australia's most successful bowler of the tour, but Toshack's ongoing knee problems resulted in Victoria's Bill Johnston taking on a main bowling role.[28]

**"I stayed on 35 for a long time."**

Ernie Toshack, a former railway gang labourer, became a Sydney building company executive after he retired from the game.

## 171. MORRIS, A.R. (Arthur) : 1922—.
Tests (46)
3533 runs at 46.48
2 wickets at 25.00

A champion left-handed opening batsman who, as an 18 year old, placed his name firmly in Australian cricket's record books when he scored a century for NSW against Queensland in each innings of his first class debut match.

Shortly after achieving world wide recognition for this feat, Morris served with the Australian Army in New Guinea for the next

28. Pollard, 1982, p995

six years, but in the first series after hostilities ceased, Arthur Morris scored three Test centuries in the series against Hammond's 1946–47 English team. Success continued on the 1948 tour of England, where the unflappable and sportsmanlike left-hander added two more Test centuries to his growing tally, and he headed the Test aggregates. Ironically the unassuming Morris scored 196 when Bradman was dismissed for a duck in his final Test. Most cricket fans are aware of Bradman's fate, but few realise how well Morris performed in that same memorable Test match.

Morris captained Australia twice in his long career, he toured England again in 1953, and he confronted the old foe again on home soil when England retained the Ashes in 1954–55. By then his arch rival and close friend Alec Bedser was dismissing Morris more regularly, but the accomplished Australian opener had also plundered many runs from the great English medium pacer in their many enthralling duels.

In 1955 Morris' wife Valerie contacted cancer, and he retired to care for her welfare after scoring eight of his 12 Test centuries against English teams. He re-married 12 years after the 33 year old Valerie died, and in recent times Arthur Morris has been an active member of the SCG Trust.

**Ironically the unassuming Morris scored 196 when Bradman was dismissed for a duck in his final Test.**

## 172. TRIBE, G.E. (George) : 1920—.

Tests (3)

35 runs at 17.50

2 wickets at 165.00

An unorthodox left arm spinner and forceful Victorian batsman who spent his most productive years of cricket playing in Lancashire League ranks and for Northamptonshire in English county cricket.

War interrupted the 19 year old Tribe's ascendancy in cricket, but he still managed to play Australian Rules professionally while he was on active service. Encouraging all-round performances for Victoria rejuvenated his cricket prospects in 1946–47, but after Tribe played three Tests against England that summer with modest success, he became a professional player with Lancashire League clubs.

During the winter months in England George Tribe pursued his engineering career, and he combined his twin roles of engineering and cricket when he settled in Northampton. In county cricket Tribe was a dominant player, gaining the double of 100 wickets and 1,000 runs in a season on seven occasions. Tribe also toured India twice with strong Commonwealth teams, and in retirement he became a respected cricket coach.

## 173. FREER, F.A.W. (Frederick) : 1915–88.

Tests (1)

28 runs at n.a.

3 wickets at 24.66

An impressive Victorian opening bowler who unluckily played in the same era as Lindwall, Miller and Johnston.

Fred Freer performed well in his only Test of the 1946–47 Ashes series when he replaced an injured Lindwall, but he was unable to retain his place in the strong Australian team.

He enjoyed all-round success with Lancashire League clubs and touring Commonwealth teams, and Fred Freer was also well known in both South Africa and India where he coached during English winters.

## 174, DOOLAND. B. (Bruce) :
## 1923–80.
Tests (3)
76 runs at 19.00
9 wickets at 46.35

A quality leg spinner who only represented Australia in three Tests, but was still chosen in 1954 by the esteemed "Wisden" magazine, to be one of the five cricketers of the year.

Dooland was selected in South Australia's team at the age of 17, but was refused leave from work by his bank employers. War then interrupted his cricket, but after serving as a commando in the Pacific conflict, Dooland collected a hat trick in Sheffield Shield ranks and played two Tests against Hammond's 1946–47 team. He later opposed India in one Test, but in 1948 Dooland decided to pursue a cricket career in England.

In both Lancashire League ranks and in county cricket with Nottinghamshire Dooland was a star, collecting 368 wickets with Notts in just two seasons. "Wisden" recognised his fine achievements in 1954, and there was disappointment at Trent Bridge when Dooland decided that his children would be educated in Australia. His family and he returned home in 1957, and Bruce Dooland passed away in 1980.

## 175. HARVEY, M.R. (Mervyn) :
## 1918—.
Tests (1)
43 runs at 21.50

Mervyn Harvey was the eldest of six cricketing brothers, four of whom scored Sheffield shield centuries, while Mervyn and the more famous Neil represented Australia.

Mervyn Harvey was an audacious stroke-player who was capable of dominating high quality attacks if luck was on his side. He scored 12 and 31 in his only Test against Hammond's English tourists in 1946–47, and during his state cricket career Mervyn Harvey scored three centuries.

## 176. HAMENCE, R.A. (Ronald) : 1915—.

Tests (3)
81 runs at 21.50

A reliable batsman who served South Australian cricket admirably and represented Australia on three occasions.

Between 1935 and 1951 Ron Hamence scored 11 centuries for South Australia, and this tally included at least one three figure score against every other state. He scored a valuable 30 not out in the Fifth Test of the 1946–47 season against Hammond's English team, and Hamence also played in two Tests against India.

On the 1948 tour of England he scored 532 runs at an average of 32.33, and his illustrious Australian teammates were disappointed when the popular Hamence missed a tour century by one run against Somerset at Taunton.

## 177. JOHNSTON, W.A. (William "Bill") : 1922—.

Tests (40)
273 runs at 11.37
160 wickets at 23.91

A tall Victorian who was pencilled in as

being only a reserve bowler when Bradman's 1948 team began its English tour. However Johnston finished that northern summer sharing the honour with the great Ray Lindwall of being the leading wicket-taker in the Test series. Some English opponents found Johnston's late swing and disconcerting bounce more difficult to counter than the speed of Lindwall or Miller. The gangly left hander's ability to also bowl competent spinners added to his impressive versatility.

Bill Johnston grew up on a dairy farm near rural Colac, and he made slow progress at first in his quest for higher cricket honours. However strong performances against the 1947–48 Indian touring team gained him English tour selection in 1948, and he continued to represent Australia with distinction against all major cricketing nations of the world until the 1954–55 season. His best Test performance against England was match figures of 9/183 from a marathon 84 overs at Trent Bridge in 1948.

The easy going Johnston received only one criticism from his great Australian teammate Bill "Tiger" O'Reilly. "As a bowler he (Johnston) has one failing – he hasn't a temper." Fellow players chortled at Johnston's antics in the field and his abysmal performances with the bat, but the amiable Victorian had the last laugh on two occasions in Test cricket with his batting performances.[29]

On January 4th 1952 Bill Johnston and Doug Ring snicked and slogged Australia to an unlikely victory at the MCG against the West Indies when they added a match winning 38 runs in a last wicket partnership. Furthermore Johnston, the acknowledged batting dunce of most Australian teams, topped

29. Pollard, 1982, p558

Johnston, the acknowledged batting dunce of most Australian teams, topped the batting averages at the end of the 1953 tour of England!

the batting averages at the end of the 1953 tour of England! Johnston's final average was an unbelievable 102, with 28 not out being his highest score in his aggregate of 102 runs. He was only dismissed in one innings.

To this day that 1953 achievement remains Bill Johnston's favourite cricket memory.

## 178. HARVEY, R.N. (Neil) : 1928—.
Tests (79)
6149 runs at 48.41
3 wickets at 40

The star member of a talented cricketing family, who became one of the most brilliant batsman and fieldsman to ever wear "the baggy green".

The star member of a talented cricketing family, who became one of the most brilliant batsman and fieldsman to ever wear "the baggy green". Neil Harvey, who batted left-hand, and threw with his right, scored 21 centuries and accepted 64 catches at Test match level between 1948 and 1963, and he remains one of Australia's leading run-makers in Test cricket.

At 19 Harvey guaranteed his place in Bradman's 1948 English touring team after he scored a brilliant 153 in his second Test match against India. Then at Leeds he had a dream Ashes debut when he scored a crucial 112 in his first encounter with England. The elegant, fast scoring Victorian, who was the youngest member of the "The Invincibles" team by seven years, finished fourth in the Test averages and scored 1129 runs at 53.76 on his first of ten overseas Australian cricket tours, four of which were to England.

The nimble footed left-hander continued to plunder runs from South African, West Indian, Indian and Pakistani Test teams, and in 1961 he captained Australia to a victory in England on the only occasion that he was the Test skipper. It must have been disappointing for Harvey when first Ian Craig and then Richie Benaud were appointed as Australian captains ahead of him, but he remained a fine team player and a valued vice-captain of the national teams in the late '50s and early '60s.

Neil Harvey served as a national selector after he retired as a player at the end of the 1962–63 season. He is still a much respected figure in the game, and now resides in Sydney.

## 179. JOHNSON, L.J. (Leonard) : 1922—.
### Tests (1)
### 25 runs at N/A
### 6 wickets at 12.33.

This lively fast medium bowler was the spearhead of Queensland's attack between 1946 and 1953, but he only gained Test selection once due to the presence of Lindwall, Miller and Johnston in Australian teams of his time.

Len Johnson, like the more celebrated speedster Craig McDermott, was raised in Ipswich. He played his only Test against India in 1946–47, and he performed creditably, returning match figures of 6/74.

## 180. LOXTON, S.J.E. (Samuel) : 1921—.
### Tests (12)
### 554 runs at 36.93
### 8 wickets at 43.62

A popular, belligerent Victorian all-rounder, who became a valued stop gap player when any of the esteemed batting or bowling specialists in Bradman's 1948 team were injured.

Sam Loxton earned a place on that tour to England after he scored an undefeated 232 against Queensland in his Sheffield Shield debut. A swashbuckling 93, which included five towering 6s in the Fourth Test match at Leeds, was the highlight performance of his tour. During the following season in South Africa at Johannesburg Loxton scored his first and only Test century.

After retiring from the game, Sam Loxton enjoyed a distinguished public career. He was the Liberal Party Whip in the Bolte and Hamer Victorian state governments, he served as the MLA for Prahran for 25 years, and he has been a Victorian and Australian cricket selector. Loxton now resides on Queensland's Gold Coast.

## 181. RING, D.T. (Douglas) : 1918–2003.
Tests (13)
426 runs at 22.42
35 wickets at 37.28

A large man who bowled competent leg spinners and hit the ball long and hard. Doug Ring played first class cricket for Victoria over 15 summers between 1938 and 1953, and he toured England in both 1948 and 1953.

Australia's reliance on its speed bowling attack left Ring with few opportunities in England, though his bowling lacked the flight and imagination expected of quality spinners.

Ring only scored one first class century, probably because of his tendency to loft the ball when he batted, He and tail ender Bill Johnston remain famous for their last wicket stand of 38 which produced an unexpected Test victory against the 1951–52 West Indian team.

## 182. SAGGERS, R.A. (Ronald) : 1917–1987.
### Tests (6)
### 30 runs at 10.00
### dismissals 24 (16 catches, 8 stumpings)

A stylish wicketkeeper who was an outstanding stumper. He performed well when he replaced the injured Tallon in the Leeds Test of the 1948 English tour, where Saggers finished with the same number of tour dismissals as Tallon.

When Tallon was unavailable to tour, Ron Saggers displayed excellent form in all five Tests of the 1949–50 South African series. After he returned the tall Sydneysider retired from first class cricket to concentrate on his insurance career.

# PLAYERS BETWEEN THE BRADMAN AND BENAUD ERAS

## 183. MORONEY, J. (John,"Jack") : 1917–99.

Tests (7)
383 runs at 34.81

A competent NSW batsman who scored a century in each innings of a Test and represented Australia against three different countries.

Jack Moroney gained selection in Hassett's 1949–50 team which visited South Africa after scoring 655 runs at 72.77 in the 1948–49 domestic season, and he was an outstanding success on tour. At Johannesburg in the Fourth Test he scored 118 and 101, and he amassed six centuries in total on the tour.

On returning to Australia Moroney was an automatic selection for the First Test against England at the Gabba in 1950–51. However a pair of ducks forced the Sydney school teacher out of the Test team until he was included one more time against the 1951–52 West Indies team.

Moroney consistently scored heavily at a state level, but after his success in South Africa he became a stodgy batsman which possibly counted against him with Test selectors.

## 184. NOBLET, G. (Geoffrey) : 1916—.

Tests (3)
22 runs at 7.33
7 wickets at 26.14

A South Australian medium pace swing

bowler and off-spinner who represented Australia briefly in the 1950s.

Geoff Noblet was an outstanding state player claiming 236 wickets for the cost of only 18.92 apiece. His action was unusual, and controversial to some observers, but he was passed by all umpires, and was well respected for his persistency and accuracy.

Noblet played one Test in South Africa with Hassett's team, he was chosen for a home Test against the West Indies in 1951–52, and his final appearance at this level occurred in 1952–53 against the touring South African team. In retirement he served for some time as vice-president of the South Australian Cricket Association (SACA).

## 185. IVERSON, J.B. (John "Jack") : 1915–73.

Tests (5)
3 runs at 0.75
21 wickets at 15.23

**A clumsy Victorian player who briefly enjoyed fame in Test cricket, because he developed a mystery delivery which initially confused some of the best players of his time.**

A clumsy Victorian player who briefly enjoyed fame in Test cricket, because he developed a mystery delivery which initially confused some of the best players of his time.

Iverson perfected the delivery with table tennis balls during his war service stint in New Guinea. His unusual technique, which was basically copied by John Gleeson two decades later, consisted of flicking the ball from his middle finger, and varying positions of his thumb produced indistinguishable spin from either the off or leg side.

When key Australian players were absent on South African Test duties in the 1949–50 season, Jack Iverson baffled Victoria's inter-state opponents so much that he captured an impressive 46 wickets at 16.60 in the Sheffield Shield competition. Visiting English batsmen in Freddie Brown's 1950–51 team were also bewildered, and Iverson captured the superb figures of 6/27 in one Test, and an imposing 21 wickets for the series.

However the talented and experienced NSW duo of Miller and Morris unravelled the inexperienced Iverson when they faced him in a Shield match. Both the Australian Test stars unnerved the newcomer by facing up a metre outside leg stump. The temperamental Iverson lost his accuracy, Miller and Morris hammered his bowling, and at the end of the 1950–51 season Iverson declared himself unavailable for state selection until he had overcome his bowling problems.

Jack Iverson struggled with depression problems in retirement, and he tragically took his own life in 1973.

## 186. ARCHER, K. A. (Kenneth) : 1928—.
### Tests (5)
### 234 runs at 26.00

An aggressive opening batsman who represented Australia in five Test between 1950 and 1952.

As an 18 year old Ken Archer debuted for his state in the 1946–47 season, and he toured South Africa in 1949–50 where he was 12th man in all five Tests. When he finally debuted against England in 1950–51, Archer scored 26 and 46. He also played two Tests against the 1951 52 West Indian side. Ken Archer captained Queensland on 20 occasions, and opened his state team's batting for 11 years.

After retiring from the first class scene, Ken Archer continued to develop his radio management career.

## 187. BURKE, J.W. (James, "Jim") : 1930–79.
Tests (24)
1280 runs at 34.59
8 wickets at 26.75



A brave but stodgy opening batsman who played some defiant innings for Australia, but irked many spectators with the slowness of his scoring. He once took 250 minutes to score 28 not out, so it is no wonder that an irate spectator once yelled "I wish you were a statue and I was a pigeon, Burke", during one of his prolonged stays at the wicket.[30]

Jim Burke debuted for NSW at the age of 18, and a year later he scored a debut Test century against Freddie Brown's 1950–51 touring team. Burke later scored Test centuries in India and South Africa but his most successful season occurred during the Ashes' tour defeat of 1956 in England, when he headed the Australian Test and tour averages. Burke's solid opening partnerships with Colin McDonald was one of the highlights of a dismal English summer for the "baggy greens".

In an age when 'chucking' was a hot debating point Burke bowled his off-spinners with a very jerky action. He was never called by umpires, and once captured 4/37 in a Test match.

Jim Burke was a genial companion off the field, so it profoundly shocked the cricket world when temporary financial problems induced him to commit suicide at the age of 49.

30. Pollard, 1982, p215

# 188. HOLE, G.B. (Graeme) :
# 1931–1990.
## Tests (18)
## 789 runs at 25.45
## 3 wickets at 42.00

A middle order batsman for NSW, South Australia and Australia who was given many chances to succeed at Test level, but fell short of expectations.

Graeme Hole played the 1949–50 season with his home state of NSW before moving to Adelaide to improve his prospects. He first gained selection with Australia in the Fifth Test of the 1950–51 series against England, and scored 63 in the second innings. However after displaying indifferent form against the touring West Indians and South Africans, Hole slipped out of the Test team despite accumulating large totals in state cricket.

Hole scored a century against Worcester-shire to start the 1953 tour of England promisingly, but again his form fell away and he only scored 273 runs from ten innings in the Tests. Alec Bedser claimed his wicket five times in the series. When the Englishmen retained the Ashes in the 1954–55 series in Australia, Frank "Typhoon" Tyson became Hole's new nemesis, as he bowled him for low scores in three successive innings.

Tyson's speed virtually ended Graeme Hole's Test career. He continued to perform well in state matches until the 1957–58 season, and most of his 11 first class centuries were scored with South Australia. He died in Adelaide at the age of 59.

## 189. LANGLEY, G.R.A. (Gilbert) : 1919—.

Tests (26)
374 runs at 14.96
dismissals 98 (83 catches, 15 stampings)

A wicketkeeper who lacked the polish of Oldfield or Tallon, but whose average of four wickets a Test made him one of Australia's most reliable players behind the stumps.

Gil Langley established himself as South Australia's keeper in the 1947–48 season, and he was understudy to Ron Saggers on the 1949–50 Australian tour of South Africa. In Sagger's absence, Langley gained Test selection against the West Indies at Brisbane in the 1951–52 series, and his seven dismissals in that game was a record for a debut Test keeper. His final tally of 21 dismissals for the series provided longevity for Langley, because he stood behind the stumps in most Tests for Australia until his retirement following the 1956 tour of England. That losing series provided a personal highlight for the popular Langley, as in the Lords fixture he became the first wicket keeper to dismiss nine batsmen in a Test.

The thickset Langley was also an excellent Australian Rules footballer, who represented South Australia 15 times. For over 20 years he was a state parliamentarian, and he served as Speaker in the South Australian House of Assembly.

# THE BENEFITS OF BENAUD

Australia gradually lost ground in Ashes contests after Bradman and other members of the famous 1948 team drifted into retirement. England humbled "baggy green" Test teams at home in 1953 and 1956, and in Australia during the 1954–55 series.

The 1953 Tests provided a close contest, but the fast bowling duo of Tyson and Statham at home in 1954–55, and the spinning wiles of Laker and Lock in England during the 1956 series, decisively swung the pendulum England's way.

Australia embarked on a rebuilding program, and it started on the 1957–58 tour of South Africa. Bob Simpson, Wally Grout, Ian Meckiff and Lindsay Kline all made their Test debuts, and the team was led by 22 year old Ian Craig, Australia's youngest ever captain.

The youthful NSW pharmacist proved to be an excellent leader. Team spirit was strong, the selectors' patience with Richie Benaud was finally rewarded with match winning all-round performances, and the team won all of its tour matches.

However further problems presented themselves before the eagerly awaited 1958–59 Ashes Tests began in Australia. A new Test captain was unexpectedly needed when Craig was struck down with a severe bout of hepatitis.

International games were also becoming dreary affairs and starting to lose popularity. In the First Test at Brisbane England only scored 134 runs on the opening day, Australia struggled to reach 148 runs on day two, and the meagre total of 228 runs was ground out on days three and four.

England's Trevor "Barnacle" Bailey was the main culprit, scoring 68 runs in a mind numbing 6 hours and thirty minutes, and when he reached 50 it was the slowest half-century recorded in Test history. Australia's Jim Burke was little better, labouring to 28 not out in 250 minutes on the final day.

The batting boredom extended to other parts of the cricket world. In the Third Test of the 1959–60 series in Pakistan the home side only scored 104 runs in a day against Australia. It then took an agonising 318 minutes for Shoji udo-Din to score 45 in the Second Test of that dreary series.

The game badly needed rejuvenating, and Australia found the saviour cricket needed in its captaincy choice for the 1958–59 Ashes series.

# PLAYERS OF THE ERA

## 190. BENAUD, R. (Richard "Richie") : 1930—.
### Tests (63)
### 2,201 runs at 24.45
### 248 wickets at 27.03

Richie Benaud has made an immeasurable contribution to cricket during his long involvement in the game. As a player he was a world class all-rounder – a superb gully fields-man, an attacking batsman, a shrewd and for-midable leg spinner and one of Australia's greatest captains. He went on to become a respected cricket columnist. Today he is the acknowledged guru of all the celebrity com-mentators who bring international cricket via the television screen to thousands of homes, pubs and clubs.

Benaud's early progress in the game was slow. Our national selectors noted the 21 year old NSW all-rounders' potential when they included him in Australia's Test team which played the West Indies in the 1951–52 series, and Benaud was persevered with on English tours in 1953 and 1956. There were many early failures among a few glimmers of hope for future success in these developmental years, and on the 1957–58 tour of South Africa the selector's faith was rewarded.

Benaud became a world class all-rounder in that Test series, and between 1958 1964 he consistently produced outstanding perform-ances. He joined the ranks of elite all-rounders when he captured more than 200 wickets and scored over 2000 runs, and his final tally of 248 Test wickets remained a world record for 16 years. Richie Benaud also scored three cen-

**Benaud shook the game out of the doldrums with his attacking and innovative leadership**

turies and accepted 65 catches in his 63 Test match career.

However it was his inspirational captaincy that moved Benaud into the legendary class. With the ready co-operation of West Indian captain Sir Frank Worrell, Benaud shook the game out of the doldrums with his attacking and innovative leadership during the 1960–61 Test series in Australia. Enthusiastic crowds returned to the Tests, and the popular visitors from the Caribbean were given a ticket tape farewell in the streets of Melbourne at the end of the tour.

Benaud's elevation to the captaincy before the 1958–59 Ashes series surprised most fans, as long serving vice-captain Neil Harvey appeared to be the obvious choice. However the selector's gamble with Benaud was a spectacular success. He moulded his teams into closely knit groups, and he seldom erred in his game tactics.

As the team leader he displayed team loyalty and an impressive ability to deal with a hostile English media when accusations of "chucking" were levelled at Australian bowlers Meckiff, Rorke, Slater and Burke. During his captaincy years Benaud only lost four of his 27 Tests, and this outstanding achievement has only arguably been equalled in recent times by Ian Chappell, Mark Taylor, Stephen Waugh and Ricky Ponting.

In 1977 there were rumblings of disagreement in established cricket circles when Benaud became the public relations consultant with WSC. However the diplomatic skills of the ever suave Benaud helped heal the wounds between the rival factions, and the healthy state of cricket today owes much to the substantial and varied contributions of Richie Benaud.

## 191. McDonald, C.C (Colin) : 1928—.
### Tests (47)
### 3106 runs at 39.32

A tenacious opening batsman who stood firm against the most hostile bowlers and gave Australia many solid starts in his Test career which lasted over a decade.

McDonald first donned "the baggy green" cap against the West Indians in 1951–52, the first of his five home Test series. McDonald also toured India, Pakistan, South Africa the West Indies and England in 1953, 1956 and 1961. He was Australia's leading batsman in the 1958–59 home series against England, and McDonald's determined approach was never more evident than in the Manchester Test of 1956 when English spinner Jim Laker snared a match winning 19 wickets.

Colin McDonald, despite battling injury, scored 32 and 89 while Australian wickets fell all around him. In total the gritty Victorian scored five Test centuries and 17 scores over 50, and it was his slashing cut shot behind point that brought him  many of his runs.

In retirement McDonald has been an insurance broker, and he also served as the Executive Director of the Lawn Tennis Association of Australia.

## 192. THOMS, G.E. (George) : 1920—.
### Tests (1)
### 44 runs at 22.00

An opening batsman who featured in many excellent opening batting partnerships for Victoria with Colin McDonald. George Thoms scored three first class centuries, and he represented Australia at the SCG against the West Indies in the Fifth Test of the 1951–52 series.

## 193. ARCHER, R.G. (Ronald) : 1933—.
Tests (19)
713 runs at 24.58
48 wickets at 27.45

A talented all-rounder, who retired prematurely at the age of 25 from first class cricket because of knee and spine problems. At one stage he was touted as being the next Keith Miller before injuries and increasing weight ended that possibility.

Ron Archer followed his older brother Ken into Queensland and Australian cricket, and he toured England twice in 1953 and 1956. Ron Archer had the ability to move the ball sharply either way, but his new ball opportunities were limited by the presence of Lindwall, Miller and Johnston in Australian teams of that era. Archer's best figures in Tests was achieved at The Oval in 1956 when he captured 5/53. His only Test century was scored at Kingston, Jamaica during the 1954–55 tour of the West Indies.

Ron Archer increased his involvement in media work when he retired from first class cricket, and he became the manager of a Brisbane television station.

## 194. CRAIG, I.D. (Ian) : 1935—.
Tests (11)
358 runs at 19.88

Ian Craig remains the Peter Pan of cricket, the ever youthful slip of a boy who danced fleetingly into cricket record books before prematurely vanishing into retirement. He is the youngest player to ever represent NSW, the youngest player ever to be awarded the coveted "baggy green" cap, and Australia's youngest ever captain.

Craig was born in the southern NSW town of Yass, and after a series of impressive batting performances in Sydney schoolboy and grade cricket games, he was chosen in the state team at the age of 16 years 249 days. Soon after Ian Craig scored a dashing 213 not out for NSW against the 1952–53 touring South African team, and his esteemed state captain was most impressed.

"For a boy of his age it was unbelievable," enthused Keith Miller. "He hit every shot in the meat of the bat... and had composure through it all that many veterans could not have matched."[31]

This performance elevated Ian Craig into Australia's Test side at the tender age of 17 years and 239 days, and a composed innings of 53 and 47 on debut against South Africa, gained him selection in Hassett's 1953 English touring team.

By then Craig was a sporting celebrity with sportswriters covering every move he made in England, and the pressure of expectations began to affect the shy, reserved young man. He only scored 429 runs at 16.50 on the tour, and on returning to Australia Ian Craig began studying to be a pharmacist and placed his cricket career on hold for two seasons.

Craig's good form in the domestic season of 1955–56 saw him return to England with Ian Johnson's 1956 team. However like many of his experienced teammates he was baffled by Jim Laker's sharply spinning off-breaks. Craig still fared better than in 1953, scoring 872 runs at 36.33. A Test score of 40 against

31. Pollard, 1982, p194

**Ian Craig remains the Peter Pan of cricket, the ever youthful slip of a boy who danced fleetingly into cricket record books before prematurely vanishing into retirement.**

India on the return trip home encouraged the Australian selectors to activate the Craig experiment to another level.

With many of the post-war stalwarts moving into retirement a rebuilding process began with the Test team, and Ian Craig was surprisingly chosen ahead of the experienced Neil Harvey to captain an inexperienced Australian team to South Africa in 1957–58. The 22 year old skipper coped admirably with the huge task. He won the respect of his experienced players, he developed a strong spirit within the touring group, and Australia was undefeated in the five Tests. Craig himself again performed disappointingly with the bat, but his captaincy success seemed to guarantee his immediate future before fate struck him a cruel blow.

Just prior to the eagerly awaited 1958–59 Ashes Tests began in Australia, Ian Craig was struck down by a severe bout of hepatitis, and he was replaced by Richie Benaud who became entrenched in that position when Australia  regained the Ashes. Craig returned successfully to state cricket after he recovered. However his pharmaceutical marketing commitments and marriage responsibilities prevented a comeback to Test cricket.

Ian Craig scored 15 first class centuries between 1951 and1962, and he gained the respect of all who were associated with him in cricket. If his health had been stronger, if his commitment to cricket had been fiercer, and if the national selectors had not rushed his advancement in the game, then Ian Craig may be remembered today as one of Australia's great players.

## 195. DAVIDSON, A.K. (Alan "Dave") : 1929—.

Tests (44)
1,328 runs at 24.59
186 wickets at 20.58

A match winning all-rounder who became the spearhead of Australia's attack after Lindwall, Miller and Johnston retired from Test cricket. The tireless NSW left-hander, moved the ball late in either direction from a lively pace, he scored vital runs in the late order, and he raked in some superb catches during his 44 match Test career.

Alan Davidson was raised near Gosford, and played his first Test against England on the 1953 tour. He took only eight wickets on his initial tour, but in future Ashes Tests Davidson became a formidable force. In the 1958–59 series in Australia he captured 24 wickets, his haul on the 1961 English tour was 23, and on home grounds in 1962–63 Davidson claimed 24 wickets.

The 1961 tour also produced Davidson's most memorable batting performance when Graham McKenzie and he shared a vital last wicket partnership of 98 runs in the Manchester Test. Davidson contributed an unbeaten 77, and earlier that year he blasted a typically aggressive 80 in the tied Test match against the West Indies. In that historic game Davidson became the first player to score 100 runs and take 10 wickets in a Test match.

On the field Davidson often hobbled back 15 paces to the start of his run-up, and his impish teammates on the South African tour presented him with his own massage table so that the team table would become more readily available. However Alan Davidson was a lion hearted performer on the field and a great team man. In retirement he

173

became director of Rothman's National Sports foundation, President of the NSWCA and a national selector.

## 196. HILL, J. C. (John "Jack") : 1923–74.
Tests (3)
21 runs at 7.00
8 wickets at 34.12

A quickies Victorian leg spinner who represented Australia in three overseas Tests, two in Hassett's 1953 team in England, and one on the 1954–55 tour of the West Indies.

Hill played for Victoria between 1945 and 1956, and his figures of 7/51 against South Australia in 1952–53 were a career best. Jack Hill captained his club side St. Kilda for seven years, and he died at the age of 51 in 1974.

## 197. DE COURCY, J.H. (James "Jim") : 1927–2000.
Tests (3)
81 runs at 16.20

A classy batsman from Newcastle who played all his club cricket in his home city. Jim de Courcy represented NSW for ten seasons, and after scoring runs consistently in county fixtures on Australia's 1953 tour of England, he played in the last three Ashes Tests of the series. A sparkling knock of 41 at Old Trafford raised the hopes of his fans in the Hunter Valley, but de Courcy failed in the other five innings.

Jim de Courcy was a very private person who started many innings well but only scored six first class centuries during his career. Many believe that his obvious talent would have developed more if he had played a higher standard of club cricket.

## 198. FAVELL, L.E. (Leslie) : 1929–87.

Tests (19)
757 runs at 27.03

Les Favell's cavalier approach to opening the batting delighted many spectators around the world. It also contributed to some premature dismissals, and may partly explain why this talented stroke-player only scored one Test century, and was never selected to tour England during his 19 years of first class cricket.

Favell moved from Sydney to Adelaide to improve his prospects, and in his debut state game he scored a dashing 164 against his former NSW mates. He went on to amass a formidable 12,379 runs in first class matches, which included 91 half-centuries and 27 hundreds. His only Test century of 101 was achieved in India in 1959–60, and Les Favell also toured South Africa, New Zealand and the West Indies with Australian teams.

The popular Favell captained his state on 95 occasions, and in 1963–64 he led South Australia to its first Sheffield shield title in 11 seasons. Les Favell's refreshing approach to cricket and his good sportsmanship won the applause of all who knew him. It shocked the cricket world when he died tragically from cancer at the age of 56.

> **Les Cavell's refreshing approach to cricket and his good sportsmanship won the applause of all who knew him, and it shocked the cricket world when he died tragically from cancer at the age of 56.**

## 199. MADDOCKS, L. V. (Leonard) : 1926—.

Tests (7)
177 runs at 17.70
dismissals 19 (18 catches, 1 stumping)

A competent Victorian wicket-keeper who was regarded as the second choice for that position in Australian teams for much of the 21 years of his playing career.

Len Maddocks first represented Victoria in 1946–47, two years before his brother Dick gained selection. Dick Maddocks scored two Shield centuries for the Vics in his 21 games, while Len notched five hundreds for his state, and a valuable 69 for Australia against the speed of Tyson and Statham at Adelaide in the Fourth Test of the 1954–55 series.

The ever-cheerful Maddocks toured the West Indies, England, New Zealand and India with Australian teams, and he also became a respected Tasmanian coach for six years.

Len Maddocks has remained actively involved in the game since he retired as a player. He handled the difficult job of being the team manager of many future WSC players well during the 1977 tour of England, and he has also served as an Australian selector.

## 200. BURGE, P.J.P. (Peter) : 1932–2001.
Tests (42)
2,290 runs at 38.16

An effective and hard hitting middle order batsman who scored heavily for Queensland and finally matured into a damaging player for Australia.

Peter Burge debuted for his state at the age of 20, and two years later he gained selection for Australia against the triumphant 1954–55 English team. On subsequent tours of the West Indies and England he made little impact at a Test level, but he came of age as a quality batsman during the 1961 English trip.

The burly Burge blasted an undefeated 37 at Lords to power Australia to victory when the game was in the balance, and he ended the series by scoring his first Test century at the Oval. That innings of 181 was one of four Test 100s scored by Burge, all of which were registered against England. Burge also scored a superb 160 at Headingly in 1964, and in Melbourne, during the 1965–66 series, he blasted 120.

Burge's batting was characterised by strong drives on either side of the wicket, as well as fierce pulls and hook shots. He scored 24 centuries for Queensland including a mammoth innings of 283 against NSW in the 1963–64 season. Burge was an accountant, a cricket commentator, a devotee of trotting race meetings and a match referee at many international cricket matches before he passed away in 2001.

## 201. WATSON, W.J. (William "Willie") : 1931—.
### Tests (4)
### 106 runs at 17.66

A capable NSW opener who toured the West Indies with Ian Johnson's 1954–55 team but failed to impress at Test match level.

Watson scored 155 in his second first class game against England, which resulted in him again confronting Len Hutton's 1954–55 team in the final Test. On that occasion he made 18 and 3.

During his visit to the Caribbean in 1955 Watson's top score in Tests was only 30. He continued to play well for NSW totalling six centuries before a family bereavement forced him out of first class cricket in the late 1950s.

For many years Willie Watson continued to play the game in suburban Sydney.

## 202. CRAWFORD, W.P.A. (Patrick) : 1933—.
Tests (4)
53 runs at 17.66
7 wickets at 15.28.

A tall NSW fast bowler who appeared at one stage to be the heir apparent to Ray Lindwall in the Test team, but whose career was thwarted by muscular problems. Pat Crawford began impressively in state cricket, claiming match figures of 12/114 against Queensland in his 1954–55 debut season. He then toured England in a very wet summer with Ian Johnson's 1956 team, but found it difficult to generate the same pace from the softer pitch surfaces. In his only Test appearance on tour at Lords, Crawford pulled a muscle after delivering 29 balls, and he played no further part in the match.

Crawford did play in all three Tests against India on the way home, but was not suited by the matting pitches and did not perform well.

## 203. MACKAY, K.D. (Kenneth "Slasher") : 1925–82.
Tests (37)
1,507 runs at 33.48
50 wickets at 34.42

A gum chewing Queenslander with an ugly but effective batting style which netted him 23 first class centuries and 13 scores over 50 in Test cricket. The sarcastic nick name of "Slasher" was given to him because of his cautious approach to batting, and a columnist from the "Manchester Guardian" aptly described one of his less inspiring performances by saying "Mackay is like the common cold. There is no cure for either." Nevertheless Mackay toured England twice, he played in two series at home against the Ashes rivals and one against the West Indies, and he also visited South Africa, India and Pakistan with Australian teams.[32]

At home he was much admired for his stoic performances. In the 1961 Fourth Test at Adelaide against the West Indies "Slasher" Mackay and number 11 batsman Lindsay Kline enabled Australia to secure an unlikely draw after they shared an unbroken scratchy last wicket stand of 66 runs in 100 minutes. Mackay let the final searing delivery from Wes Hall thud into his ribs rather than take the risk of offering a catch, and the two unlikely heroes enabled Australia to escape with a draw.

Under the inspired captaincy of Richie Benaud, "Slasher" also became an effective medium pace bowler. He restricted England's run scoring effectively in the 1961 series, and proved to be a match winner on a Test matting wicket in Pakistan.

Ken Mackay wrote an entertaining book titled "Slasher Opens Up" after he retired, and he died prematurely in 1982 at the age of 56.

### 204. RUTHERFORD, J.W. (John "Pythagoras") : 1929—.

Tests (1)

30 runs at 15.00

1 wicket at 15.00

A gritty opening batsman who was the

32. Pollard, 1982, p672

first Western Australian selected for a major tour and also the first to play Test cricket. John Rutherford gained his selection in Australia's side after scoring four excellent centuries for W.A. between 1953 and1955.

Rutherford, who taught mathematics at a Perth school, was given the nickname "Pythagoras" by Keith Miller when they were teammates on the 1956 tour of England. Rutherford scored a pleasing 98 on his first appearance at Lords, but overall he performed disappointingly on tour, scoring 640 runs at 22.86. On the way home the stocky opener played in a Test in India, and after registering his sixth century for WA in the 1957–58 season John Rutherford dropped out of first class cricket.

## 205. WILSON, J.W. (John "Jack") : 1922—.

Tests (1)
1 wicket at 64.00

A left-arm spinner who represented South Australia between 1950 and 1957, after moving across from Victoria. Wilson's cleverly flighted deliveries gained him selection in Ian Johnson's 1956 team, and he did enjoy one exceptional game on tour against Gloucestershire when he captured the memorable match figures of 12/61.

Overall, however, Jack Wilson experienced little success in England, taking only 43 wickets for the summer on pitches unsuited to his style of bowling. He did play a Test in India on the return trip, and after one more season in the Sheffield Shield competition, Jack Wilson became actively involved in cricket administration.

## 206. GROUT, A.T.W. ("Wally", "The Griz") : 1927–68.
### Tests (51)
### 890 runs at 15.08
### dismissals 187 (163 catches, 24 stumpings)

A Queensland and Australian wicket-keeper who resembled his idol Don Tallon in his style. "I don't know if Tallon was an inspiration to Grout or a model which he copied," mused Sir Donald Bradman, when asked to comment on Grout's performances. "But without doubt their glovework was very similar."[33]

Wally Grout was the heir apparent to Don Tallon in his state team for over seven seasons, before the Bundaberg legend retired from the first class scene shortly after the 1953 tour of England. Grout's international chance came later when he gained selection in the 1957–58 Australian team which toured South Africa. He made the most of his late opportunity at Test level by claiming six opposition batsmen in an innings at Johannesburg.

Between 1958 and 1964 Grout built an enviable reputation as Australia's Test keeper. He toured England in 1961 and 1964, and he also visited the West Indies, India and Pakistan. In the epic 1960–61 series against the West Indies Wally Grout gained 23 dismissals, and in Australia against England in 1958–59 he dismissed 20 opposition batsmen. On two occasions he snared eight victims in Test matches.

Grout had secretly suffered health problems for years before he died prematurely at the age of 41. Prior to the 1964–65 tour of the West Indies he had suffered a heart attack, and he knew then that his days were numbered.

33. Pollard, 1982, p460

Sadly he was also a heavy gambler, and after his death his former teammates rallied around Wally Grout's widow and family and provided financial support.

## 207. KLINE, L.F. (Lindsay) : 1934—.
Tests (13)
58 runs at 8.28
34 wickets at 22.82

A Victorian left arm off-break and googly bowler who once captured a much coveted Test match hat trick. However, he is better remembered for the time he scored 15 not out against the 1960–61 West Indian team in Adelaide.

Between 1955–1962 Lindsay Kline was a valued member of Victoria's bowling attack, and he toured New Zealand, South Africa, England, India and Pakistan in Australian teams. In the Second Test against South Africa at Cape Town in the 1957–58 series, Kline captured a Test hat trick, and he topped the Test bowling averages for the series after claiming 15 wickets at 16.33. Against England he appeared in two Tests in the 1958–59 series, but failed to gain Test selection on the 1961 tour of England.

Kline was a genuine number 11 batsman. Consequently when he took guard against the formidable West Indian attack in the 1960–61 Adelaide Test, with two hours of play still remaining and only one wicket in hand, some of his Australian teammates started to pack up for an early departure. However against all odds, Kline and the equally resolute Ken Mackay successfully defied the visitors' hostile bowling until stumps were drawn, and enabled Australia to salvage an unlikely draw. At stumps Lindsay Kline remained 15 not out,

and to this day that modest score is still vividly recalled when cricket fans meet this successful Melbourne businessman.

## 208. MECKIFF, I. (Ian) : 1935—.
Tests (18)
154 runs at 11.84
45 wickets at 31.62

A Victorian left-arm fast bowler who was
cheered to the echo on his 24th birthday after
gaining the superb figures of 6/38 against
England in the Melbourne Test of the
1958–59 series, but labelled a cheat and
forced out of the game five seasons later.

Ian Meckiff came into Test cricket under
one law. He was later banned after administra-
tors changed that law, because of fears that the
international game was being harmed by the
controversy about "chucking" or bowling the
ball illegally.

There was no hint of the impending storm
of controversy when the friendly and outgoing
South Melbourne player first entered first class
cricket. Meckiff graduated from Sheffield
Shield ranks to a tour of New Zealand with an
Australian second X1 side. His promising
career continued to prosper when he captured
11 wickets from the four Test matches he
played in South Africa with Ian Craig's
1957–58 touring team. Ian Meckiff then
played a valuable role when Australia regained
the Ashes from England in the 1958–59 series,
collecting 17 wickets, and he gained 12 further
Test wickets on the 1959–60 tour of India.

Meckiff's consistent form then fell away
when he took only two wickets in the series
against the 1960–61 West Indian touring
team, and injury removed him from calcula-

tions for the 1961 tour of England. At this stage Meckiff had participated in five Test series, and he had never been called for throwing. In light of the media criticism that later surrounded Meckiff, it would have been interesting to observe the English umpires' reaction to his whippy action if he had been selected to tour in 1961.

However after Ian Meckiff was called twice for throwing in a 1962–63 Shield match, the public and media pressure began to mount more for action to be taken. Finally, at the Gabba, in the opening Test of the 1963–64 series against South Africa, Meckiff was called for throwing by umpire Col Egar. Australia's captain Richie Benaud appeared to concur with Egar's decision, as he opted to be a bowler short for the remainder of the match, and did not bowl Meckiff at either end when Australia was in the field.

Meckiff's career in first class cricket was over, and the shattered Victorian retired to recover from his ordeal in the privacy of normal life. Today Ian Meckiff is employed by a business that is often prominent at Test match venues, and the amiable Victorian appears to hold no grudges. Arguably there were genuine concerns about his controversial action, but the tardy way in which Ian Meckiff was forced out of the game is still open to criticism.

**But the tardy way in which Ian Meckiff was forced out of the game is still open to criticism.**

## 209. SIMPSON, R. B. (Robert "Bob", "Simmo") : 1936—.

Tests (62)
4,869 runs at 46.81
71 wickets at 42.26

Bob Simpson was one of Australia's best opening batsman. He was also a superb slips fieldsman, a handy spin bowler, an astute captain and an excellent coach. However "Simmo" is best remembered for returning to Test cricket six years after he first retired to rebuild Australia's faltering team after WSC had lured away most of the best players.

Simpson began playing Sydney first grade cricket with Petersham-Marrickville when he was just 15, and a year later he was chosen as 12th man in the NSW team. When he substituted for a player at the SCG his state captain Keith Miller laconically waved him into the slips area, where he had never fielded previously. Half an hour later the teenage Simpson had taken two blinding catches and he remained in that fielding position for the rest of his career.

Despite five reasonably successful seasons with NSW Simpson failed to gain a Test place, so he moved to Western Australia in 1956 to increase his opportunities. At that stage, following Jim Burke's retirement, Australia needed a new opening batsman. Simpson followed the advice of Neil Harvey and took on that role in the West.

The move up the order proved to be enormously successful. At one stage in the 1959–60 season Bob Simpson had the mammoth batting average of 300 after 902 runs in six innings, and when he went to England with the 1961 team, he scored 1947 runs on the tour. Simpson's insatiable appetite for runs continued. After returning to NSW he scored his third double century in Sheffield Shield ranks, and in that same 1963–64 season he plundered 359 against Queensland. When Benaud retired that summer Simpson replaced him as Australia's captain.

At that stage a Test century had eluded him, but that changed dramatically when Bob

Simpson's team retained the Ashes on the 1964 tour of England. The Aussie skipper batted for two days in the Fourth Test at Old Trafford, and his mammoth score of 311 clinched the Ashes for Australia. Further Test double centuries and centuries followed against the West Indies, South Africa and India. When Simpson retired to a successful business career at the end of the 1967–68 season, he had amassed an impressive 4131 runs in Test cricket at an average of 48.60.

He did continue in Sydney grade cricket, and it was the 41 year old Bob Simpson that the Australian selectors turned to as captain when most of leading players were deemed ineligible for Test cricket, after they defected to WSC in 1977. Simpson achieved credible results with his inexperienced team, leading Australia to an exciting 3:2 series victory against India, and he averaged 53.90 in a middle order batting position. Against the pace of the West Indians in the Caribbean in 1978 though, the aging Simpson faltered. He retired again as a player from the Test scene after the Board of Control would not guarantee him selection against the 1978–79 touring English team. When he finally departed as a player Bob Simpson had amassed ten Test centuries and taken a record breaking 110 catches

However Bob Simpson's amazing longevity in the game has continued. He introduced the rigorous training drills and fitness needs that are required for the modern game when he coached Australian teams for the decade between 1986 and 1996, and his success rate in that role was most impressive. A World Cup victory in 1987, four triumphant Ashes series, and a superb series victory in the Caribbean in 1995, resulted in Australia becoming the leading Test nation during Simpson's tenure as coach.

**It was the 41 year old Bob Simpson that the Australian selectors turned to as captain.**

Simpson's all-absorbing commitment to the game has continued, as he still continually bobs up in Bermuda, India and other parts of the cricket world in coaching and advisory roles.

## 210. GAUNT, R. A. (Ronald) : 1934—.

Tests(3)
6 runs at 3.00
7 wickets at 44.28

A strong fast medium bowler whose success was impeded by the high percentage of no balls he bowled when he dragged his foot over the bowling crease.

Ron Gaunt hailed from Western Australia, and the red haired opening bowler played successfully with his home state from 1955 to 1960. He toured New Zealand and then South Africa, where he played one Test match in the 1957–58 series, and in 1960–61 he transferred his cricket career to Victoria. Strong performances with the Vics saw him chosen in the 1961 Australian team that toured England.

Gaunt topped the tour averages that summer, but he only appeared in the final Test at The Oval where he captured 3/53. Ron Gaunt's final Test selection occurred against South Africa in the 1963–64 season.

## 211. O'NEILL, N.C. (Norman) : 1937—.

Tests (42)
2,779 runs at 45.55
17 wickets at 39.23

A handsome, well built NSW batsman who was labelled another Bradman after he scored over 1000 runs in the 1957–58

Sheffield Shield season. However, the pressure of expectations resulted in him becoming tense at the batting crease, especially at the start of his innings.

Norman O'Neill was always a powerful and accomplished shot maker, and he was predicted to be Australia's big hope against the 1958–59 visiting English team when he made his Test debut at the age of 22. He began promisingly, scoring 34 and 71 not out, averaged 56.40 for the series, and was a brilliant fieldsman in the covers region. O'Neill went onto score centuries against all the major Test playing nations except South Africa. He also toured England, New Zealand and India twice, as well as visiting the West Indies, Pakistan and South Africa. When knee problems forced him out of first class cricket after 12 seasons in the game, Norman O'Neill had the impressive Test batting average of 45.55 in his 42 appearances for Australia.

O'Neill unfortunately had acrimonious relationships with both cricket authorities and Keith Miller towards the end of his career, which ended his cricket days on a sour note. Since his retirement Norman O'Neill has had several business interests, and he has also been a cricket commentator on ABC radio. His son, Mark O'Neill, was a useful all-rounder with Western Australia and NSW.

**Norman O'Neill had the impressive Test batting average of 45.55 in his 42 appearances for Australia.**

## 212. SLATER, K.N. (Keith) : 1935—.
Tests (1)
1 run n.a.
2 wickets at 50.50

A moderately performed Western Australian all-rounder who was targeted by the English press as being one of the "chuckers" in

Australian first class cricket when the topic of illegal bowling was exhaustively debated during the 1958–59 Australian/England series.

Our national selectors added to the furore when they called the off-spinner up for Test duty for one match that summer, but the ever cheerful Slater had little impact in his only appearance at this level.

Keith Slater was also an ·outstanding Australian Rules footballer and baseballer, and in recent times he has commentated on ABC radio.

## 213. RORKE, G. F. (Gordon) : 1938—.

Tests (4)

9 runs at 4.50

10 wickets at 20.30

One of the most controversial fast bowlers of all time who was labelled a "chucker" and a "dragger" by the English press, especially after he experienced success in the 1958–59 Ashes series. Unquestionably Rorke did drag his foot well down the pitch before he delivered the ball, and concern about that aspect of his bowling led to the controversial front foot rule being applied at the end of the '58–59 season. This irritating law has been a problem to cricket umpires and players ever since.

Rorke was a giant of a man who bowled with tremendous pace when the rhythm was right in his bowling run-up. He comprehensively bowled the English captain Peter May with a real thunderbolt in a tour game. Later, when the NSW speedster made his Test debut in Adelaide, he performed well in very hot conditions, taking 5/101 off 52 overs .

However the popular fast bowler contacted hepatitis during the 1959–60 tour of India and

Pakistan, and when he was sent home early the seriously ill young man had lost over 10 kilograms in weight.

Gordon Rorke never regained his rhythm and pace after that setback. He dropped out of first class cricket after being omitted from the NSW squad in 1964.

## 214. STEVENS, G. B. (Gavin) : 1932—.
Tests (4)
112 runs at 16.00

Another whose promising career was ruined by severe hepatitis which shortened his 1959–60 tour of India and Pakistan.

Prior to then Gavin Stevens had been a prolific run scorer for South Australia.. He scored three successive centuries in Shield cricket in 1958–59, and during that same stellar season the strongly built opener hammered 259 not out against NSW.

Selection for the sub-continental tour followed, with Stevens opening up with  Colin McDonald in four Tests for understandably modest results, considering his state of health. At 28 Gavin Stevens' promising career was over after he scored seven centuries for his state between 1954 and1960.

## 215. Jarman, B.N. (Barrington "Barry") : 1936—.
Tests (19)
400 runs at 14.81
dismissals 54 (50 catches, 4 stumpings)

A burly but agile wicket-keeper who was understudy to the great Wally Grout on five overseas tours, and the number one keeper on four tours.

Barry Jarman first represented South Australia in the 1955–56 season, and he played his first Test at Kanpur in India during the 1959–60 tour of the sub-continent. Another three seasons passed before a second Test chance came Jarman's way, but he continued to keep and bat well for South Australia and played a significant role in the state team's Sheffield Shield title in 1963–64.

Jarman toured England three times in 1961, 1964 and 1968, and on his third trip he took over the reigns of captaincy in the Headingley Test after Bill Lawry was injured. Jarman took a brilliant catch down the leg-side to dismiss Keith Fletcher in that Test, and the tour vice-captain was at the helm when Australia retained the Ashes. Barry Jarman toured India, Pakistan and New Zealand twice, and he also went to South Africa and the West Indies.

Barry Jarman declared himself unavailable for the 1967–68 South African tour. Two seasons later, after gaining an impressive 560 dismissals and scoring five centuries in first class cricket, he retired from the game to devote more time to his Adelaide sporting goods business.

## 216. MARTIN, J.W. (John) : 1931–92.

Tests (8)

214 runs at 17.83

17 wickets at 48.94

A perky little left-arm unorthodox spinner and hard hitting late order batsman, who clouted at least 200 sixes for the Petersham club in Sydney as well as quite a few in first class cricket arenas around the world.

He was affectionately known as "the mayor of Burrell Creek," which is a NSW

**He was affectionately known as "the mayor of Burrell Creek".**

hamlet where he spent a large part of his life as the local post master. Johnny Martin had a chequered career in Sheffield Shield cricket with both NSW and South Australia, and he did not gain Test selection until the Melbourne fixture of the 1960–61 series against the West Indies.

Martin made a sensational Test debut, scoring 55 in a ninth wicket partnership of 97 with "Slasher" Mackay, and later removing the famous trio of Kanhai, Sobers and Worrell in the space of just four balls. Martin played three Tests in that memorable series, and he also played at this level against India, Pakistan and South Africa without ever having the impact that he achieved in his first Test match.

The enthusiastic but erratic spinner also toured England in 1964, but was not called upon in the Test series. In November 1971, after he returned to Burrell Creek to lick stamps, the 40 year old Johnny Martin suffered a heart attack. His health problems were ongoing, and he died at the age of 60.

## 217. MISSON, F.M. (Frank "Tarzan") : 1938—.
Tests (5)
38 runs at 19.00
16 wickets at 38.50

A determined Sydney fast medium bowler who modelled his fitness program on the schedules adopted by Olympic swimmers, and followed a diet that included vast quantities of honey, nuts and fruit.

Frank Misson collected the wicket of West Indian opener Conrad Hunte with his second delivery in Test cricket in the 1960–61 series in Australia, and selection for the 1961 English touring side followed. There he played a vital batting role in the Second Test, assisting Ken Mackay in a crucial 49 run stand for the tenth wicket. However the rapid development of Graham McKenzie and a series of ankle injuries hindered Misson's international prospects, and he only played in five Test matches.

Back in Australia Misson continued in Shield cricket until the 1963–64 season, and he also participated in Sydney grade and Lancashire League competitions for some years.

## 218. HOARE, D. E. (Desmond) : 1934—.
### Tests (1)
### 35 runs at 17.50
### 2 wickets at 78.00

A strongly built Western Australian fast-medium bowler who was a high achiever for his state but only played in one Test for Australia during his ten years of first class cricket.

Hoare started his Adelaide Test debut well against the 1960–61 West Indian team when he removed Conrad Hunte cheaply, but his final match figures of 1/156 finished any future Test aspirations.

## 219. LAWRY, W. M. (William "Bill", "The Phantom") : 1937—.
### Tests (67) plus one abandoned
### 5,234 runs at 47.15

One of Australia's most accomplished openers who was chosen as a developmental player for the 1961 tour of England, but ended up being a hero of an Ashes victory.

Bill Lawry debuted for Victoria in the

**Seeing Lawry bat "was like watching a corpse with pads on".**

1955–56 season at the age of 18. Five seasons later, after scoring a timely 206 against NSW, he clinched selection in the 1961 Australian team that toured England.

Lawry enjoyed a superb northern summer. He topped the batting averages, he became only the third post-war Australian to top 2,000 runs on an English tour, and he scored two Test centuries. His debut hundred, when he scored a gallant 130 against a hostile English attack on a bowler-friendly Lords' pitch, is still regarded as one of the classic knocks of all Ashes Tests.

In 1962–63 Bill Lawry was appointed captain of his state, and he led Victoria to a Shield victory for the first time in 12 years. Centuries continued to flow from his bat, and by the time Lawry returned to England as vice-captain of the 1964 team, he and Bob Simpson had formed one of Australia's best opening partnerships. The tall left-handed opener again performed well in England, though his six hour innings of 108 in the Fifth Test evoked the comment from one pressman that seeing Lawry bat "was like watching a corpse with pads on".[34]

Bill Lawry took over the Australian captaincy when Simpson first retired in 1967–68, and the ex-plumber and racing pigeon owner at first enjoyed great success in this role. Australia retained the Ashes in England in 1968, and it gained victory against a strong West Indies team at home in 1968–69. Lawry led from the front scoring three excellent centuries against Gary Sobers' team from the Caribbean, and he was a cheerful and popular leader.

However team spirit in the Australian side declined during the arduous 1969–70 tour of

34. Pollard, 1982, p624

India and South Africa. Lawry appeared to be impatient when his players made mistakes, he clashed with umpires and spectators, and he became somewhat of a recluse from the rest of the team group.

Australia received a 4:0 drubbing from a strong South African team, and when Ray Illingworth's English team easily regained the Ashes before the 1970–71 series in Australia was even completed, the national selectors dropped Lawry from the team and appointed Ian Chappell as captain for the final Test in Sydney. It is the only time that selectors have replaced a captain during a Test series, and a shocked Bill Lawry was also omitted from the 1972 Australian team which toured England.

Bill Lawry captained his country 25 times for nine wins, eight draws and eight losses. Despite the furore that occurred regarding the manner of his dismissal, history vindicated the need for change. Ian Chappell inspired a pre-viously dispirited team and became one of Australia's finest captains.

Lawry finished his career with an enviable batting record, scoring 13 centuries and 27 fifties in Test matches against all the major countries. In retirement he has become an enthusiastic and long serving cricket commen-tator, with a ready wit that seems far removed from the morose and tetchy figure he became when the pressures of captaincy weighed heav-ily on him.

**It is the only time that selectors have replaced a captain during a Test series.**

### 220. McKENZIE, G.D. (Graham "Garth") : 1941—.
Tests (60) plus one abandoned
945 runs at 12.27
246 wickets at 29.78

An excellent Western Australian fast-medium bowler who became the youngest Australian to capture 100 Test wickets, a goal he achieved in three years and 165 days.

Graham McKenzie's potential was first noticed at a Perth net practice by the West Indian captain Sir Frank Worrell, and the strongly built 19 year old became the "baby" of the 1961 Australian team which toured England. There he shared a crucial last wicket stand of 98 runs with Alan Davidson, which was instrumental in Australia winning the Manchester Test.

McKenzie toured England again in 1964 and 1968, and between 1964 and 1970 he also played in India, Pakistan, the West Indies and South Africa. In the losing Australian team that opposed South Africa in 1969–70, the late outswing and durability of McKenzie was one of the few highlights for Australia, and he won the respect of his dominant opponents.

Graham McKenzie was two wickets short of Richie Benaud's Test record haul of 248 victims, when he retired from international cricket. He could have become the new record holder if he had not previously been left out of two Test teams against the struggling 1967–68 Indian team. McKenzie had captured ten wickets in the previous Test against the visitors from the sub-continent, and it appears that he was controversially omitted so that untried candidates for a 1968 English tour could display their bowling talents.

McKenzie continued to play English county cricket with Leicester after ending his Test career, and he also participated in South African domestic cricket.

# 221. BOOTH, B.C. (Brian "Sam") : 1933—.
## Tests (29)
## 1,773 runs at 42.21
## 3 wickets at 48.66

A fluent and elegant stroke-player who was renowned for his fine sportsmanship.

Brian Booth was also a national hockey player who was unavailable for Sheffield Shield cricket when he represented Australia at the 1956 Olympic Games. At that stage the tall upright player from the NSW country town of Bathurst had played one season with NSW, and his steady progress gained him a tour berth in the 1961 Australian team which toured England where he played in two Tests.

Booth served as vice captain on the 1964 English tour, and he occupied that role again in the Caribbean in 1964–65. He also captained Australia in two Tests when Simpson was ill or injured. In the 1962–63 season he registered successive centuries against England, but his finest Test innings occurred in the Caribbean where he scored a gritty 117 against the formidable pace bowling attack of Wes Hall and Charlie Griffith.

Booth was at his best in a crisis, and after this man of strong religious convictions scored a gutsy century for Australia, sportswriter Robert Gray called him "Sam Booth, Australia's one-man Salvation Army."[35]

Brian Booth scored five Test hundreds and he represented NSW on 93 occasions. During his many cricket tours he often attended church services and fund raising activities for charities, with local Test stars such as the Reverend David Shepherd and Conrad Hunte.

35. Pollard, 1982, p164

**"Sam Booth, Australia's one man Salvation Army."**

## 222. GUEST, C.E.J. (Colin) : 1937—.
Tests (1)
11 runs at 11.00
0 wickets for 59

A Victorian and Western Australian cricketer who shared the fast bowling responsibilities with Davidson and McKenzie in just one Test against Ted Dexter's 1962–63 English team. "I think I got picked so 'Davo' could have a rest now and then," commented Guest wryly in recent times.[36]

Colin Guest captured five wickets or more in innings five times in first class cricket and he also represented Western Australia in baseball. He has coached state junior teams in the West, and managed an Australian Under 18 cricket team that toured America in 1979.

## 223. SHEPHERD, B.K. (Barry) : 1938—.
Tests (9)
502 runs at 41.83

**A burly left-handed batsman from Western Australia who kept the hands of fielders warm with the power of his shots.**

A burly left-handed batsman from Western Australia who kept the hands of fielders warm with the power of his shots.

At the age of 18 Barry Shepherd scored 103 not out in his state debut match, and his three double centuries and 10 centuries were all scored representing Western Australia. Shepherd also captained his state team 39 times, a record that was finally surpassed by John Inverarity.

Barry Shepherd scored an undefeated 71 in his first Test match at Sydney against the 1962–63 English side, but after two more games he was dropped from the Australian team, and only played in six other Test match-

36. Pollard, 1982, p461

es against English, Pakistani and South African opponents. Barry Shepherd's highest Test score was 96 against South Africa in the 1963–64 series. He toured the West Indies in 1964–65, but was not selected in Test matches.

### 224. HAWKE, N. J. N. (Neil) : 1939–2000.
Tests (27)
365 runs at 16.59
91 wickets at 29.41

A powerful medium-pace bowler who bowled late in-swingers and cut the ball sharply off the pitch. He played for three states and represented his country in 27 Tests, before a recurring football injury, and a dispute with his Australian captain Bill Lawry, saw him finish his career in Lancashire League ranks.

Neil Hawke was a champion Australian Rules footballer, and in his youth he successfully combined both cricket and football. He first played state cricket for Western Australia for one season, before returning to his native state of South Australia in 1960–61. After producing excellent Sheffield Shield performances in the 1962–63 season, Hawke made his Test debut against England in the final fixture of the summer, and he cemented his position during the following season against South Africa when he captured 14 wickets.

In 1964 Neil Hawke headed the Australian bowling averages in England, and played exceptionally well in Tests at Headingley and The Oval, where he returned the respective figures of 5/75 and 6/47. His finest performance, however, occurred in the West Indies in 1964–65 where his 24 Test wickets made him the leading wicket-taker of the series.

An unhappy tour of 1968 under Lawry's captaincy caused Hawke to stay in England where he played seven seasons with various Lancashire League clubs. In the Australian summers this globe-trotting sportsman with the playboy image also played in Tasmania. After returning to Adelaide in 1980 Neil Hawke married for the third time, and his latest wife cared for him constantly when he became dangerously ill. Hawke returned to public speaking engagements after he appeared to make a complete recovery, but in recent years his health declined once more and he died in the year 2000 at the age of 61.

## 225. CONNOLLY, A.N. (Alan) : 1939—.
Tests (29)
260 runs at 10.40
102 wickets at 29.22

**He once bowled until there was blood inside his boots.**

A durable fast medium bower who improved noticeably when he slowed his pace and concentrated on being an accurate swing and seam bowler. Alan Connolly gave such committed service to Victoria and Australia, that Bill Lawry recalled that he once bowled until there was blood inside his boots.[37]

Connolly was first selected for his state in 1959, but he matured slowly and did not clinch a position in Australian teams until he went to England in1964. The fast bowling Test places were then occupied by McKenzie, Hawke and Corling, but Connolly performed well in Tests against India and Pakistan on the journey home.

Once again the big Victorian was left out of national teams in series against the West Indies, England at home and South Africa,

37. Pollard, 1982, p285

but he performed well enough at home against India in 1967–68 to tour England again. There he showed that he had become a more accurate and cunning bowler, and Connolly headed the averages and captured 23 Test wickets in the 1968 series. Success continued at home where he gained 20 wickets for the series against the West Indies. Alan Connolly then produced his finest performances on his last overseas tour.

In South Africa in 1968–69 Connolly obtained his best Test figures when he captured 6/47 at Port Elizabeth in a match that Australia still lost by 323 runs. Once again he won the bowling average, taking 20 wickets in the series, but after Alan Connolly signed to play as a professional with Middlesex in 1969, back troubles forced him out of his three year contract after two seasons.

Alan Connolly finished his 12 year first class career with the proud record of being a member of three winning Victorian Sheffield Shield teams, and his 6/6 wickets for his state was a record making achievement.

## 226. VIEVERS, T.R. (Thomas) : 1937—.

Tests (21)
813 runs at 31.26
33 wickets at 41.66

One London cricket scribe wrote that Tom Vievers looked like a koala, but the cheerful Queensland off-spinner used other images to describe his craft.

"The successful off-spinner needs the dedication of a hot gospeller, the physical endurance of a long distance runner, and the hide of a rhinoceros."[38]

Tom Vievers needed all these qualities

**"The successful off-spinner needs the dedication of a hot gospeller, the physical endurance of a long distance runner, and the hide of a rhinoceros."**

when he bowled his marathon spell of 95 overs, which included 36 maidens, when he captured 3/155 against England in the 1964 Test against England at Manchester. Vievers' Herculean effort was only 17 balls short of the all-time record set by the West Indies spinner Sonny Ramadhin, and this performance indicated that Tom Vievers was a very economical bowler. However, he lacked the penetration to remove top quality batsmen.

The Queensland all-rounder became the best off-spinner that played for Australia since Ian Johnson. He captured 52 wickets and scored 725 runs on the 1964 tour, and he visited all of the major cricket countries of that time except the West Indies.

In Test matches his best bowling figures were 4/68, and his highest score was 88. For Queensland Tom Vievers captured 104 wickets and scored four centuries, before he retired at the age of 30 to devote more time to being an executive of a Brisbane radio station. He has also represented the Labor Party in the Queensland State Parliament.

## 227. REDPATH, I.R. (Ian "Redders") : 1941—.

Tests (66) plus one abandoned
4,737 runs at 43.45

A resolute and dependable Victorian batsman who played over a decade of Test cricket between1963–1976 against all the top cricket nations.

Ian Redpath became Bill Lawry's opening partner with Victoria after Colin McDonald retired, and he scored 97 in his debut Test against South Africa at the MCG in the

38. Pollard, 1982, p1035

1963–64 season. He was then dropped from the Australian team until the 1964 tour of England when he scored a valuable 58 not out in the Trent Bridge Test, and totalled 1075 runs for the season.

At this stage Redpath was persevered with as an opener, but his Test selection was spasmodic until the 1966–67 tour of South Africa when he batted down the order. On his return to England in 1968 Redpath's best Test score was 92. He recorded his first century at this level during the following season against the West Indies at home.

By then Ian Redpath was an accomplished player of spin bowling, and his duels with Lance Gibbs, the great West Indian off-spinner, were engrossing both then and when Australia toured the Caribbean in 1973. His highest score against England came in the 1970–71 season when he reached 171 in the Perth Test, but Redpath still missed selection for the English tour that followed in 1972. Another Test century against England was registered in 1974–75. Ian Redpath also scored a Test "ton" against New Zealand, another opposed to Pakistan, and three further centuries against the West Indies.

Redpath came briefly out of retirement to join WSC, but tore an Achilles tendon and soon returned to his antique shop in Geelong.

### 228. CORLING, G.E. (Graham) : 1941—.
#### Tests (5)
#### 5 runs at 1.66
#### 12 wickets at 37.25

A product of the NSW city of Newcastle who performed promisingly as a 22 year old in all five Test matches of the 1964 tour of England, but then disappeared from international cricket.

Graham Corling had a classical action for swing bowling, and he was well suited to English conditions where he bowled well in partnership with his new ball comrades McKenzie and Hawke.

In the usual sunny conditions that prevail in Australia, it was believed that he was not as effective at Test match level, and he soon returned to Newcastle where he became involved in club administration.

## 229. COWPER, R. M. (Robert "Bob", "Wallaby") : 1940—.
Tests (27)
2,061 runs at 46.84
36 wickets at 31.63

An excellent Victorian and Australian all-rounder of the early 1960s who scored a marathon 307 against England at the MCG in the 1965–66 season

Bob Cowper's family had a strong connection with Australian Rugby Union, which is why he was given he nickname "Wallaby". His brother David managed a Wallaby tour of England, and he also kept wickets at state level for Victoria.

Bob Cowper had scored five first class centuries when he was chosen to tour England in Australia's 1964 team, and he made his Test debut in the Fourth Test at Leeds. In the Caribbean the following season, Cowper blossomed into a world class player, topping the Australian averages and scoring two Test centuries against the feared West Indian fast bowlers.

Further centuries in the domestic season back home convinced some observers that Bob Cowper would one day captain Australia, but the talented left handed batsman too often allowed himself to become bogged down while batting. The Australian selectors dropped him from the Fourth Test against England in the 1965–66 after Cowpcr took four hours to score 60 in Sydney, but the determined left-hander responded with his triple century in the Fifth Test. His long innings occupied a mind boggling 12 hours and seven minutes of batting time, and included 20 boundaries.

Cowper developed his off-spin bowling skills on a successful 1966–67 tour of South Africa. After retiring from a Test career which yielded five centuries and ten scores over 50, he became a successful investment councillor who negotiated on behalf of many WSC cricketers at ACB meetings.

## 230. SELLARS, R.H.D. (Reginald "Rex") : 1940—.

Tests (1)

0 runs

0 wickets for 17

An Indian-born leg spinner who represented South Australia for five seasons between 1959–64 and gained selection in the 1964 Australian team which toured England.

Rex Sellars made slow progress in South Australia's team until the 1963 64 season when he captured 48 first class wickets. This performance gained him selection in Bob Simpson's Australian team which toured England in 1964, but the tall, loose-limbed

Sellars failed to adjust to a very wet summer in England. He also had a cyst removed from his spinning finger, which forced him out of cricket for much of the tour.

The finger operation was not entirely successful so Rex Sellars retired from first class cricket after returning home, and in the late 1970s he served as a South Australian selector.

# CHAPPELL'S CHALLENGE

Australian cricket endured a bleak period in the late 1960s and early 1970s. In South Africa the 1969–70 touring team received a 4:0 thrashing. Then in 1971–72 Ray Illingworth's English tourists convincingly regained the Ashes, in a series that was extended to seven Tests after continual heavy rain caused the Melbourne Boxing Day Test to be abandoned.

Team morale had declined so markedly that the national selectors took the unprecedented step of stripping the captaincy from Bill Lawry before the 1971–72 series had ended. The new captain who undertook the enormous challenge of rejuvenating the Australian team was Ian Chappell.

# PLAYERS OF THE ERA

### 231. CHAPPELL, I.M. (Ian "Chappelli")
### : 1943—.
Tests (75) plus one abandoned
5,345 runs at 42.42
20 wickets at 65.80

**Ian Chappell was born with cricket throbbing through his veins.**

A feisty and talented batsman, an outstanding slips fieldsman, a handy change bowler, and possibly Australia's greatest captain before his argumentative nature began to tarnish his fine achievements.

Ian Chappell was born with cricket throbbing through his veins. His grandfather was the former Australian captain Victor Richardson, and his father Martin Chappell was a competent Adelaide club player. Greg, the second son in the Chappell family, later became an Australian captain, and Trevor Chappell, the youngest of the three sons, also played Test cricket.

Ian Chappell debuted with South Australia as an 18 year old in 1962–63, and towards the end of that summer he scored his first century in Shield cricket. Chappell made his Test debut in 1964–65 against Pakistan, and on his first tour of England in 1968 Ian Chappell topped the Australian batting averages, scoring 1,261 runs at 48.50. In the following summer the new vice-captain of the "baggy greens" caught the attention of the cricket world when he scored five centuries against the touring West Indians, including two in successive Tests.

The arduous 1969–70 tour of India and South Africa followed this home series success, but after "Chappelli" scored 138 and then 99 in Tests against India, his captain Bill Lawry placed unnecessary pressure on the still inexperienced batsman. Before the South African series began, Lawry declared that "Ian Chappell was the best batsman in the world on all types of pitches".[39]

Chappell's run surge faltered against the impressive South African pace attack, he endured a poor series, and Australia was thrashed 4:0 in the Tests. Following that disappointment, and the subsequent defeat of Australia in the Ashes series at home, Ian Chappell replaced Lawry as captain on February 3rd 1971 before the final Test of the summer commenced.

The Chappell era had begun, and the new skipper immediately displayed his strong team ethic by criticising the tardy way his predecessor had been dismissed. Under Ian Chappell the Australians showed more fight in the last Test in Sydney, and on the following 1972 tour of England the raw but revitalised Australian side drew the series against Ray Illingworth's strong team.

Over the next few years Ian Chappell developed a great Australian team. Despite Dennis Lillee succumbing to a serious back injury, and Bob Massie losing form on that same 1973 Caribbean tour, Chappell guided his depleted and inexperienced team to a 2:0 series victory against the West Indies. Australia then defeated New Zealand in the 1972–73 summer, thumped England 4:1 in the home Ashes series, retained that coveted trophy on the 1975 tour of England, and thrashed a strong West Indian team in the 1975–76 home series.

Australia was undisputed champion of world cricket, but discontent was festering about some aspects of the strong Chappell

39. Pollard, 1982, p261

influence. Sledging of opponents in highly personal terms became more prevalent on the field, dress for official functions was sloppy, and Chappell's colourful language was not appreciated in some quarters. Even one of Chappell's greatest admirers, the revered commentator Alan McGilvray, who rated Chappell's captaincy ahead of both Bradman and Benaud, concluded that "many of the things that Ian has done were completely unnecessary."[40]

Ian Chappell inspired fierce devotion from his own team. However the abrasive, non-conforming South Australian continued to clash with cricket officials and umpires before, during and after the WSC years, until he retired as a player in 1980.

Since then Ian Chappell has become a well known television cricket commentator. He was once suspended from this role for using unacceptable language while on air, but overall Chappell provides well balanced and perceptive commentary for the thousands of viewers who watch international games throughout the world.

## 232. SINCOCK, D.J. (David "Stumps") : 1942—.

Tests (3)
80 runs at 26.66
8 wickets at 51.25

An erratic South Australian left-arm googly bowler, who was capable of bowling unplayable deliveries, but who also copped some fearful hidings from his Pakistani, West Indian and English opponents in Test match fixtures.

At the age of 19 David Sincock impressed

*"Many of the things that Ian has done were completely unnecessary."*

40. Pollard, 1982, p258

the West Indian players at an Adelaide nets practice, and a week later he captured a stunning 6/52 from 13 overs in his first state game against NSW. However at the end of that 1960–61 season the red-haired dental student withdrew from top cricket to complete his studies.

After returning to the first class scene, Sincock made his Test debut against Pakistan in 1964–65, and he represented Australia again that season in the Second Test in Trinidad when he toured the Caribbean. In that Test Sincock dismissed Sobers cheaply, but overall his bowling was too loose and he was punished accordingly.

After failing again in a 1965–66 Test against England, David Sincock fell out of favour with the national selectors and he retired in 1973 at the age of 31. His brother Peter played five games with South Australia, while his cousin Andrew Sincock was often selected in Sheffield Shield games, and captured a hat trick for his state team against the 1977–78 Indian team.

## 233. MAYNE, L.C. (Laurence) : 1942—.

Tests (6)

76 runs at 9.50

19 wickets at 33.05.

A Western Australian opening bowler who was given opportunities to cement a place in Australian Test teams, but lacked the penetration to regularly take the wickets of quality batsmen.

Laurie Mayne's best performance occurred in his debut Test against the West Indies at Kingston, Jamaica in 1965 when he returned the encouraging match figures of 8/99 from 41 overs.

He also toured India and South Africa in 1969–70, and during his Sheffield Shield career Laurie Mayne captured 118 wickets at 31.21 for W.A.

## 234. PHILPOTT, P.I. (Peter "Percy") : 1934—.

Tests (8)
93 runs at 10,33
26 wickets at 38.46

One of the most travelled players of all time who gained his first "baggy green" cap in his 30s, and later became a world respected cricket coach.

Peter Philpott was only a teenager when he debuted for NSW in the 1954–55 season. For the next 13 years cricket then dominated the leg spinning all-rounder's life. He performed in Lancashire League ranks during most winters, and played and coached in Australia, South Africa, New Zealand and South-East Asia during the English off-season.

At the age of 29 he retired briefly because of tendon problems to his bowling hand, but returned again so successfully that the dream of every player was at last achieved by "Percy" Philpott; he was chosen in an Australian team! Philpott later graphically described that euphoric moment when his selection was announced.

"Tension. The announcer's calm disciplined voice. One by one the names were read but mine did not come in alphabetical order as it should have if I was chosen…A crushing disappointment.. and then that marvellous announcer's voice apologised and added 'Peter Philpott, New South Wales.'[41]

"That moment, that wonderful, blissful

fraction of time was worth every sacrifice, every hard day of practice, all the concentration on correcting my faults and learning tactics."

The happy dream continued. On that 1964–65 tour of the West Indies Philpott captured 49 wickets, which was record for any Australian bowler in the Caribbean. He also played in all five Tests of the series, and when "Percy's" Test dream came to an end his best figures were the 5/90 he obtained at Brisbane in the 1965–66 series against England .

After retiring as a player the Sydney English and History master coached the New South Wales state team. After Peter "Percy" Philpott recovered from an open heart surgery operation in 1980, he became the team manager of the 1981 Australian team which toured England.

## 235. THOMAS, G. (Grahame) : 1938—.
Tests (8)<br>325 runs at 29.54

A gifted Sydney batsman who produced some brilliant innings in Shield cricket, but who was thwarted by the depth of players available for Australia at that time, as well as bouts of homesickness when he toured overseas.

Grahame Thomas debuted for NSW at the age of 20, and at the end of the 1959–60 domestic season, he toured New Zealand with an Australian Second X1, where his batting technique improved. However, after being pipped by Bill Lawry for selection in the 1961 English touring team, Thomas was also overlooked for the 1964 series in England when Ian Redpath was preferred. But the dashing NSW opener kept reeling off impressive scores, and he was rewarded with a place in

41. Pollard, 1982, p798



"That moment, that wonderful, blissful fraction of time was worth every sacrifice, every hard day of practice, all the concentration on correcting my faults and learning tactics."

Bob Simpson's team which toured the Caribbean in 1964–65.

Thomas held his place in the Test team against the West Indies for the entire series, and scored 61 in his second Test match. A superb score of 219 against Victoria at the MCG in the following summer gained him selection in three of the 1965–66 Tests against England, and the swarthy opener scored two half-centuries. He toured South Africa in 1966–67, but malicious local media gossip about his racial origins distracted the young man, who lost form and was not chosen in the Test series.

Following that unhappy experience, Grahame Thomas retired when he returned to Australia after scoring 17 first class centuries.

## 236. ALLAN, P.J. (Peter) : 1935—.
Tests (1)
Did not bat
2 wickets at 41.50

A prolific wicket-taker for Queensland, who captured 10/61 from 126 balls against Victoria in the 1965–66 season. Ironically the fast medium bowler had been shunned by the Vic state selectors when work commitments previously took him to Melbourne for three seasons, so Allan's memorable feat at the MCG gave him special satisfaction.

In that same season Allan represented Australia at the Gabba in his first and only Test, and returned the moderate figures of 2/83. Peter Allan toured the West Indies in 1964–65, but was hospitalised with illness for much of the trip and played in no Tests. He was regularly selected in Queensland teams between1963 and 1969 and performed consistently well for his state.

## 237. WALTERS, K.D. (Doug "Freddie") : 1945—.
### Tests (74) plus 1 abandoned
### 5,337 runs at 48.26
### 459 wickets at 29.08

One of the most popular players to ever represent Australia, who scored four Test hundreds at home against England, but none on the four occasions he was picked for Ashes tours.

Kevin Douglas Walters was raised on a dairy farm in the Hunter Valley region of NSW, from where he was picked in the NSW Colts team. Walters scored an undefeated 140 against the Queensland Colts, and one six he hit from the middle of the SCG No. 2 Oval landed in a lake 60 metres outside the ground.

Three centuries and a double century at Sheffield shield level at the start of the 1965–66 season gained him Test selection at the Gabba against the visiting English team, and Walters performed brilliantly.

On debut he scored a dashing 155, he scored another century in the Second Test at the MCG, and to round off a superb summer Doug Walters made 60 and captured 4/53 with his medium pace swing deliveries in the final Test of the series.

Then, when Walters was being compared to the greats of cricket, he was lost to the game for two years while he performed Army national service duties. During that time some observers believe that Walters' batting technique suffered permanent damage. On hard, predictable surfaces his well timed drives, neat cuts and powerful hooks still made him a match winner. However on wet pitches and in overcast conditions that often prevail in

England, Walters appeared to play across swinging and seaming deliveries, which made him vulnerable to behind the wicket catches.

Statistics support the notion that Walters was an inferior player in England. On four trips there in 1968, 1972, 1975 and 1977 this normally high scoring batsman failed to register 1,000 runs on any of the tours, and his statistics there were well below his overall Test average. Despite such damaging evidence there was a huge public outcry when Walters was left out of the 1981 English touring team. Supporters who had created "the Duggie Walters Stand" banner which was displayed on the famous Sydney Hill, organised protest marches, and questions regarding his omission were asked in parliament. One selector even received death threats. Walters himself appeared to be bemused by all the fuss, and calmly accepted the decision.

His medium pace bowling often broke troublesome opposition partnerships, but it was Doug Walters' batting achievements that made him a champion. He had the ability to alter the course of a game, and was always a crowd pleaser. Walters played a typically blazing knock at the WACA against the 1970–71 English team, and the six that he struck off Bob Willis on the last ball before the tea interval, scored him 100 runs for the session. In all Test matches K.D. Walters scored 15 centuries, and when he retired from first class cricket after representing NSW a record breaking 103 times, he had scored 6,612 runs for his state team. Little wonder that the NSWCA provided "Duggie" Walters with a testimonial season, which had never been granted before in 123 years of state cricket administration.

This generous gesture was typical of the

warm response that Doug Walters evoked in people. He always laconically accepted both fame and failure, he was much admired for being the relaxed Australian who loved a beer and a cigarette, and people laughed when they heard that his pre-match "warm ups" consisted of throwing darts at a board before he joined the cricket action.

He was the ordinary person's hero, and when he was told that England's losing margin of 45 runs in the 1977 Centenary Test equalled their losing margin of the very first Test in 1877, Doug Walters delivered this classic "one liner": "The Poms haven't learnt much in 100 years!"[42]

**"The Poms haven't learnt much in 100 years!"**

## 238. STACKPOLE, K.N. (Keith "Stacky") : 1940—.
### Tests (43) plus 1 abandoned
### 2,807 runs at 37.42
### 15 wickets at 67.73

An entertaining Victorian and Australian opening batsman who struggled to make an impact for some time, but went on to become vice-captain of the national team.

Keith Stackpole carried the same Christian name as his father, who scored two centuries for his state team in the post World War II years, and Keith junior followed that path when he broke into the Victorian side in the 1962–63 season. After Stackpole scored a century against NSW in the 1964–65 season he surpassed his Dad's feats, as he gained a "baggy green" cap against Mike Smith's English team.

The robust Victorian made an encouraging debut, scoring 43 and collecting 2/33 with

42. Ferguson, 1996, p40

his handy top spinners. Stackpole was then selected to tour South Africa in 1966–67, and in the Cape Town Test he scored a defiant 134 against the host teams' hostile fast bowlers.

Despite gaining his first Test century, Keith Stackpole was dropped from the Australian side in the domestic series that followed against India, and he was not chosen to tour England in 1968. At this stage "Stacky" was considered to be a middle order batsman, but once he began opening the innings for Victoria his form lifted. After winning back his Test spot, Keith Stackpole became entrenched as Australia's opener for 25 consecutive Tests, and his powerful hooks and cuts became the platform on which many large totals were built

In 1970–71 Stackpole reached his highest Test score when he bludgeoned 207 against England at Brisbane. "Stacky" headed the Australian averages in that series, and when the 32 year old toured England for the first time in 1972, he repeated the achievement, and scored more runs than any other Australian player. Keith Stackpole scored his seventh Test century against New Zealand in 1973–74, and he retired from the first class scene at the end of that season.

Since then the amiable "Stacky" has become a popular radio special comments person at first class venues, and he has also hosted many international trips for cricket tourists to Test match countries.

## 239. RENNEBERG, D. A. (David) : 1942—.

Tests (8)
22 runs at 3.66
23 wickets at 36.08

A big, strong NSW fast-medium bowler, whose lack of shoulder and body movement hindered him against top class batsman.

Dave Renneberg made his Test debut in South Africa, where he played the entire 1966–67 series and captured 11 wickets in the five fixtures. He also toured England in 1968, but failed to gain Test selection. His best performance at this level occurred in Australia against the 1967–68 Indian team, when he captured 5/39 in the Adelaide Test.

Renneberg was a stalwart of the NSW team. He represented "the Blues" 54 times and captured 190 wickets at 30.48.

## 240. TABER, H.B. (Brian) : 1940—.
Tests (16)
353 runs at 16.04
dismissals 60 (56 catches, 4 stumpings)

A neat and highly efficient wicketkeeper who accepted eight catches in his debut international match at The Wanderers ground in Johannesburg. He later revealed it was the first Test game he had ever attended!

Brian Taber was raised in the Wollongong suburb of Fairy Meadow, and he commenced playing Sheffield Shield cricket in 1964–65. After claiming 66 dismissals in his first two seasons, Taber became Australia's keeper in South Africa when the usual incumbent, Barry Jarman, was unavailable for the 1966–67 tour.

The NSW keeper was Jarman's deputy for the Ashes tour of 1968, and during the following domestic season Brian Taber equalled the world record for dismissals when he caught nine and stumped three South Australian batsmen in a 1968–69 Shield fixture. In that same season Taber scored 48 and

**He accepted eight catches in the first Test game he had ever attended.**

snapped up six catches in his only Test appearance against the touring West Indians.

Just prior to the 1969–70 tour of India and South Africa Brian Taber contracted a lung infection which affected his health for some time. He did keep efficiently in all Tests of that gruelling tour, but in the 1970–71 season Taber was replaced by Rodney Marsh as Australia's keeper.

## 241. WATSON, G.D. (Graeme "Beatle") : 1945—.
Tests (5)
97 runs at 10.77
6 wickets at 42.33

**In a memorable sporting career Graeme Watson was once close to death after being struck in the face while batting.**

An energetic "triple treat" all-rounder who represented three states, played in three Sheffield Shield winning teams, and toured three countries with Australian teams. In a memorable sporting career Graeme Watson was once close to death after being struck in the face while batting, he played WSC cricket, and he represented Melbourne in Australian Football.

Watson's career began in Victoria, and after the opening batsman and brisk medium pacer scored a century and captured six wickets in an innings against Queensland, he was chosen in the Australian team which toured South Africa in1966–67. At Cape Town he scored 50 in his first Test, and his career continued to develop when he toured New Zealand with Sam Trimble's Australian team in 1968.

A move to Perth in 1971–72 produced both worthwhile and disturbing outcomes for Graeme Watson. He did play in three winning Sheffield Shield teams in four seasons, but

Watson also required heart massage and mouth to mouth resuscitation to keep him alive after his nose and cheekbone was shattered by a Tony Greig delivery in January 1972. Doctors at the Perth hospital advised Graeme Watson to retire from the game, but he refused.

Instead he went to England with Ian Chappell's 1972 team where he scored 176 against Hampshire, when Keith Stackpole and he shared a record breaking opening stand of 301 runs. Watson played in two Tests on the tour, but made little impact.

In 1976–77 Watson transferred as a marketing executive to Sydney, and played five games for NSW. He then linked up with WSC, and his colourful career ended when settlement was reached between the rebel group and the ACB.

## 242. GLEESON, J.W. (John "Cho") : 1938—.
Tests (29) plus one abandoned
395 runs at 10.39
93 wickets at 36.20

A bush cricketer who did not begin his Test career until he was in his 30th year, but still managed to confuse the world's leading batsmen with his unorthodox spinning deliveries.

John Gleeson was a postal technician from Tamworth who toured the world twice with a group of bush cricket addicts called the Emus. On those tours he was a wicket-keeper, but he switched to bowling after he perfected Jack Iverson's grip, and became hugely successful. Gleeson never obtained the spin that Iverson produced, but he bowled more accurately and with more guile.

In Sydney Gleeson won Balmain's bowling average in 1966–67, and the following season he topped the Sheffield Shield averages in his first season of state cricket. After enjoying further success on a New Zealand tour, John Gleeson played his first Test against India in 1967–68, and performed well enough to gain a tour spot to England in 1968. His tally of 58 wickets was more than any other Australian bowler.

He continued to be a valuable bowler in Tests at home against the West Indies, and on the Indian and South African tour in 1969–70. However, it gradually became evident that this likeable character and competent bowler lacked the flight and deception that great spinners possess.

Gleeson's best Test figures of 5/61 occurred against the West Indies in 1968–69, and in 1974–75 he finished his playing career in South African domestic cricket where he represented Eastern Province.

Like Bob Cowper, John Gleeson was a strong advocate for players' rights, and he served in an honorary capacity on the first WSC governing committee.

## 243. SHEAHAN, A.P. (Paul) : 1946—.
Tests (31)
1,594 runs at 33.91

A player that was always a joy to watch in the field, but whose stylish batting fell a little short of the high expectations many held.

Paul Sheahan was the great-grandson of William Cooper who toured England with the 1884 Australian team, and from an early age the handsome and personable Sheahan appeared to be destined for stardom. He was second in the Shield batting averages in 1966–67, and in the following season Paul Sheehan scored 81 and 35 in his Test debut against the visiting Indians.

That Adelaide Test was the first of 25 consecutive appearances in the "baggy green" for Sheahan. He toured England in 1968 and 1972, South Africa in 1970 and New Zealand in 1973–74. His two best scores against England were 88 and 44, and after Paul Sheahan scored Test centuries against India and Pakistan in the early 70s his supporters hoped that  he was at last fulfilling his potential.

However shortly after the elegant Victorian married he unexpectedly retired from the first class scene. Paul Sheahan has since become a distinguished educationalist, and he is currently the Principal of Melbourne Grammar School.

## 244. FREEMAN, E.W. (Eric) : 1944—.
Tests (11)
345 runs at 19.16
34 wickets at 33.17

A determined fast bowler and noted big hitter who was handy rather than inspired at Test level.

The strongly built South Australian toured New Zealand in 1966–67 after taking the excellent Shield figures of 7/52 against Queensland. Over the next three seasons Eric Freeman toured England, India and South Africa, and his 4/78 in England on the 1968 tour was his most valuable contribution in Tests. The powerful South African batting line-up punished Freeman's bowling in1969–70,  and he dropped out of international cricket soon after the tour ended.

Eric Freeman was also a champion Australian footballer, and today he is often the Adelaide special comments person on radio sports programs.

## 245. JOSLIN, L.R. (Leslie) : 1947—.
Tests(1)
9 runs at 4.5

A Victorian left handed batsman who made a promising start in big cricket, but did not last long in the upper echelons of the game.

Les Joslin scored two Sheffield Shield centuries before playing his only Test against India in 1967–68. Despite failing in that fixture, Joslin gained selection in the 1968 Australian team which went to England, but only scored a disappointing 344 runs at 21.50 on tour. He dropped out of first class cricket during the 1968–69 season.

## 246. INVERARITY, R.J. (John) : 1944—.
Tests (6)
174 runs at 17.40
4 wickets at 23.25

A dour batsman, a useful left-arm slow bowler, and a shrewd captain who led Western Australia to four Sheffield Shield titles in six seasons.

His father Merv also represented the state in cricket, and John performed consistently for "the Sandgropers" before making his Test debut for Australia on the 1968 tour of England. His score of 56 in the final international fixture was his highest Test score.

Inverarity was a tour selector in Ian Chappell's 1972 English touring team, and he played in three further Tests. At times his cautious batting became so slow that English critic Jim Swanton dubbed him "Inforeverity".[43]

He later returned to England in a teaching role, and after John Inverarity became Deputy-Headmaster of an Adelaide school in 1980, he captained South Australia at times in Sheffield Shield games.

## 247. MALLETT, A.A. (Ashley "Rowdy") : 1945—.
### Tests (38) plus one abandoned
### 430 runs at 11.62
### 132 wickets at 29.84

The most successful off-spinner Australia has produced both in the Sheffield Shield competition and in the Test match arena.

Ashley Mallett moved to Adelaide to pursue his cricket dreams from his native state of Western Australia, and the tall, shy young man quickly became called "Rowdy" because of his quiet demeanour. He soon played for South Australia and in 1968 he went to England where he took 44 wickets on tour and played his maiden Test at the end of the series.

When Ian Chappell succeeded Bill Lawry as captain, "Rowdy" Mallett became a key player in Australia's successful sides. He was invaluable as an accurate stock bowler when Lillee or Thomson were rested, and he raked in some superb catches in the gully region. Mallett toured England again in 1972 and 1975. He retired in 1976 but returned to Test cricket briefly after the rift between the WSC and the ACB was healed.

His impressive haul of 344 Shield wickets has only been bettered by the great Clarrie

43. Pollard, 1982, p530

Grimmett. In recent times Ashley Mallett has played a valuable coaching role for young spinners emerging in the game.

## 248. JENNER, T.J. (Terry "TJ") : 1944—.
Tests (9)
208 runs at 23.11
24 wickets at 31.20

An able leg spin bowler and useful late order batsman who was involved in controversy both on and off the ground, but who has now won lasting respect as a well regarded coach of Shane Warne and other current spin bowlers.

Terry Jenner came across to Adelaide from Perth with his friend Ashley Mallett to further his cricket opportunities, and after gaining state selection with South Australia "TJ" performed well on the 1969–70 Australian "B" team's tour of New Zealand.

In a controversial incident in his second Test against the 1970–71 English tourists, Jenner had his head badly gashed by a John Snow bouncer, and crowd anger over this incident induced the English captain Ray Illingworth to lead his team from the field until order was restored. In another Ashes Test in 1973–74 Terry Jenner struck an aggressive 74 against Mike Denness' English team, which was his highest Test score. He also performed well with Ian Chappell's 1973 Caribbean touring team, and captured 5/90 with his well flighted deliveries in the Trinidad Test against the West Indies.

However after he departed from the game Terry Jenner became addicted to gambling, and he served a gaol sentence for embezzlement. To his credit he has since re-habilitated himself well, and he has become well known for his cricket commentary work on radio, his entertaining speaking engagements and for his successful tutoring of the great leg spinner Shane Warne.

## 249. MARSH, R.W. (Rodney "Bachus") : 1947—.
Tests (97) plus one abandoned
3,633 runs at 26.52
dismissals 355 (343 catches, 12 stumpings)

A Western Australian who was given the disparaging nickname of "Irongloves" during his shaky Test debut in 1970, but who went on to become one of the greatest wicket-keeper batsmen in the history of the game.

Rod Marsh scored 104 on debut for West Australia against the 1968–69 West Indian team, but the national selectors surprised most pundits when they later chose him as wicket-keeper instead of the more favoured Brian Taber for the opening Test of the 1970–71 Ashes series, However Marsh improved both his fitness and his glove work, and when he scored an undefeated 92 in the Melbourne Test, it helped secure his position in the team.

The acrobatic catches taken by Marsh off Dennis Lillee's bowling in England on the 1972 tour, started a famous partnership between the Western Australian pair. In the first Test at Manchester Marsh equalled the record for an English–Australian Test when he accepted five catches, and he ended the tour with 23 Test victims.

In 1972–73, after twice scoring 90s in Test cricket, Rod Marsh became the first Australian keeper to notch a Test century

The acrobatic catches taken by Marsh off Dennis Lillee's bowling in England on the 1972 tour, started a famous partnership between the Western Australian pair.

when he hammered 118 against Pakistan. In later Tests Marsh added two further hundreds to his Test record, when he scored 132 against New Zealand and 110 not out against England in the 1977 Centenary Test.

After performing well in WSC ranks, Marsh rejoined traditional cricket, and in 1981 he became the most successful keeper of that time when he passed Alan Knott's record of 263 Test victims.

Rod Marsh joined Greg Chappell and Dennis Lillee in retirement after the 1983–84 series against Pakistan. Since then he has become enormously successful in cricket management and coaching. He established excellent cricket academies in both Australia and England, and is still much sought after by all the major cricket countries.

## 250. THOMSON, A.L. (Alan "Froggy") : 1945—.

Tests (4)
22 runs at 22.00
12 wickets at 54.50

An extroverted and unorthodox Victorian opening bowler, who started his first class career in emphatic style, but slipped out of Test calculations when his lack of genuine pace became evident.

Thomson caught the imagination of the public when he aggressively launched his state cricket career with the Victorian team in the 1968–69 season. He was seen as Australia's new fast bowling hope after he captured match figures of 9/181 against the 1970–71 MCC touring team. In the Test series, however, Thomson posed little threat, and his best figures for the series were 3/79. Thomson continued to represent Victoria until 1974, but he was not selected again in the Australian team.

Alan Thomson was a Melbourne school teacher, and he also officiated as a boundary umpire in VFL Australian Football fixtures.

## 251. CHAPPELL, G. S. (Gregory) : 1948—.
### Tests (88) plus one abandoned
### 7,110 runs at 53.86
### 47 wickets at 40.70

The second son in the family of three boys that dominated Australia's cricket landscape for 15 years. Greg Chappell was a more elegant and classical batsman than his extroverted older brother, but he lacked the aggressive leadership qualities that Ian Chappell brought to the captaincy position.

Greg Chappell commenced playing interstate games at the age of 18, and two seasons with Somerset in English county cricket further tightened his graceful batting technique. At the age of 22 the tall South Australian scored a fighting 108 in his debut Test match against the 1970–71 English team in Perth, and from that time he became one of the world's premier batsman.

On his first English tour in 1972, Greg Chappell topped the batting averages and scored two superb Test centuries. A year later he became the first Australian to score more than 1,000 runs on a Caribbean tour, and in the following summer in New Zealand Greg Chappell pounded 247 not out and 133 in the same Test match. His outstanding form also helped Australia enjoy series' victories against England at home in 1974–75, and again in England in 1975.

The second son in the family of three boys that dominated Australia's cricket landscape for 15 years.

Greg Chappell succeeded his older brother as Australian captain in 1975–76, and he also skippered Queensland after being lured north by an attractive financial offer. At this stage he and many other leading players were at loggerheads with cricket authorities over financial rewards from the game, and when Greg Chappell was leading the Australian team on its 1977 tour of England, it was prematurely announced that he and most of his team had signed lucrative contracts to play with WSC. From that point on morale became poor in the Australian team, and England easily regained the Ashes.

Both Greg and Ian Chappell were key figures in the success of the WSC 'rebel" matches, but when disputes were resolved with the governing authorities of the game, Greg Chappell regained the Australian captaincy position in the 1979–80 season. Before long, however, the strains of leadership, the constant media pressure, and the demands of both Test cricket and one day internationals, began to weigh on a weary looking Chappell, and culminated in a decision which angered and shocked the cricket world.

**Greg Chappell instructed his brother Trevor to bowl an underarm delivery on the last ball of the match.**

In the final limited overs fixture of the 1980–81 season at the MCG against New Zealand, Greg Chappell instructed his brother Trevor to bowl an underarm delivery on the last ball of the match, so that the Kiwis would be unable to score the six runs needed for victory. Cricket identities, political figures and the general public were outraged, and a contrite Greg Chappell later admitted "it is something that I would not do again."[44]

He was unavailable for the 1981 English tour, but resumed as captain again in 1981–82, and led Australia against Pakistan, the West

44. Pollard, 1982, p257

Indies and New Zealand. Prior to the 1984–85 Caribbean tour, Greg Chappell retired from first class cricket with the enviable record of having scored 20 Test centuries, which included one in his first Test and one in his last Test against Pakistan in 1984. His aggregate of over 7000 runs surpassed the record of Sir Donald Bradman, who admittedly played 24 fewer Tests. His haul of 122 catches was also a world record and he secured 47 Test wickets with his handy medium-pace deliveries .

In recent times Greg Chappell has been prominent in the media, he has coached South Australia, and he is currently the coach of India.

## 252. DUNCAN, J.R.F. (Ross) : 1944—.

Tests (1)
3 runs at 3.00
0 wickets for 30

A stocky opening bowler who represented Queensland, Victoria and on one occasion, Australia.

Ross Duncan represented his home state Queensland with distinction for six seasons until he transferred to Victoria in 1971–72. Outstanding match figures of 13/125 for Queensland against Victoria gained him selection for one Test against the 1970–71 English touring team, but he bowled 14 unsuccessful overs, and was not chosen for Australia again.

## 253. O'KEEFE. K.J. (Kerry "Skull") : 1949—.

Tests (24)
644 runs at 25.76
53 wickets at 38.08

A quickish leg break bowler, a useful late

order batsman and a brilliant gully fieldsman who was a fringe Test player for most of his career.

Kerry O'Keefe impressed critics when he debuted for NSW in his late teens, and he widened his experience by playing two seasons with Somerset. He later toured England with Greg Chappell's 1977 team, and finished second in the team's batting averages. O'Keefe also toured New Zealand three times, and he was a useful member of Ian Chappell's victorious 1973 team in the West Indies. He spent some time in Lancashire League ranks and with WSC, until he retired from first class cricket in 1981.

Kerry O'Keefe recently emerged as a cricket media celebrity, and "Skull's" zany sense of humour and outrageous comments are much appreciated in guest speaking engagements.

## 254. LILLEE, D.K. (Dennis "Fot" ) : 1949—.

Tests (70)
905 runs at 13.71
355 wickets at 23.92

"Lill-ee! Lillee!" the crowd chanted when the charismatic fast bowler began his menacing charge to the wicket.

Dennis Lillee, who was arguably the greatest fast bowler of all time, had the personae of a movie star in the 1970s and early 80s, and drama always lurked nearby when the aggressive Western Australian was involved.

Dennis Lillee began in state and Lancashire League cricket as an erratic, tearaway fast bowler, and it was these qualities that first caught the attention of Australian selec-

**Dennis Lillee, who was arguably the greatest fast bowler of all time, had the personae of a movie star in the 1970s and early 80s, and drama always lurked nearby when the aggressive Western Australian was involved.**

tors when the 1970–71 English pace attack dominated the Ashes series. The new express bowler captured five wickets in his Adelaide Test debut, and during the following summer Lillee cut a swathe through international cricket's best batsmen when he captured the superb figures of 8/29 against the Rest of the World X1 in Perth.

Success continued on the 1972 drawn Ashes series in England, where Lillee captured 31 Test wickets. Locals in the Caribbean then eagerly awaited the arrival of the new fast bowling sensation when he arrived in Jamaica for the 1973 series against the West Indies. Unfortunately Lillee was sidelined for most of the tour by stress fractures to his back, which at one stage threatened his career.

However once the plaster was removed from his injury Lillee commenced a demanding exercise routine which saw him ready to start the 1974–75 Ashes series in Brisbane. He defied the sceptics who doubted his ability to return, and Dennis Lillee and Australia's newest express bowler Jeff Thomson formed one of the most lethal fast bowling attacks ever. Australia crushed England 4:1 in the six Tests, and Lillee captured 25 wickets in his triumphant return to international cricket.

A string of Australian victories continued against the major cricket countries of the world, and Lillee reserved his best performance for the big stage of the MCG's Centenary Test when he captured 6/26 and 5/139. However even as he was being applauded for his great efforts, Lillee withdrew from the 1977 tour of England so that he could rest his suspect back.

Dennis Lillee then starred in WSC fixtures, and after he returned to the Test scene he was a different bowler. The searing pace

Dennis Lillee and Australia's newest express bowler Jeff Thomson formed one of the most lethal fast bowling attacks ever.

had diminished, but Lillee was now a craftier exponent of swing and seam bowling, and his success rate actually improved in his later years of Test cricket. In the 1980–81 series against India he became Australia's greatest wicket taker when he claimed his 249th wicket. In the following home series against the West Indies he became the highest wicket taker in world cricket, and by the time he retired in 1983–84 Dennis Lillee's world record had grown to an imposing 355 Test wickets

The fiercely competitive Lillee was inclined to showcase his temperament as much as his talent. In the 1981 Perth Test against England he strode out to the wicket with an aluminium bat that he was sponsoring, only to be informed by the umpire that he could not use it in his innings. On the same ground in the next series against Pakistan, umpire Crafter bravely stepped between Lillee and the equally volatile Javed Miandad when a mid-pitch altercation between the two appeared likely.

Today Dennis Lillee is recognised as being an international expert on the art of fast bowling. He has greatly improved India's resources of new ball bowlers, and he is frequently consulted by other fast bowlers throughout the world.

## 255. DELL, A.R. ( Anthony, Tony) : 1947—.

Tests (2)

6 runs n.a.

6 wickets at 26.66

A huge Queensland left-arm new ball bowler, who moved the ball disconcertingly on the few occasions his run up and delivery technique worked smoothly.

Tony Dell captured six wickets in an innings on five occasions in his five seasons of state cricket, and he also opened Australia's bowling in Test matches against England in 1970–71 and New Zealand in 1973–74.

## 256. EASTWOOD, K.H. (Ken) : 1935—.

Tests (1)
5 runs at 2.50
1 wicket at 21.00

The choice of Eastwood for his only Test at the age of 35 was one of the strangest selections ever, though he had scored two double centuries for Victoria before he replaced Bill Lawry in the seventh Test against England in 1971.

Ken Eastwood scored nine Shield centuries during his 42 matches for his state, and he probably deserved his chance in an Australian side at a younger age. The evergreen veteran was still amassing huge scores in Melbourne club cricket when he was in his late 40s.

> **The choice of Eastwood for his only Test at the age of 35 was one of the strangest selections ever.**

## 257. COLLEY, D.J. (David) : 1947—.

Tests (3)
84 runs at 1.00
6 wickets at 52.00

A gifted all-rounder whose talent was largely untapped because of a nagging back injury and poor motivation.

Dave Colley was only 15 when he captured a hat trick in his debut game with Mosman in Sydney grade ranks, but spasmodic performances kept him out of the state team for seven seasons.

Colley was a surprise selection for the 1972 Australian touring team, but his bowling was more hostile in English conditions and he also produced some strong batting performances. Dave Colley's valuable innings of 54 in the Trent Bridge Test was his best effort in the three international games he played.

On return Colley did captain NSW with flair on four occasions, but a decline in his commitment to the game together with persistent back injuries, ended his Test career.

## 258. FRANCIS, B.C. (Bruce) : 1948—.
Tests (3)
52 runs at 10.40

A determined NSW opening batsman who scored heavily at state and county level but was found wanting in Test matches.

Bruce Francis played on 32 occasions with NSW, he had one season of Lancashire League, and he was with Essex in English county cricket in 1971 and 1973. He scored 210 against a Combined Oxford and Cambridge team in Ian Chappell's 1972 Australian touring team, but failed in his three Test appearances.

Francis graduated in Economics from Sydney University, and he pursued a career in the business world when his first class cricket career ended.

## 259. EDWARDS, R. (Ross) : 1942—.
Tests (20)
171 runs at 40.37

A valuable team player who scored two excellent Test centuries when Australia was in dire straits, and saved numerous runs with his inspirational fielding.

Ross Edwards' father, E.K. Edwards, kept wickets for Western Australia in 1948–49, and his son also donned the wicket keeping gloves for his state when he debuted in 1964–65. Ross Edwards batted at number 10 in his initial first class game, but he improved his batting so much that he scored four centuries for W.A. in the 1971–72 season.

This run of good form gained Edwards selection in the 1972 Australian team which toured England. After Bruce Francis fell ill before the Third Test at Trent Bridge, Ross Edwards scored a magnificent 170 as a stopgap opener. Edwards also became the first Western Australian to score a century in his own state when he contributed 115 runs in Perth in the 1974–75 Ashes series.

Ross Edwards was a qualified accountant, and when he lost his Sydney job after touring England with Australia in 1977, he retired to more predicable employment after his stint with WSC ended.

## 260. MASSIE, R.A.L. (Robert, Bob) : 1947—.
### Tests (6)
### 78 runs at 11.14
### 31 wickets at 20.87

A Western Australian swing bowler who captured a record breaking 16 wickets in one Test match, but whose form slipped so badly that he was later omitted from his state side.

Bob Massie failed in his bid to be signed by Northamptonshire when he was playing Scottish League cricket, and he gained no wickets when he debuted for W.A. in the 1965–66 season. However the excellent figures of 7/76 against the rest of the World X1 in 1971–72, gained him a trip to England with Ian Chappell's Australian team.

There in the Lords Test, Massie was virtually unplayable In conditions that favoured swing bowling, he moved the ball late either way, and bowled Australia to a stunning victory by taking 8/84 in England's first innings and 8/53 in the second. His superb performance bettered Spofforth's 14 wickets in a match, while Jim Laker (19 wickets) and S.F. Barnes (17) were the only English players who ever topped that achievement in Tests.

Then Bob Massie's mastery of swing deserted him. He had a disappointing tour of the West Indies in 1973, and after "the miracle of Lords" Massie only took another 15 Test wickets before he dropped out of first class cricket. Today Bob Massie's thoughtful comments are often heard on ABC radio when first class cricket games are staged in Perth.

## 261. BENAUD, J. (John) : 1944—.
Tests (3)
223 runs at 44.60
2 wickets at 6.00

The younger brother of the famous Richie Benaud was also an adventurous captain when he led NSW, but John Benaud's career was shortened when a career in journalism became his priority.

John Benaud toured the West Indies with Ian Chappell's 1973 team, and he scored one Test century (an aggressive knock of 142 against Pakistan in 1972–73), after being informed that he had been dropped for the following Test in Sydney!

John Benaud later became a newspaper

editor.

### 262. THOMSON, J.R. (Jeffrey "Thommo") : 1950—.
Tests (51)
679 runs at 12.81
200 wickets at 28.01

A NSW, Queensland and Australian fast bowler who bowled with ferocious pace. "Lillee n' Thomson" became the most feared opening bowlers in the game, and in their prime years in the '70s the Aussie duo left a spate of injuries and wickets in their wake. Jeff Thomson never worried about subtleties such as swing when he bowled — he was primarily a shock bowler whose pace and bounce intimidated the best batsmen in world cricket.

"Thommo" was picked for Australia against Pakistan in the 1972–73 season after producing some hostile spells for NSW, but he reportedly played with a broken bone in his foot, and was dropped after collecting the unflattering figures of 0/110. He moved to Queensland where he regained his form, but selectors' still gambled when they chose him for the First Test of the 1974–75 Ashes series in Brisbane.

Jeff Thomson vindicated his selection emphatically, capturing the telling match figures of 9/105 and sidelining two key English batsmen with hand injuries from his thunderbolt deliveries. 33 wickets fell to "Thommo" in four Tests from that series, he collected another 16 wickets in England on the 1975 tour on slow pitches, and a series winning 29 wickets against a powerful West Indian team in 1975–76.

In their prime years in the '70s the Aussie duo left a spate of injuries and wickets in their wake.

His match-winning form was halted in the Adelaide Test of the 1976–77 series against Pakistan, when he dislocated his right collarbone after colliding in the field with teammate Alan Turner. The injury put Thomson out of the series as well as the 1977 Centenary Test, but he toured England again later that year where he captured 23 wickets.

After performing well at home against India in 1977–78 and in the Caribbean in 1978, Thomson signed with WSC. On his return to traditional cricket, the old spite and lift seemed to have waned from Thomson's bowling, and he was dropped from Tests against the West Indies at home and for the 1981 tour of England. However Thomson soldiered on until the end of the 1985 Ashes series in England, where his disappointing figures of 3/275 in two Tests persuaded him to finally hang up the boots.

Since then Jeff Thomson has coached Queensland, and he has often commentated for a cable television network on international cricket matches.

## 263 WALKER, M.H.N. (Maxwell "Tangles") : 1948—.

Tests (34)
586 runs at 19.53
138 wickets at 27.47

A jovial medium pace swing bowler whose awful action inspired the nickname "Tangles", but who provided valuable support for Lillee and Thomson in Australia's attack, and was invaluable in times of crisis.

Max Walker primarily moved from Tasmania to Victoria to study architecture and play Australian Football with Melbourne, but the big man who bowled huge inswingers found himself playing cricket for Victoria in 1968–69. Three seasons later he debuted for Australia against Pakistan in Melbourne.

"Tangles" proved to be a willing warrior in his second Test in Sydney, where he and Dennis Lillee dismissed the Pakistanis for a lowly 106, when they only required 159 runs for victory. Walker's superb figures of 6/15 guaranteed him selection in Australia's team which visited the Caribbean in 1973, and he became Australia's leading bowler on the tour.

After Lillee was sidelined with a back injury, and Bob Massie lost all form, it was Walker who spearheaded the depleted attack, and big "Tangles" responded magnificently to the challenge. He captured 26 Test wickets at 20.73 which greatly influenced the outcome of the series. Success continued in the 1974–75 home series against England, where his haul of 23 wickets included the figures of 8/143 when Lillee and Thomson were unavailable for the final Test.

Max Walker toured England in 1975 and 1977, where he was not as successful because he tended to pitch the ball too short, though he did claim 14 Test wickets on each tour. He became a popular WSC player, and when agreement was reached between the two rival authorities, "Tangles" played again for Victoria until the 1982–83 season.

Max Walker has since become an author of some very funny sporting books. He is also seen frequently on television advertisements and sports shows, and is still much sought after as a public speaker at dinners, receptions and fund raising functions.

> **After Lillee was sidelined with a back injury, and Bob Massie lost all form, it was Walker who spearheaded the depleted attack, and big "Tangles" responded magnificently to the challenge.**

**264. WATKINS, J.R. (John) : 1943—.**
Tests (1)
39 runs at 19.50
0 wickets for 21



The Newcastle leg spinner's selection for Australia was a disaster and the amiable wharf worker soon disappeared from first class cricket.

John Watkins had taken only ten wickets in a total of five first class games when he was chosen for the last Test of the 1972–73 series against Pakistan. The nervous debut player sent down a succession of wides in his three embarrassing overs, but he did bat solidly, and his score of 36 not out greatly helped Australia's cause.

Watkins toured the West Indies soon after, but only played four matches in the Caribbean before fading out of big cricket.

**265. HAMMOND, J.R. (Jeffrey "Bomber") : 1950—.**
Tests (5)
28 runs at 9.33
15 wickets at 32.53

A South Australian fast bowler whose promising career was ruined by injury.

Jeff Hammond headed the Australian bowling averages in his second season of Shield cricket in the 1970–71 season, and he was the youngest member of the 1972 Australian team which toured England. Hammond's progress on tour was restricted by a back injury, but he played all five Tests on the 1973 tour of the West Indies and captured 15 wickets.

A broken foot and continued back problems restricted him to a few state games after he returned. In retirement Hammond moved to Darwin and became a prominent figure in Northern Territory cricket.

## 266. DAVIS, I. C. (Ian "Wizard") : 1953—.
### Tests (15)
### 692 runs at 26.61

A slightly built NSW opening batsman who first represented Australia at the age of 20, but failed to secure a Test position because of his inability to amass large scores.

Ian Davis debuted for both NSW and Australia in the 1973–74 season, and his elegant stroke making enthused cricket pundits. However he continued to slip in and out of the Test side, though he did score his maiden century against Pakistan in 1976–77. He also scored 68 in the second innings of the 1977 Centenary Test against England.

Davis toured England in 1977 where he scored a disappointing 107 runs in his three Tests. After the series ended he joined WSC, but when differences were settled between the rival groups, Ian Davis did not regain his place in the Australian team.

## 267. GILMOUR, G. J. (Gary "Gus" ) : 1951—.
### Tests (15)
### 483 runs at 23.00
### 54 wickets at 26.03

An exceptionally gifted left-handed all-rounder who lacked the necessary commitment to fully realise his potential.

Gary Gilmour captured four wickets in four balls for Western Suburbs in a 1972–73

Sydney grand final, after blazing a century in his Sheffield Shield debut at the age of 20. He played his first Test against New Zealand in 1973–74, and went on to play 15 in total, and participate in two tours to New Zealand and one to England.

On the 1975 English tour, "Gus" Gilmour produced a devastating spell of swing bowling against the host nation in a World Cup semi-final, which propelled Australia into the final against the powerful West Indian team. After narrowly losing that exciting game, "Gus" was queried about the best way to bowl to the West Indian powerhouse batsman Clive Lloyd. "Wear a helmet", was Gilmour's succinct advice, as he recalled Lloyd's thundering straight drives.[45]

**"Wear a helmet," was Gilmour's succinct advice.**

Gilmour's best Test achievements were the 6/85 he took against England at Leeds in 1975, and the 101 he scored in Christchurch New Zealand in 1977. After he finished WSC cricket Gilmour only played for a short time with NSW, before he returned to his home city of Newcastle. There he has been involved in the sports retail industry, and he has followed the fortunes of the local Rugby League club with great fervour.

In recent months Gary Gilmour was gravely ill, and required a kidney transplant. He appears to have now recovered.

## 268. DYMOCK, G. (Geoffrey) : 1945—.
Tests (21)
236 runs at 14.45
78 wickets at 27.11

A left-arm swing bowler who became Queensland's greatest wicket taker, and served Australia with distinction in the difficult years

45. Age newspaper, 2006

when the best players had been lost to WSC.

Geoff Dymock, a Maths teacher from rural Maryborough, honed his bowling skills in the Lancashire League before he gained state selection in 1971–72. In his Test debut against New Zealand in 1973–74, Dymock captured match figures of 7/102, and when Australia's leading bowlers defected to WSC, the determined veteran gratefully accepted the unexpected opportunity to be a Test new ball bowler.

Dymock bowled well against England in 1978–79, he had a very successful tour of India in 1979, and he produced a match-winning performance of 6/34 in the 1979–80 Test against England in Perth. During his Test career Geoff Dymock once took ten wickets in an innings, and the best figures he obtained were 7/67.

## 269. HURST, A.G. (Alan) : 1950—.

Tests (12)

102 runs at 6.00

43 wickets at 27.90

A Victorian fast bowler who some rated as quick as Lillee when his rhythm was right, but who too often strayed in his accuracy.

The Melbourne teacher made his Test debut against New Zealand in 1973–74. Before the advent of WSC, the presence of Lillee, Thomson, Walker, Gilmour and Malone restricted his opportunities, but from the start of the 1978–79 season Alan Hurst became a formidable fast bowler.

He performed with greater accuracy, and the addition of a superb leg cutter to his bowling repertoire gained Hurst 40 wickets in eight Test matches. Hurst was chosen for the 1979 World Cup in England, but back injuries made it more difficult to compete with Lillee, Hogg, Pascoe and Lawson for a Test place. Alan Hurst retired from first class cricket at the start of the 1980–81 season.

## 270. WOODCOCK, A.J. (Ashley) : 1947—.

Tests (1)
27 runs at 27.00

A stylish South Australian opening batsman who failed to produce big scores when Test opportunities seemed available.

Woodcook, an Adelaide physical education teacher, scored 56 against India in his first state game in 1967–68, and after registering three first class centuries he played his only Test against New Zealand in 1973–74. Woodcock was dropped after scoring 27, but he toured New Zealand with Ian Chappell's team later that summer.

## 271. EDWARDS, W. J. (Walter) : 1949—.

Tests (3)
68 runs at 11.33

Wally Edwards scored over 50 eleven times for Western Australia, but the left-handed opener only scored two centuries in three seasons of first class cricket.

He was selected for the first three Tests of the 1974–75 season against England after scoring 153 against NSW, but was omitted after only managing a top score of 30. Edwards dropped out of top cricket after the 1975–76 season, but continued in Perth club ranks for some years.

# 272, McCOSKER, R. B. (Richard, Rick)
## : 1946—.
### Tests (25)
### 1,622 runs at 39.56

The graphic photographs of this cricket warrior with a broken jaw striding painfully to the batting crease in the second innings of the 1977 Centenary Test in Melbourne, capture a vivid memory that remains with many cricket followers.

Rick McCosker had his jaw broken by a Bob Willis bouncer when he was dismissed in Australia's first innings for four. He only scored 25 in the second innings of that historic match, but batting again after he was seriously injured was a brave act that was greatly admired.

McCosker was nearly 27 before he first played for the state team, but after scoring two Shield centuries in the 1974–75 season, he was chosen for the unaccustomed role of an opening batsman for the Third Ashes Test in Sydney. He scored a fine 80 on debut.

Rick McCosker's success continued on the 1975 tour of England where the consistent opener notched scores of 59, 79, 95 not out and 127 in the Test matches, and finished second overall to Doug Walters in the tour averages. He then visited New Zealand, and after touring England again in 1977 Rick McCosker linked up with WSC.

After appearing in seven Super Tests with his new cricket employers, McCosker became captain of NSW, for whom he continued to be a major run maker until he retired to his Newcastle law and accounting office in the early 1980s.

The graphic photographs of this cricket warrior with a broken jaw striding painfully to the batting crease in the second innings of the 1977 Centenary Test in Melbourne, remains a vivid memory to all who follow Tests between Australia and England.

### 273. TURNER, A. (Alan) : 1950—.
Tests (14)
768 runs at 29.54

A NSW left-hand opening batsman who struggled to cement a Test place in the 1970s because of his inability to compile large scores.

Alan Turner scored 89 on debut for NSW in 1968–69, and the following season he had moderate success with Sam Trimble's Australian team in New Zealand. On return his consistent batting earned the swarthy dark-haired opener a place in the 1975 Australian team which toured England, where he played in three Test matches.

Turner's best Test performances came in the 1975–76 home series against the West Indies when he compiled scores of 81, 53 and then 136 in the Fourth Test in Adelaide. Turner toured New Zealand again in 1976–77, and retired the following season after scoring seven first class centuries.

### 274. COSIER, G.J. : 1953—.
Tests (18)
897 runs at 28.93
5 wickets at 68.00

A red-haired powerhouse batsman who was 12th man for Victoria at the age of 17, and went on to score a Test century for Australia on debut. However, his first class career in three states was over before he was 30.

Gary Cosier always seemed to be a potential match-winner with his prodigious hitting, handy medium pace bowling and sharp catching, but after three seasons with Victoria he moved to South Australia to launch his future Test career. After scoring over 1500 runs in 23 matches for his new state, Cosier became the11th Australian to score a Test century on debut when he smashed 107 against the 1975–76 West Indian team at the MCG.

The inconsistent Cosier then endured a lean patch of form, managing only 80 runs in eight Sheffield Shield innings at the start of the 1976–77 season. However, the national selectors' faith in him was vindicated for a time when he scored 168 against Pakistan in the 1977 Melbourne Test. Two months later he played in the Centenary Test against England, and at the start of the 1977–78 season he signed a reportedly lucrative ten-year contract to play for Queensland.

For a short time Cosier was Australia's vice-captain, but failures continued to mount both in the West Indies in 1978, and in England for the 1979 World Cup. By 1980–81 he was back in Melbourne, but out of the state team by the end of the season. Gary Cosier scored seven centuries in 91 first class matches, but his first class career ended at a young age.

## 275. YALLOP, G.N. (Graham) : 1952—.
Tests (39)<br>2,756 runs at 41.13

A stylish left-handed Victorian batsman who scored impressive Test centuries and captained Australia in seven Tests, but still found it difficult to impress selectors, especially when the WSC players returned to established cricket.

Graham Yallop made his debut with Victoria in 1972–73, and that winter he started a three season stint in English League cricket. In Australia he soon began amassing big scores, contributing 121against India in 1977–78, and topping the averages in Bob Simpson's ill-fated side that toured the West Indies in 1978, despite missing matches with a broken jaw.

In 1978–79 Graham Yallop replaced Simpson as captain after the latter could not come to terms with the Board of Control, and in his debut match as skipper he scored 102 against England at the Gabba. However his relationship with key bowler Rodney Hogg and other teammates became testy, as did his communications with the media. After he lost six of the seven Tests he captained, Yallop was replaced by Kim Hughes for the 1979 tour of India. Yallop scored 167 as an opener in the Calcutta Test on that trip, but was dropped again from the team soon afterwards

Yallop had previously guided Victoria to two Shield victories, but in the 1981–82 season he lost the state captaincy to Richie Robinson. Despite that setback, Yallop continued to produce some excellent innings. At Birmingham on the 1981 tour of England he scored 114, and at the Boxing Day Test at the MCG in 1983 Graham Yallop scored a magnificent 268 against Pakistan. In that same season he broke Bill Ponsford's 55 year old Victorian record when he scored 1,254 runs for his state.

Yallop went to South Africa on "rebel"tours between 1985 and 1987, which caused him to be suspended by the ACB. After the tours ended he continued to play Melbourne District cricket until 1991. He has since been engaged in various business enterprises and is currently president of the Casey-South Melbourne Cricket Club.

**In that same season he broke Bill Ponsford's 55 year old Victorian record when he scored 1,254 runs for his state.**

## 276. HOOKES, D.W. (David "Hooksey") : 1955–2005.
### Tests (23)
### 1,306 runs at 34.37

David Hookes was a charismatic but sometimes abrasive personality who experienced his share of highs and lows, before he was tragically killed in an altercation with a Melbourne hotel bouncer in 2005.

At 21 Hookes made his international debut when he gained selection in Australia's team for the 1977 Centennary Test in Melbourne, and the tall left-handed batsman from Adelaide made a sensational entry to the big stage of international cricket.

After coming to the crease when Australia was struggling on 3/53, "Hooksey" struck five successive boundaries with superlative drives from the bowling of the English all-rounder Tony Greig, and the crowd heralded a new hero of the game after he scored an exhilarating 56. Prior to his Test selection, Hookes had plundered four centuries in 11 days for South Australia, and the brash young man appeared to be on the brink of stardom.

However his exciting promise as a player faltered. Hookes only scored 283 runs in nine Test innings on the 1977 English tour, and after he joined WSC at the end of that summer, he had his jaw badly broken by a Andy Roberts' bouncer. On returning to traditional cricket David Hookes was dropped from Australia's team when he failed in the First Test of the 1979–80 series against the West Indies, and he scored a pair of ducks in the only Test he played in Pakistan in 1980.

After missing selection in the 1981 team which toured England, Hookes was appointed

David Hookes was a charismatic but sometimes abrasive personality who experienced his share of highs and lows, before he was tragically killed in an altercation with a Melbourne hotel bouncer in 2005.

as South Australia's captain. "The Redcaps" had finished in sixth position the previous season, and still appeared to be under-manned, but the confident Hookes was not deterred. He proved to be an inspiring leader and led his young side to an unexpected Shield victory.

David Hookes continued to remain on the fringe of Test selection for the rest of his playing days. In 1982–83 he performed solidly against England, averaging 49.14 in Tests, and at the end of that season he blazed 143 against Sri Lanka in Kandy. However his form was disappointing on the 1984 West Indian tour, and he also failed in home series against India and New Zealand before his Test career came to a close.

In recent years David Hookes moved to Melbourne where he became a TV cricket host at international games, and a popular celebrity on talk-back radio programs. He also inspired the 2003–04 Victorian side to a brilliant Shield victory when he accepted the state coaching position. He was socialising with Victorian and South Australian players when he was fatally injured in his 50th year.

## 277. PASCOE, L.S. (Formerly Durtanovich) (Leonard) : 1950—.
Tests (14)
106 runs at 10.60
64 wickets at 26.06

A powerful NSW speedster who changed his name but not his intimidating pace or quick-fire temper during his volatile career.

Lennie Pascoe grew up in the same area of Sydney as Jeff Thomson, and the performances of "Thommo" inspired this son of a Yugoslav migrant to emulate his fast bowling deeds. He debuted for NSW in 1974–75, and when he was irked by Ian Chappell's sledging in a 1980 Shield fixture, Pascoe produced a match winning burst of fiery fast bowling that removed the South Australian team for the lowly total of 69. Big Lennie captured the magnificent figures of 7/18.

He made his Test debut at Lords in 1977 before joining WSC for two seasons. Knee injuries then plagued Len Pascoe for much of his remaining career, though he did collect 28 Test wickets against India and New Zealand in 1980–81. However, his nagging problem caused him to be unavailable for the 1981 tour of England. Pascoe faded from the Test scene after only collecting four wickets against the 1981–82 touring West Indian team.

### 278. ROBINSON, R.D. (Richard "Richie") : 1948—.
Tests (3)
100 runs at 16.66
dismissals 4 catches

A tall Victorian wicket-keeper whose quick reflexes and useful batting skills made him a valuable all-round player in Australian touring teams.

Richie Robinson first played for his state in 1971–72, and he was Rod Marsh's understudy on the 1975 tour of England. Back home in 1976–77 Robinson's batting showed considerable improvement, and he scored four Shield centuries. This led to Robinson playing three Tests in England as a specialist batsman in 1977, and at the end of the series he joined WSC.

Richie Robinson took over the reins of captaincy for Victoria again in 1979–80, before he retired to become a publican in rural Victoria during the 1981–82 season.

### 279. SERJEANT, C. S. (Craig) : 1951—.
Tests (12)
522 runs at 23.72

A player who was first given opportunities in Test cricket when WSC swooped on Australia's best talent, but who struggled to maintain his spot once those players returned.

Craig Serjeant made an impact in his first season with W.A. when he averaged close to 50 runs per innings, and at the end of that summer he was chosen in Australia's 1977 touring team, even though he had only played ten first class matches. In the First Test against England at Lords the strong driving Seajant top scored with 81, but he was only selected for three Tests on tour.

Although he scored a robust 85 in one Test against the visiting Indians in a 1977–78 Test his overall form was disappointing, but after Craig Serjeant scored 124 at Georgetown against the West Indies in 1978 it seemed that he had cemented a Test place. However once more his form slumped, and he was not chosen against the 1978–79 touring English team.

The reserved Perth pharmacist continued to perform well at state level, and in 1981–82 Craig Serjeant was appointed captain of W.A..

### 280. BRIGHT, R.J. (Raymond "Candles") : 1954—.
Tests (25)
445 runs at 14.35
53 wickets at 41.13

A Victorian left-arm orthodox spinner who bowled long accurate spells, but lacked the variety and penetration to be a major wicket-taker at Test level.

Ray Bright first represented Victoria at 18, and a year later the small, solidly built spinner was a shock choice in Ian Chappell's 1974 team which toured New Zealand. After being overlooked in Australian teams in 1976–77, the selectors again surprised when they picked Ray Bright for the 1977 English tour, where he made his Test debut. Bright performed well that northern summer, winning the bowling averages, and he then had two successful seasons with WSC.

On resuming in established cricket, Bright obtained his best Test figures when he captured 7/87 in the Karachi Test of the 1980 series in Pakistan, and in the three Test fixtures he snared 15 wickets. Bright then toured New Zealand again in 1982, he appeared again in Test series against both the Kiwis and India, and he became a key figure in the 1986–87 tour of India, especially in the dramatic tied Test at Madras.

Bright played a pivotal role in that unforgettable contest, claiming match figures of 5/94 from 25 overs, which remains the highlight of his long career. Bright remains involved in the game, and his name has been suggested as a future Australian selector.

# THE 1977 CRICKET REVOLUTION

Following the euphoric success of the 1977 Centenary Test in Melbourne, the 17 man Australian squad flew out for the Ashes tour in England with high expectations. However, given the events that soon transpired in that northern summer of discontent, it is not surprising that the 1977 "baggy greens" produced the worst Australian result in England since 1886, for a cricket revolution broke out early in the tour that threatened the very existence of the game.

The mastermind behind the revolt against established cricket was the Australian television mogul and millionaire businessman Kerry Packer, who saw the great commercial benefits that cricket could provide. Since the early 70s the match winning deeds of players such as Dennis Lillee, Jeff Thomson and the Chappell brothers had brought crowds surging into the Test grounds to watch their heroes perform. Gate receipts for state cricket authorities then grossed a staggering $1.9 million.

However the cricketers who brought the crowds back to the game were not sharing in the financial benefits. Fringe players such as Richie Robinson received $ 80 for a four-day Sheffield Shield contest, and an established star was paid a paltry $400 to represent Australia in a five-day Test match. The security of player contracts was non-existent.

For years the Australian Cricket Board (ACB) showed a contemptuous and paternalistic attitude to the players' pleas for more secu-

However, given the events that soon transpired in that northern summer of discontent, it is not surprising that the 1977 "baggy greens" produced the worst Australian result in England since 1886, for a cricket revolution broke out early in the tour that threatened the very existence of the game.

**"The players are not professionals... they were invited to play and if they don't like the conditions there are 50,000 other cricketers in Australia who would love to take their places."**

rity and a fairer share of profits from the game.

"These (the players) are not professionals... they were invited to play and if they don't like the conditions there are 50,000 other cricketers in Australia who would love to take their places." These were the dismissive words of Alan Barnes, who was secretary of the ACB in 1975.[46]

Frustrated players such as Ian Chappell believed that the ACB was hopelessly out of touch with modern cricketers' needs. The average age of Board members was over 60, and there appeared to be little empathy between the players and the 14 stockbrokers, businessmen, tax assessors and retired men of leisure who decided the economic and social welfare of Australian cricketers.

The situation was ripe for a promoter's picking, and the entrepreneurial instincts of Kerry Packer were aroused He reportedly offered the ACB $500,000 dollars for the exclusive rights to televise Tests. It allegedly took six months for the Board to decline the offer because of their perceived media obligations to the ABC. Packer also asked for future venue details of international games, but never received a reply. A confrontation between the two conflicting interests was inevitable.

Packer secretly gained the support of influential cricket identities such as Richie Benaud, Tony Greig, Ian Chappell and Clive Lloyd, and the discreet recruitment of established players began. Rumours about unrest continued to grow, and in early May, shortly after the 1977 Australian tour of England began, rising speculation forced Tony Greig to release major details about the plan that would soon cause the biggest divisions in the game's history.

46. Beecher, 1978

It was confirmed that Kerry Packer had already contracted 35 of the world's leading players to play matches in Australia beginning in the summer of 1977–78, and that they would not be available to participate in games that clashed with WSC fixtures. Players' remuneration would range from $16,500–$35,000 a season, and they would have the security of contracts and receive injury benefits.

The world media, cricket authorities and many in the general public reacted angrily to the impending cricket revolution. The players deserting the established game, which soon grew to over 50 in number, were denounced by one newsman as the "Dogs of Cricket". Most national authorities banned the "cricket mercenaries" from Tests, other first class games and even club fixtures. Thirteen of the 17 Australian players in England had signed with Packer, and the media and public furore gravely affected both team morale and performances. Richie Robinson offered this explanation to the many fans who felt that they had been betrayed by their heroes.

"I know people say we have no loyalty, but loyalty won't get my sons a good education. That takes money, and Packer was offering it at the right time."

In the face of all the conflicting arguments, supporters of the sport wondered anxiously what the outcome would be. Would cricket overcome this dark period of uncertainty and evolve into a different but richer game, or would this period of division tear the game apart?

The final answer to this dilemma was still some years away.

> "I know people say we have no loyalty, but loyalty won't get my sons a good education. That takes money, and Packer was offering it at the right time."

# POST-REVOLUTION RECOVERY YEARS

Australia ultimately lost its best 18 cricketers to WSC, so it is little wonder that the national team floundered as it began a massive rebuilding program.

Under the captaincy of the recalled veteran Bob Simpson the novice "baggy greens" started promisingly, accounting for India 3:2 in an exciting home series. However a full strength West Indian team thrashed the inexperienced Aussies in the first two Tests of the 1978 series in the Caribbean, and the hosts hung on to win 3:1 after their main stars were also banned from established cricket.

The 41 year old Simpson then made way for Graham Yallop, but after he led Australia to six losses in seven Tests the Australian selectors turned to player

# PLAYERS OF THE HUGHES–BORDER ERAS

**281. HUGHES, K. J. (Kimberly) :
1954—.**
Tests (70 )
4,415 runs at 37.42

A brilliant but erratic player who enjoyed some magic moments in Test cricket with the bat, but whose career was prematurely shattered by the burdens of captaincy.

Kim Hughes was earmarked for stardom from an early age, and in the 1975–76 season he made an eye-catching debut when he scored 119 and 60 against NSW in Perth. Centuries against West Indian and Pakistani touring teams followed, and he toured New Zealand and England in 1977 but did not make his international debut against England until the final Test at The Oval. In 1978–79 he scored a measured 129 at Brisbane opposed to the visiting English team, which was the first of ten centuries that he scored in Tests.

Hughes stood in as captain for the injured Graham Yallop in the 1978–79 season in Perth, and led the Australians to a stirring win. The morale of the team picked up so much under Hughes' youthful leadership, that he continued in that role for the 1979 World Cup and the tour of India in the same season. He scored 594 runs in six Tests on the sub-continent, and performed so well as captain that there was some speculation that he would be preferred to Greg Chappell when he and the other WSC players returned to established cricket.

That situation did not eventuate, but

Hughes became Chappell's vice-captain ahead of the experienced pair of Marsh and Lillee, and Hughes was also appointed captain of W.A.. He produced some scintillating batting form in this period, being named Man of the Match at the Lords Centenary Test in 1980 after scoring 117 and 84, and in January 1981 Kim Hughes celebrated the birth of his twin sons by blazing a magnificent 213 against India in Adelaide. A superb 100 not out against the feared West Indian pace attack in the Melbourne Test of 1981–82 was also a gem of an innings.

Over the years Hughes' Australian captaincy credentials were eroded when Greg Chappell, the selector's first choice as leader, chose not to be available for certain tours, so the ever-available Western Australian was constantly seen as being only a substitute captain. This may have partly caused the lack of leadership success that gradually evolved with Kim Hughes' teams between 1981 and 1984, especially against the all-conquering West Indian teams.

Australia failed to win a Test against the powerful world champions in the Caribbean campaign of 1983–84, and after the West Indies thrashed the "baggy greens" in the Brisbane Test of the 1984–85 series, a tearful Kim Hughes resigned from the post of Australian captaincy at the after-match press conference. Hughes did continue to play under Alan Border's leadership for three more Tests that summer, but the woeful form of this traumatised player resulted in him being dropped for the final Test.

Hughes, who had remained steadfastly loyal to established cricket during the tumultuous WSC years, then captained a "rebel" Australian team which toured South Africa

**A tearful Kim Hughes resigned from the post of Australian captaincy at the after-match press conference.**

between 1985 and 1987, before he retired from the game. Today his cheerful media personality often comes to light in Western Australian sporting programs, and Kim Hughes appears to harbour no lasting bitterness about the way his promising cricket career became derailed.

## 282. MALONE. M. F. (Michael "Mick") : 1950—.

Tests(1)
46 runs at 46.00
6 wickets at 12.83

An impressive medium-pace swing bowler, who joined WSC when he was in his prime, a decision which cost him many Test appearances.

Mick Malone gained selection with W.A. in 1974–75, and debuted for Australia in style, capturing 5/63 and scoring 46 in the final Oval Test of the 1977 series. His swing and accuracy made him a valuable addition to WSC games and later one day fixtures for Australia, and after disputes between WSC and the ACB were settled, Malone toured Pakistan with Australia's 1980 team.

In his early years Mick Malone was a champion full back in Australian Football , but he abandoned the winter game to concentrate on cricket. He finished his first class career as a valued player with Lancashire, for whom he once took 7/69 in a county game against Nottinghamshire.

## 283. CLARK, W.H. (Wayne) : 1953—.

Tests (10)
98 runs at 5.76
44 wickets at 28.75

A seam and swing bowler from W.A, who performed well when the advent of WSC gave him an unexpected opportunity to play Test cricket

Wayne Clark, who was similar in style and durability to the great Graham McKenzie, broke into first class cricket in the 1974–75 season, and within three years he was in Australia's Test team. He performed quite well on the 1978 tour of the West Indies, taking 15 Test wickets, but after doubts were voiced about the legality of his bouncer, Wayne Clark lost his place in the Australian team to Rodney Hogg.

He still continued to perform well in the Sheffield Shield competition for some time, and in recent years held the position of state coach. Wayne Clark's son, Michael, has also represented W.A..

## 284. HIBBERT, P.A. (Paul) : 1952—.

A dour Victorian left-handed opening batsman who gained Test selection against India in 1977–78 at the Gabba, but lost his place after only one match.

Paul Hibbert also played English League cricket in 1977, and he continued to represent Victoria in the early '80s. In recent years he and former Test player Ian Callen became partners in a cricket bat production business.

## 285. MANN, A.L. (Anthony "Tony") : 1945—.

Tests (4)
189 runs at 23.62
4 wickets at 79.00

A West Australian leg spinning all-rounder

who represented his state for nearly two decades, and scored a famous century for Australia after he was sent in as a nightwatchman.

Tony Mann debuted in Perth grade cricket at the age of 14, and he was still a teenager when he was chosen in the state side in 1963–64. His appearances in the Sheffield Shield competition were sporadic, but occasionally good performances kept him on the fringe of Australian selection. In 1970–71 Tony Mann registered a century against the English touring team, and three seasons of English League cricket improved the flight and guile of his leg spinners.

At the age of 32 Mann was called into Australia's side when the 1977–78 team was weakened by the exodus of leading players to the Packer camp. On his WACA home ground the cheerful veteran scored a memorable 105 against India after captain Bob Simpson sent him in as nightwatchman.

Mann played for his state until the early 1980s, and today he is employed in the family's wine growing business in the Swan Valley.

## 286. OGLIVIE, A.D. (David) : 1951—.

Tests (5)
178 runs at 17.80

A red-haired Queensland batsman who started promisingly in first class cricket, but lost his confidence after he was struck on the head by fast bowler Bob Willis when the 1978–79 English team was touring Australia.

David Ogilvie went into the Queensland team in the 1974–75 season, and the excellent technique of this Brisbane school teacher impressed experts. Ogilvie scored six first class centuries in 1977–78, and in that same year he played in Tests at home opposed to India, and in the Caribbean against the West Indies. His highest Test score was 47.

## 287. RIXON, S.J. (Stephen) : 1954—.
Tests (13)
341 runs at 21.31
dismissals 35 (31 caught, 4 stumped)

A neat NSW wicketkeeper from the border town of Albury, who mostly played Test cricket during the WSC days, and who is now keenly sought for his coaching ability.

Steve Rixon gained NSW selection after Brian Taber retired as wicketkeeper in 1973–74, and in 1977 he joined his Western Suburbs teammate Bob Simpson in an Australian side which had been much depleted by defections to WSC. Rixon made a promising start against India, claiming 22 victims for the series and scoring a Test 50, and he then gained 13 victims and scored another Test half-century in the Caribbean series of 1978.

Once the WSC players returned Rixon became Rod Marsh's understudy on tours of Sri Lanka and England in 1981, and his keeping in Shield games continued to be of a high standard. In 1984–85 Rixon returned to the Test scene for thee matches against the West Indies, and he then ended his playing career in South Africa where he participated in "rebel" tours between 1985 and 1987.

Steve Rixon has since built a fine reputation as a coach, and has enjoyed success with the NSW state team, the New Zealand national team, and the English county side, Surrey. Rixon is sure to be seriously considered for the Australian coaching position when it next becomes vacant.

**A neat NSW wicketkeeper from the border town of Albury, who mostly played Test cricket during the WSC days, and who is now keenly sought for his coaching ability.**

## 288. TOOHEY, P.M. (Peter) : 1954—.
Tests (15)
893 runs at 31.89

A dashing batsman and fine fielder from the NSW rural town of Blayney whose attacking stroke play drew comparisons with Doug Walters.

Peter Toohey scored six centuries in his first 50 innings for NSW, and he was named man-of-the-match after he scored 82 and 57 in his first Test against India in 1977–78. The Indian captain Bishen Bedi nominated Toohey as being "the find of the series", and the slightly built right hander then toured the Caribbean where he scored 122 and 97 in the final Test at Kingston.

Toohey then endured a lean season against the 1978–79 English team, apart from one innings of 81 not out in Perth, and he missed selection in Australian teams which toured India, Pakistan and England in 1981.

In recent years Peter Toohey resided in Sydney, where he worked as a food technologist.

## 289. DYSON, J. (John) : 1954—.
Tests (19)
779 runs at 25.13

A dour batsman from NSW who could bat attractively, but often became bogged down in his role as an opener.

John Dyson was labelled "a stroke less wonder" after his first laborious century in state cricket, but the Sydney physical education teacher was called up for Test duty in three matches against India in 1977–78 when many highly rated players were with WSC .[47]

After he topped the NSW batting averages in 1979–80 Dyson played in the 1980 Lords Centenary Test. He played regularly in Tests against the Indians in 1980–81, but failed to impress on the 1981 tour of England, though he did score a stubborn 102 in the Leeds Test. The following season was memorable for John Dyson because he scored an undefeated 127 and raked in one of the "catches of the century" to dismiss West Indian Sylvester Clark in the Sydney Test.

Dyson finished his playing career with Tests against New Zealand, England and the West Indies in the early 80s, and in recent years he coached the Sri Lankan national team.

**He scored an undefeated 127 and raked in one of the "catches of the century" to dismiss West Indian Sylvester Clark in the Sydney Test.**

## 290. GANNON, J.B. ( John "Sam") : 1947—.

Tests (3)
3 runs at 3.00
11 wickets at 32.82

A tall, left-handed fast-medium bowler, who spent four seasons out of first class cricket, before returning to the Western Australian team and forcing his way into Australia's Test team during the WSC period.

Sam Gannon came into his state team in 1966–67, but the presence of Lillee, Massie and Ian Brayshaw made it difficult for him to gain regular selection until the Packer defections opened up better opportunities. Gannon played in three Tests against the 1977–78 Indian team and claimed 11 wickets.

## 291. CALLEN, I.W. (Ian "Mad Dog") : 1955—.

Tests (1)
26 runs, n.a.
6 wickets at 31.83

47. Pollard, 1982, p328

A tall, unpredictable Victorian fast bowler who bowled admirably in his only Test, but who then faded from the scene because of injury and behavioural problems.

Ian Callen was born in the Victorian hamlet of Yarck, and he burst onto the first class cricket scene when he captured 31 wickets in six Shield games during the 1976–77 season. He made his Test debut against India at Adelaide during the following season, and captured six wicket in a brave 55 over spell when Jeff Thomson was unable to bowl.

Callen then toured the West Indies, but took little part in the 1978 Caribbean action after he injured his back when he fell from a coconut tree. This mishap forced him to withdraw from his contract to play county cricket with Somerset, but he did play Lancashire League cricket in 1981. Callen returned briefly to the Australian team for the 1982 tour of Pakistan.

In recent years Ian Callen has been involved in various business enterprises.

**Callen took little part in the 1978 Caribbean action after he injured his back when he fell from a coconut tree.**

## 292. DARLING, W.M. (Warwick "Rick") : 1957—.
Tests (14)
697 runs at 26.80

A dashing batsman of high quality whose Kamikaze running between wickets, his nervous disposition, and his tendency to be a compulsive hooker, resulted in a shortened Test career.

Rick Darling, a great nephew of the former Australian captain Joe Darling, was born in the South Australian Murray River town of Waikerie, and he commenced playing Adelaide club cricket at a young age. He scored 65 and 56 in his 1977–78 Test debut against India at home, and he toured India with Kim Hughes' Team in 1979. Darling previously visited the Caribbean in 1978, and he played Test matches against England and Pakistan. During those years Darling was regarded as being the best cover fieldsman in the country.

During the 1979–80 home Ashes series, Darling scored an entertaining 91 in the Fourth Test at the SCG, but in the following fixture in Adelaide Rick Darling was struck a near fatal blow above the heart from a Bob Willis delivery. The gum that Darling was chewing lodged in the back of his throat, and only prompt action from close-in English fieldsman John Emburey cleared the obstruction, and enabled Darling to resume breathing.

**The gum that Darling was chewing lodged in the back of his throat, and only prompt action from close-in English fieldsman John Emburey cleared the obstruction, and enabled Darling to resume breathing.**

## 293. WOOD, G.M. (Graeme) : 1956—.
Tests (59)
3,374 runs at 31.83

The other "Kamakaze Kid" in the Darling-Wood opening combination, which gave teammates and spectators much cause for anxiety when they ran suicide singles between wickets.

Graeme Wood grabbed his opportunity to play for Western Australia when many established players defected to WSC, and he finished second in the Shield averages in that 1977–78 season. He debuted with Australia in the final Test of the home series against India, and in 1978 he played in all five Tests in the Caribbean. In the third Test against the West Indies Graeme Wood scored a stylish 126, which impressed WSC organiser Ian Chappell so much that he tried to woo the taciturn

Perth physical education teacher into the Packer camp.

Doubts about his running between wickets surfaced during the next series at home against England, and Wood then endured a disastrous tour of India before missing selection for the 1979 World Cup and 1979–80 tour of Pakistan. After the Indian tour the left-handed opener was dropped from both the state and national teams, but he resourcefully fought his way back into Australia's team for the 1980 Centenary Test at Lords, where he scored 112. Further Test centuries against New Zealand and India over the next two years strengthened his place in Australia's team. Wood's second century against New Zealand on the tour of '82 placed him second in the tour averages behind Greg Chappell.

Wood reached three figures once more against Pakistan in 1982–83. He also played other home Tests against the West Indies, and he toured the Caribbean and appeared in a Test in Sri Lanka in 1984, as his international career started to wind down. Graeme Wood finished Test cricket in fine style by registering his highest Test score of 172 against England at Trent Bridge in 1985.

## 294. YARDLEY, B. (Bruce "Roo") : 1947—.

Tests (33)
978 runs at 19.56
126 wickets at 31.63

A combative warrior of Australian cricket, who was undeterred by selectors' whims, terrible lapses in form, or head wounds from fast bowlers; "Roo" Yardley just kept on coming back for more.

Bruce Yardley began his cricket life as an opening bowler, but could not maintain his place in the W.A. team when star players returned from Test duty. On the advice of his club coach, Yardley switched to off-spin. He still used the fast bowler's run up that he was comfortable with, but was able to drift the ball away from right handed batsmen and then cut it sharply back.

Within two years Bruce Yardley was playing state cricket again, and he was considered unlucky not to tour England in 1977. However he made his Test debut in the final match of the 1977–78 summer in Adelaide, and captured 4/134 from 43 overs against India. This performance clinched him a place in the 1978 Australian touring team to the Caribbean.

Yardley experienced an eventful series against the West Indies. A week before the Third Test in Georgetown he was poleaxed by a Colin Croft bumper which split his skull. Blood poured from his head as he was assisted from the field, and the jagged wound was stitched in a local hospital. However the determined "Roo"'was back in the field against Guyana within two hours. He took 3/96 in the Test that followed, and hit the winning runs when Australia enjoyed a three wicket victory. Other highlights of Bruce Yardley's memorable tour included a final haul of 15 Test wickets, and he also contributed aggressive innings of 74 and 43 at vital times in the series.

He returned to Australia as a confirmed all-rounder, but still found himself in and out of the Test side. He only featured in some of the Tests against England, India and New Zealand between 1979 and 1981, but played a starring role in the 1981–82 Tests against Pakistan, returning the excellent figures of 6/84 and 7/187. The unpredictable Yardley also snared the figures of 7/98 against the West Indies that summer, and returned from New Zealand in 1982 as Australia's leading wicket taker.

Bruce Yardley also collected 22 wickets in the 1982–83 Ashes series and towards the end of his career he captured 5/58 against Sri Lanka in Kandy. The engaging "Roo" Yardley still exudes enthusiasm, and in recent times he has coached in Asia.

## 295. HIGGS, J.D. (James "Jim") : 1950—.
Tests (22)
115 runs at 5.75
66 wickets at 31.16

**A long serving Victorian leg spinner of high quality, who also achieved the dubious distinction of failing to score a run on an Australian tour of England.**

A long serving Victorian leg spinner of high quality, who also achieved the dubious distinction of failing to score a run on an Australian tour of England.

Jim Higgs was raised in the Victorian town of Kyabram, and he made his state debut in the 1970–71 season. The accurate leg spinner gained a place in Australia's 1975 touring team after he snared match figures of 11/118 against W.A., but he failed to play in the Tests against England and is best remembered on that trip for being bowled by the only ball he faced on tour.

Higgs captured 15 Test wickets with Bob Simpson's 1978 team which toured the Caribbean, and snared another 19 wickets in the Ashes home series against England in 1978–79. The following season the humorous leg spinner bowled Victoria to a Sheffield Shield title when he captured 6/57 off 20.1 overs against South Australia. In recent years Jim Higgs served as a national selector.

## 296. LAUGHLIN, T.J. (Trevor) : 1961—.

Tests (3)
87 runs at 17.40
6 wickets at 43.66

A burly, big hitting Victorian all-rounder who was a right-hand medium pace bowler and left-hand middle-order batsman.

Trevor Laughlin was born in the Murray Valley town of Nyah West, and debuted for Victoria in the 1974–75 season. He played Scottish League cricket in 1976 after scoring a swashbuckling 113 against Western Australia, and Laughlin toured the West Indies in 1978 when Australia was badly depleted by WSC defections.

In the Caribbean Trevor Laughlin made his debut in the Third Test in Georgetown Guyana. In the final Test in Kingston Jamaica, he scored 35 and captured 5/101 from 25.4 overs, before the game was abandoned after spectators rioted when Australia was closing in on victory.

Lauchlin failed to produce his best form in England's 1979 World Cup, and he lost his place in Victoria's team in 1980–81. He is now a businessman in Queensland, where his son has become a promising player in Brisbane club cricket.

## 297. HOGG, R.M. (Rodney) : 1951—.

Tests (38)
439 runs at 7.69
123 wickets at 28.48

An argumentative express pace bowler who relied on speed and accuracy rather than swing to gain wickets.

Rodney Hogg played Melbourne District

cricket with Northcote at an early age, but moved to Adelaide where more opportunities opened up. Hogg performed impressively for South Australia, and was fast forwarded into Australia's First Test team for the 1978–79 Ashes series.

It proved to be a magical summer for the tall, fair-headed speedster, as he captured a record 51 wickets in his debut season in Tests, 41 English batsmen fell to his fiery pace and accuracy, while ten Pakistani players were also dismissed by the moody fast bowler. Hogg also captured headlines because of his arguments with the Australian Test captain Graham Yallop, as well as his tendency to be off the field for lengthy sessions with illnesses that doctors were unable to diagnose.

The return of quality fast bowlers such as Lillee and Pascoe from WSC cricket represented a challenge to Rod Hogg, but he was part of the 1979 World Cup squad, he maintained his place in Australia's Test team against New Zealand and India in 1980–81, and he toured England in 1981.

Hogg disappeared briefly from the international stage to recover from injuries after playing only two Tests on that English tour, but he returned successfully in 1983–84 when he captured nine Test wickets against both Pakistan at home and the West Indies in the Caribbean. He then collected another 11 Test wickets when the powerful West Indian team toured Australia in 1984–85, before severing his ties with established cricket and playing in 'rebel' South African tour between 1985 and 1987.

Rodney Hogg now resides in Melbourne and his candid appraisals about local Pura Cup fixtures are often aired on ABC radio.

## 298. MACLEAN, J.A. (John) : 1946—.
Tests (4)
79 runs at 11.28
dismissals 18 (all catches)

A long serving Queensland player and captain who statistically was a better wicket-keeper that Tallon or Grout, but who was not chosen for Australia until he was past his prime.

John Maclean dismissed 346 batsmen in his decade of service to the Queensland state team, and the stocky civil engineer was selected as vice-captain for four Tests against the strong 1978–79 English team. He also toured New Zealand with an Australian team in 1969–70.

## 299. BORDER, A.R. (Allan "Captain Grumpy") : 1955—.
Tests (156)
11,1/4 runs at 50.56
39 wickets at 39.10

A small left-hander who became one of the giants of Australian cricket. Allan Border was initially a reluctant skipper, but he captained Australia a record 93 times in Tests, and his county's proud cricket reputation had been largely restored when he retired from the post after ten years of leadership.

Border was dubbed "Captain Grumpy" by a magazine writer after he complained about the standard of pitches and umpires that were provided on the 1988 tour of Pakistan. Many believe that more appropriate nickname for Border would have been "Captain Courageous".

In 1985 Allan Border batted for 420 min-

**A small left-hander who became one of the giants of Australian cricket.**

utes with a broken bone in his hand when he scored his seventh Test century against England at Old Trafford. The great Dennis Lillee was full of admiration when asked to comment on Border's performance.

"What a brave player this fellow is! So quiet and efficient, so determined to succeed, and so professional."

The legendary fast bowler summed up Border's batting style well. There was little style in his efficient batting, but he had fine judgement about the line and length of deliveries, his footwork and execution of shots were precise, he possessed admirable concentration and determination, and he was full of courage.

Alan Border broke into the NSW side in 1977, and he was 23 when he debuted for Australia against a dominant English team in 1978–79. Border's batting performances at international level soon improved, and in March 1979 he scored his first Test century against Pakistan.

By the 1983–84 season Border was a world class batsman. He scored 118 and 117 in the home series opposed to Pakistan, and against the feared West Indian pace bowlers in the Caribbean in 1984 his Test aggregate of 521 included a century and two 90s. An unexpected elevation to captaincy halted the run splurge somewhat against Clive Lloyd's world champions at home where he managed a modest Test tally of 246 runs, but he found his touch again when he led the Australians to England in 1985.

Allan Border amassed an imposing eight centuries on tour, and his scores of 196 and 146 were both recorded in Tests. He then averaged over 50 in Tests against both the winning New Zealand team as well as in India where he captained Australia in the memorable tied Test in Madras. Until he retired in 1994, the run glut continued for Border against all of the major countries of the world except South Africa, whom he first encountered when his illustrious career was nearing an end. He finished with 27 Test centuries (two less than Sir Donald Bradman) with eight of them being registered against England. His accurate left arm spinners were useful at times, and Allan Border enjoyed one superb Test match with the ball when he snared 7/46 against the West Indies in 1988 at the SCG.

At times during this period of personal triumphs Border appeared to be worried and perplexed, for the team that evolved under his leadership certainly experienced both agonies and ecstasies before it became an established force of world cricket.

A euphoric 1987 World Cup victory in India and Pakistan was followed by a 1:0 defeat in the 1988 Test series Pakistan. In 1989, 1990–91 and 1993 Border's men decisively won Ashes clashes, and they only narrowly lost two series against the West Indian world champions. A despondent Border nearly resigned after a Sir Richard Hadlee inspired New Zealand proved too good, but a 4:0 drubbing of India encouraged him to continue. Border's final opponent was South Africa, against whom Australia engaged in two exciting drawn series before he retired after the Kingsmead Test at Durban. His commendable record of Test captaincy included 32 wins, 22 losses, 38 draws and a tie.

Border moved from NSW to Queensland during his career, and he led "the Sunshine State" to a Shield victory before he finally left first class cricket at the age of 41. Allan Border was so often the man of the hour during his 15 years in the Test arena, and in hon-

**The team that evolved under his leadership certainly experienced both agonies and ecstasies before it became an established force of world cricket.**

our of his achievements the Allan Border Field was created as Brisbane's second main cricket venue. He still resides in Brisbane and has served Australia as a Test selector for many years.

## 300. CARLSON, P. H. (Phillip) : 1951—.
Tests (2)
23 runs at 5.75
2 wickets at 49.50

One of many players who had short Test careers when opportunities opened up during the WSC era.

Phil Carlson began promisingly in Shield cricket when he notched a century at the age of 20. Between1971 and 1981 he was an excellent all-rounder for Queensland. Carlson emulated the great George Giffen when he became the second Australian player to score a century and take ten wickets in the one Sheffield Shield game, and in that same 1978–79 season he played two Tests against the visiting English team.

Carlson was found wanting at this level, and his form deteriorated so badly that he was embarrassingly dropped from the state team in 1980–81, which Queensland Cricket had previously declared would be Philip Carlson's benefit season.

## 301. WRIGHT, K.J. (Kevin) : 1953—.
Tests (10)
219 runs at 16.84
dismissals 35 (31 caught, 4 stumped)

A competent left-handed wicket keeper for W.A., South Australia and Australia but who lived constantly in the shadow of Rod Marsh and then lost the position of Australia's reserve keeper to the NSW gloveman, Steve Rixon.

Kevin Wright first substituted for Marsh in his state side in 1974–75, and he replaced John MacLean as Australia's keeper in the Fifth Test of the 1978–79 Ashes series when Marsh was playing WSC cricket. The red-haired wicket-keeper collected six catches in his debut Test, and his impressive form continued in Tests against Pakistan, the 1979 World Cup and the six Test series in India where Wright also scored an undefeated Test half-century.

Kevin Wright performed well with South Australia when he transferred to that state after settlement was reached between the ACB and WSC, but he never gained Test selection again.

## 302. HILDITCH, A.M.J. (Andrew) : 1956—.
### Tests (18)
### 1,073 runs at 31.56

An opening batsman who captained NSW at the age of 21, but who struggled to consolidate a Test place after the WSC players returned to established cricket.

Andrew Hilditch is best remembered for his controversial dismissal for "handling the ball" in the Perth Test of the 1979 series against Pakistan. When he was at the non-strikers' end at the WACA ground he caught a gentle lob from an opposition fieldsman and tossed it helpfully back to the Pakistani bowler, Sarfraz Narwaz. The bowler appealed, and under the laws of the game the umpire had no option but to give Hilditch out for "handling the ball".

Hilditch was raised in Adelaide but was

The bowler appealed, and under the laws of the game the umpire had no option but to give Hilditch out for "handling the ball".

studying Law at Sydney University when he was appointed captain of NSW after only two first class games. He became vice-captain to Kim Hughes for the 1979 World Cup after appearing in one Test against England and two against Pakistan that season, but failed to retain his place for nearly three seasons after the WSC players returned.

His career was revived by a timely century in the Fourth Test of the 1984–85 series against the West Indies in Adelaide, which propelled him into Border's 1985 Australian Team that toured England. Hilditch started that Ashes series well, scoring 119 and 80 in the opening Test at Headingley, but his form tapered off disappointingly. He only added another 189 runs in the next five Tests.

Andrew Hilditch married one of Bob Simpson's daughters, and now resides in Adelaide from where he has served as an Australian selector for many years. He was recently appointed Chairman of the national selection panel.

## 303. SLEEP, P.R. (Peter "Sounda") : 1957—.
Tests (14)
483 runs at 24.15
31 wickets at 45.06

A durable and persistent leg spinning all-rounder who played in 13 Tests in the decade between 1979 and 1989, and is still playing club cricket today as he nears his 50th year.

Peter Sleep was raised in good red wine country in Penola near Mt. Gambier, and like the fruit of the vine he appeared to get better with age. Sleep moved from Adelaide club cricket into the South Australian team in

282

1976–77 and in the following season the developing spinner made his Test debut against Pakistan in Melbourne. The enthusiastic Sleep later broke his Lancashire League contract to join Kim Hughes' 1979–80 Australian team in India, which yielded promising results.

Sleep captured 8/145 in his two Tests and his score of 64 at Nagpur helped Australia secure a draw. When David Hookes took over the captaincy of South Australia he encouraged "Sounda" with more bowling opportunities, and the developing all-rounder helped "The Redbacks" gain the 1981–82 Sheffield Shield title.

Sleep continued to sporadically be chosen, and between the 1986–87 and the 1989–90 season he gained Australian selection on ten occasions. His best performances were a Test score of 90 against New Zealand in 1987–88, and in 1989–90 he snared five wickets in the Second Test against Sri Lanka. In that same period Sleep also appeared in Tests against England and Pakistan.

After Peter Sleep re-married he spent some years in England playing League cricket. He is now reportedly playing club cricket back in his home area of Penola.

## 304. WHATMORE, D. F. (Davenell) : 1954—.
### Tests (7)
### 293 runs at 22.54

A Sri Lankan born batsman who represented Victoria and Australia before returning to Sri Lanka to coach his native land to a thrilling World Cup victory in 1996.

Dav Whatmore debuted for Victoria in

1975–76 and played two Tests against Pakistan two seasons later after scoring well in Australian domestic cricket. He made 43 on debut, and in that same season Whatmore was instrumental in Victoria winning the Sheffield Shield. He represented Australia in the 1979 World Cup, and in the same year he played in five of his seven Tests in India with Kim Hughes' team. Whatmore's chief asset on tour was his brilliant fielding in slips, and he held six catches in the Kanpur Test.

Since he ceased playing first class cricket, Davenell Whatmore has built up an enviable reputation as a coach. He experienced much success with Sri Lanka, he has also coached in England, and currently he is coach of Bangladesh.

## 305. MOSS, J.K. (Jeffrey) : 1947—.
Tests (1)
60 runs at 60.00

A hard hitting Victorian left-handed batsman who performed particularly well for his state between 1978 and 1980 when the Vics won two Sheffield Shield titles.

After Moss scored 881 runs at 67.77 in 1978–79, he must have been close to national selection, and he was finally called into the Australian team for the final Test against Pakistan in 1979. World Cup selection in England that year then followed, but Jeff Moss lost his place in the Australian side when the WSC players returned.

## 306. LAIRD, B.M. (Bruce "Stumpy") : 1950—.
Tests (21)
1,341 runs at 35.29

A stoic opening batsman from W.A. who was at his best during his WSC career, and who blunted many formidable opening attacks with his solid technique.

Bruce Laird started impressively in his Test debut, scoring 92 and 75 against the West Indies in the 1979–80 season. The chunky opener registered at least 15 half-centuries against New Zealand, Pakistan and the West Indies, and was a model of consistency throughout his career with Australia. "Stumpy" Laird was also an excellent close-to-the-wicket fieldsman.

## 307. WIENER, J.M. (Julien) : 1955—.

Tests (6)<br>281 runs at 25.54

An attacking Victorian batsman whose consistent performances at state level gained him selection in the Australian team for the 1979–80 Ashes Test in Perth. There the blonde-haired son of Austrian migrants scored 58 in the second innings. In subsequent Tests Wiener scored 40 against the West Indies in Melbourne, and 93 against Pakistan at Lahore in Greg Chappell's 1980 team.

Julien Wiener continued to bat attractively and accumulate large scores in Shield matches, but was not chosen in Test sides again.

## 308. BEARD, G.R. (Graeme "Agatha") : 1950—.

Tests (3)<br>114 runs at 22.80<br>1 wicket for 110

A slow-medium swing and seam bowler who was nick-named "Agatha" after the crime writer Agatha Christie, because he worked hard at developing mystery deliveries to add to his bowling repertoire.

Graeme Beard was in and out of the NSW team after he first debuted in 1975, but by the 1989–90 season he was a fixture in "the Blues" best sides. He toured Pakistan in 1980 when both Jim Higgs and Ashley Mallett were unavailable for selection, and the tall, cheerful all-rounder scored useful runs in all three Tests.

At the age of 30 Beard was chosen ahead of Bruce Yardley to tour England in 1981, but his clever slow medium deliveries were not called upon in Tests. Graeme Beard retired from first class cricket in1982.

## 309. LAWSON, G.F. (Geoffrey "Henry") : 1957—.

Tests (46)
894 runs at 15.96
180 wickets at 30.56

A tall NSW and Australian opening bowler who overcame a succession of injuries early in his career to become a proven performer at Test match level.

Geoff Lawson grew up in Wagga Wagga and represented the University of NSW while he completed his optometry studies. From there he debuted with NSW in 1977–78. After capturing an impressive 34 Shield wickets in 1979–80 Lawson toured India and Pakistan, and made his Test debut against New Zealand in1980–81.

Lawson then made way for Rodney Hogg, but when Hogg was injured on the 1981 tour of England "Henry" seized his chance to impress taking 2/2 from his first 16 deliveries in the Lords Test before finishing with the fine figures of 7/81 from 43.1 overs. Injuries then interrupted Lawson's tour, and he was also sidelined for the 1981–82 New Zealand series.

Geoff Lawson returned in triumph for the 1982–83 Ashes Tests, capturing 34 wickets for 20.20 runs to be Australia's leading wicket take. He was also the premier bowler against Pakistan and the West Indies, and only Craig McDermott captured more wickets than Lawson on the 1985 tour of England. However in the home series against New Zealand in 1985–86 Lawson strained his groin which hampered his performances until the 1988–89 home Tests against the West Indies.

Lawson was looking to consolidate his place in the Australian team again, but in the first innings of the Second Test in Perth he was struck by a brutish delivery from Curtly Ambrose which broke his jaw. This further setback ended Lawson's appearances for the remainder of the series. He returned to action later that year and played a vital part in Australia regaining the Ashes in England.

Geoff Lawson captured 29 Test wickets at 27.28 in the six Tests, and his combination with new ball partner Terry Alderman was crucial in Australia's success. It was virtually the curtain call on Lawson's excellent career, as he played in no further Test after the 1989–90 season. Geoff "Henry" Lawson now resides in Sydney, and is frequently heard in the ABC commentary team at SCG matches.

## 310. ALDERMAN, T.M. : 1956—.

Tests (41)

203 runs at 6.55

170 wickets at 27.15

A W.A. and Australian fast-medium

bowler, whose technique was ideally suited to English conditions where he captured the formidable tally of 83 Test wickets during Ashes campaigns in 1981 and 1989.

Terry Alderman captured 5/65 at the SCG in his first Sheffield Shield match at the age of 18, but injuries and lack of fitness resulted in him being dropped on two occasions from the state team. His entry into the Test arena did not occur until the 1981 English tour. A stint as a professional in Scottish League cricket the year before had improved Alderman's motivation and skills, and when he reverted to seaming rather than swinging the ball in tour matches, he became the key bowler in the Ashes series.

Alderman captured match figures of 9/130 in the First Test, and he went to collect 42 wickets for the series, which broke Rodney Hogg's previous record. Back in Australia the handsome West Australian did not experience the same success, but on the softer New Zealand pitches he again came to the fore, taking eight wickets in the three Tests. After playing in the home series against Pakistan, Alderman was selected to oppose the 1982–83 English team in his home city of Perth. However on November 14th 1982 he was cruelly injured in a bizarre incident.

A larrikin crowd of English supporters invaded the playing area after England passed the total of 400, and one of them struck Alderman on the back of the head. When the furious fast bowler grappled with his tormentor, he fell and dislocated his shoulder so badly that he was out of the Test arena for two seasons.

Progress was slow for Terry Alderman when he returned to Test cricket with a modified action, but a tally of nine wickets in three

**A larrikin crowd of English supporters invaded the playing area after England passed the total of 400, and one of them struck Alderman on the back of the head.**

Tests against the visiting West Indians in 1984–85, saw him selected for the 1985 Ashes tour. However he had previously signed to participate in the 1985–86 "rebel" tour of South Africa, so Alderman missed the English series. He did not appear again in Test cricket until the next home series against the Windies in 1988–89.

Selectors thankfully remembered his previous success in England and he was chosen for his second Ashes tour in 1989. Alderman was again a resounding success, and his 41 wickets made him the main strike bowler in Australia's Ashes' triumph. Alderman continued to represent Australia in series against Sri Lanka and Pakistan, but after he was only chosen for one Test in the 1991 Caribbean series, before he retired from first class cricket.

Terry Alderman's father and brother also played first grade cricket in Perth, and his sister Denise was a high scoring batter in the Australian Women's team. Nowadays Alderman frequently commentates on ABC radio when first class fixtures are played in W.A.

## 311. CHAPPELL, T.M. (Trevor) : 1952—.

Tests (3)

79 runs at 15.80

The youngest of the three Chappells who represented three states as well as Australia for a short time, but found the challenge of living up to his older brothers' famous deeds to be a huge burden. "I'd rather be Bill Smith or just an ordinary bloke," he once admitted.[48]

Trevor Chappell was considered by his school coach to be better than his brothers at the same age, and he scored 67 on debut for South Australia in 1972–73. However for the next three seasons he was only selected on 17 occasions in the state team, and in 1976, following some winter stints with English League clubs, he moved to W.A. After experiencing modest success in four state appearances there, Trevor Chappell joined WSC, and following that two season commitment he transferred to NSW for the 1979–80 season. The youngest Chappell was valued with "the Blues" for his all-round skills which surprisingly gained him selection in the 1981 Australian team that toured England.

His parents were at Trent Bridge when the 28 year old Trevor Chappell entered Australia's record books by becoming the third member of a family to play Test cricket, and his sound innings of 20 helped to guide his team to victory. After the Ashes series ended Trevor Chappell was not chosen in Tests again. He did, however, represent his country in some limited overs fixtures, and it was in that form of the game that he became an unwilling villain in the deciding match of the 1981 World Series Cup against New Zealand at the MCG.

Trevor's brother Greg Chappell was captain of Australia at the time, and he instructed his younger sibling to bowl the final ball of the day underarm so that the Kiwis could not score the six runs that were required for victory. That decision caused uproar in sporting circles, newspapers and national parliaments on both sides of the Tasman, and sadly remains the most memorable legacy that Trevor Chappell left in his first class career.

**That decision caused uproar in sporting circles, newspapers and national parliaments on both sides of the Tasman, and sadly remains the most memorable legacy that Trevor Chappell left behind in his first class career.**

## 312. KENT, M.F. (Martin) : 1953—.
Tests (3)
171 runs at 28.50

A stylish Queensland and Australian bats-

48. Pollard, 1982, p265

man whose promising career suffered both from nagging back problems, and from being constantly shuffled around the top six batting positions.

Martin Kent was a consistent run maker from the time he scored an attractive 140 in his state debut match, but his entry into Test cricket was delayed after he signed with WSC. However he was one of the few Australians who had a successful 1981 tour of England, despite the fact that he was overlooked by selectors until the Fourth Test, and that he was not placed in a regular batting position.

Kent scored 47 and 10 batting fifth wicket down in Edgbaston, 52 and two when he was moved to third wicket down at Old Trafford, and 54 and seven when he opened in the final Test at Kennington Oval.

Back injuries prematurely forced Martin Kent from the game after the tour. He scored seven first class centuries during his career, and now occasionally commentates on Brisbane radio on first class matches

### 313. WHITNEY, M.J. (Michael) : 1959—.
#### Tests (12)
#### 68 runs at 6.18
#### 39 wickets at 33.97

A lively NSW left-arm fast bowler with an Afro haircut who first played for Australia in unusual circumstances. His longevity in international cricket continued long after many thought that he would never wear the "baggy green" cap again.

Mike Whitney was in the UK playing with Gloucestershire in 1981 when he was called up for duty with the Australian Test

A lively NSW left-arm fast bowler with an Afro haircut who first played for Australia in unusual circumstances. His longevity in international cricket continued long after many thought that he would never wear the "baggy green" cap again.

team after injuries to bowlers in the official team group called for desperate measures. Whitney captured five wickets in his two unexpected Test appearances in England, and the durable fast bowler resurfaced yet again in future years when his Test career appeared to have ended.

Seven seasons later it was Whitney who defiantly blocked out a hostile last few balls from Richard Hadlee to salvage an honourable draw for Australia against New Zealand at the MCG. In his return to Test cricket Whitney captured four wickets, and during his occasional international appearances over the next few years Mike Whitney produced two exceptional performances.

In the 1988–89 season the enthusiastic left-hander captured 7/89 against the West Indies at Adelaide, and against India in the 1991–92 series he collected a stunning 7/27. Whitney toured the Caribbean in 1991 but only played in one Test, and retired soon afterwards.

In recent years Mike Whitney has become a celebrity host on national television programs.

## 314. WELLHAM, D. M. (Dirk "Smirk") : 1959—.
Tests (6)
257 runs at 23.36

A determined batsman who gained selection in the 1981 Australian Ashes touring team after playing only five first class matches. He also achieved the rare distinctions of scoring centuries on debut at both Sheffield Shield and Test level and captaining three state teams.

Dirk Wellham is the nephew of the former NSW player Wally Wellham, and young

...also achieved the rare distinctions of scoring centuries on debut at both Sheffield Shield and Test level and captained three state teams.

Dirk burst onto the first class scene, scoring two Shield centuries and averaging 68 in his first four games for the state.. These impressive statistics gained him a trip to England, and at the age of 22 he scored 103 in the final Test at The Oval.

The euphoria of that success did not last long, as a form slump caused Dirk Wellham to be dropped from both the Australian and NSW team in the 1981–82 season. Dirk Wellham captained his home state, he also captained Tasmania, where his astute leadership of a young developing state team was highly rated, and in 1992–93 he came out of retirement to skipper Queensland.

## 315. RITCHIE, G. M. (Gregory "Fat Cat") : 1960—.
### Tests (30)
### 1,690 runs at 35.21

A wonderfully talented stroke-player who faltered in Test cricket because of  his lack of application and fitness.

Greg Ritchie's batting prowess became obvious soon after he debuted for Queensland. He was selected in the 1984 Tests in the Caribbean where he scored 78 in one fixture but only averaged 20.70 for the series. He was somewhat luckily retained in Australia's team for the 1985 Ashes' tour but the burly Ritchie was one of the success stories of the Australian team.

Ritchie scored 94 in the Lords Test, a brilliant 146 at Trent Bridge in the Test that followed, and 64 not out in the final match of the series at The Oval. His total of 422 runs at an average of 42.20 provided hope that "Fat Cat" had come of age as a batsman.

However Greg Ritchie still struggled for consistency. In the next series against New Zealand he only averaged 30 despite scoring 89 in one innings. In the home series opposed to India he again dominated, scoring 128 in Adelaide and averaging 79.50. He then tapered off once more in New Zealand and on the 1986–87 tour of India, before drifting out of Test cricket.

Greg Ritchie continued to represent Queensland for some time, and he briefly captained his state team.

## 316. RACKEMANN, C.G. (Carl) : 1960—.
Tests (12)
53 runs at 5.30
39 wickets at 29.15

A strong, blonde-headed Queensland country product who at times performed better than many of Australia's fast bowlers, but who was sidelined by injuries at crucial stages of his career.

Carl Rackemann captured 5/25 in his Shield debut season in 1979–80 , but two seasons later a back injury caused him to miss many games. He captured 2/61 at the Gabba in his debut and only Test against England in 1982–83. After he captured 16 wickets in the opening two Tests of the 1983–84 home series against Pakistan , it seemed that  his luck with injuries had changed.

Rackemann appeared to be the Pakistani's bogey-man after claiming figures of 5/32 and 6/86 in Perth followed by 3/28 in Brisbane, but his injury prone body failed him for the rest of the series. He managed to tour with Kim Hughes' 1984 team to the Caribbean, but only played in the Antigua Test where he captured 5/161.

After gaining selection for just one Test the following summer, Carl Rackemann turned his back on established cricket and played successfully in South Africa with the "rebel" tourists in 1985 and 1986. In recent years he has been involved in Queensland cricket, and occasionally commentates on Brisbane radio about state games and Tests.

## 317. WESSELS, K.C. (Kepler) : 1957—.
Tests(40)
2,788 runs at 41.00

An accomplished South African batsman who took out Australian citizenship and wore "the baggy green"in 40 Test matches, but returned home and captained South Africa once the Proteas were accepted back into world cricket.

Kepler Wessels first played in his homeland's prestigious Currie Cup competition at the age of 16, and he was only 20 when he was capped for Sussex in English county cricket. Wessels performed very successfully with WSC, and after settlement with established cricket was reached he married an Australian, played with Queensland, and took out Australian citizenship. He became a heavy runs scorer in Sheffield Shield games, and after Kepler Wessels became eligible to represent his new country in September 1982, it seemed that he would end his cricket career in a "baggy green" cap.

Wessels dominated his debut Test at the Gabba, scoring 162 and 40 against he 1982–83 English team, and his satisfying first series ended with a half-century in the final match of the series. He then compiled 141 against Sri Lanka in Kandy at the end of that season, and in the 1983–84 home series against Pakistan he scored 179 at the Adelaide Oval.

The gritty left-hander then endured a disappointing tour of the Caribbean in 1984, but he overcame that disappointment with an outstanding home series against the West Indies in 1984–85. Wessels totalled an imposing 505 runs at 56.11 in the Test series, and his scores included innings of 173, 61, 98, 70 and 90 .

After this run spurge Kepler Wessels' performance on the 1985 Australian tour of England was disappointing, as he scored a moderate 368 runs at average of 33.45. He played one more Test in the 1986–87 series against New Zealand, but after South Africa was welcomed back to the Test arena the taciturn Wessels returned to his homeland.

Kepler Wessels still resides in the Republic of South Africa. In 1982–83 he captained the Proteas in the drawn series against Australia, and he scored 50 against his former national team in the Johannesburg Test.

## 318. HOGAN, T. J. (Thomas) : 1956—.
Tests (7)
205 runs at 18.64
15 wickets at 47.07

A WA left-arm orthodox spinner and late-order batsman who had a brief Test career during the early '80s.

Tom Hogan made an inauspicious Test debut against Sri Lanka at Kandy in 1983, and had little impact at the World Cup that followed that short tour. He also had little success against the 1983–84 Pakistan team in the

Adelaide Test.

However Hogan became a useful player when the Australians toured the Caribbean in 1984. He played in all five Tests, scoring a defiant 42 not out in the opening Test in Guyana, and collecting eight wickets in the series.

Hogan was not selected in further Tests, but he toured South Africa in 1985 and 1986 with Kim Hughes' "rebel" team.

### 319. WOOLLEY, R. D. (Roger) : 1954—.

Tests (2)
21 runs at 10.50
dismissals 7 catches

The first Tasmanian born player to score a Sheffield Shield century.

Roger Woolley achieved this feat in the1977–78 season against Queensland, and in the following season the Hobart insurance broker scored 99 not out against W.A.

Woolley's wicket keeping improved so much that he kept for Australia against Sri Lanka in the 1983 Test at Kandy. He also wore "the baggy green" in the Fourth Test at St. Johns Antigua when he toured the Caribbean with Kim Hughes' 1984 team.

Roger Woolley dropped out of Test cricket following the tour, but he captained Tasmania in many Shield games before his first class career ended.

### 320. PHILLIPS, W.B. (Wayne "Flipper") : 1958—.

Tests (27)
1,485 runs at 32.28
dismissals 52 (catches)

A dashing and versatile left-handed batsman who also kept wickets for Australia, despite lacking genuine class in that specialist position. Wane Phillips debuted at 19 for South Australia, and it took him only 14 matches to reach 1000 first class runs. At that stage he had not kept wickets in first class fixtures.

In 1982–83 Phillips opened the batting against Pakistan in Perth, and scored a stylish 159. His batting average for the series was an impressive 60.33, and after he first donned the wicket-keeping gloves for Australia against the West Indies in 1984, the versatile Phillips scored an exhilarating 120 when he batted at number seven in the Third Test in Barbados. He was also called upon to open in other Tests on tour, and his form suffered from being shuffled around the batting order.

Wayne Phillips batted down the order and kept wickets in the first Test of the 1984–85 home series against the West Indies, but was only chosen for one Test. However when Steve Rixon opted to join the"rebels" in South Africa instead of touring England, "Flipper" was once again handed the wicket-keeping gloves. He performed quite well in his dual Test role in England, accepting 11 catches and averaging 35 with the bat. He retained those responsibilities in series against New Zealand and India, until the specialist WA keeper, Tim Zoehrer was preferred in the away series against New Zealand in 1985–86.

This decision effectively ended Phillips' Test career, and the amiable South Australian has since worked with the Adelaide Cricket Academy. He has also had a coaching role with the state team.

## 321. MAGUIRE, J.N. (John) : 1956—.

Tests (3)
28 runs at 7.00
10 wickets at 32.30

A fit and persistent Queensland opening bowler who appeared briefly in Test cricket during the early 1980s.

John Maguire was born in northern NSW, but played club cricket in nearby Brisbane. Some sterling performances at state level saw him selected in the Australian team for the 1983 Boxing Day Test at the MCG against Pakistan.

Maguire played in the final two Tests and captured 4/57 at Kingston Jamaica in the last match of the 1984 series against the West Indies. He later participated in "rebel" tours to South Africa between 1985–86.

## 322. MATTHEWS, G. R.J. (Gregory "Mo") : 1959—.

Tests (33)
1,849 runs at 41.09
61 wickets at 48.23

An eccentric and feisty all-rounder who produced both inspirational and poor performances during his unpredictable Test career.

Greg Matthews bristled with enthusiasm and commitment from the time he first started with NSW, and he started his Test career auspiciously by scoring 75 and capturing four wickets with his flattish off-spinners against Pakistan at the MCG in 1983. "Mo" then toured the Caribbean with Kim Hughes' team, but played in only one away Test and

**Greg Matthews bristled with enthusiasm and commitment from the time he first started with NSW.**

another Test at home against the West Indies, when they visited Australia in 1984–85. Matthews' unimpressive form then continued on the 1985 tour of England, where he again appeared in just one Test.

However just when his international career appeared to be faltering, Matthews suddenly made an impact. The left-handed middle-order batsman scored 115 against New Zealand in the1985–86 Brisbane Test, and later that season he notched 130 at Wellington and snared 4/61 at Auckland against the Kiwis. An undefeated 100 against India at the MCG was also included in Matthews' revitalised career.

The 1986–87 tour of India followed where Greg Mathews enjoyed his finest achievements in Test cricket. It was "Mo" who clinched a historic tie for Australia at Madras, trapping the Indian tail-ender Maninder Singh lbw when the scores were locked together, and the demonstrative all-rounder had a stellar match. In the stifling conditions that prevailed throughout that dramatic Test match, Matthews delivered 67.5 overs, and he captured the memorable match figures of 10/249 in his marathon performance.

Greg Matthews continued to bat consistently in series that followed but the English and West Indian teams in particular scored heavily from his bowling. He performed well in Sri Lanka in 1992, but the '93 tour of the West Indies ended his Test career after Vivian Richards and Richie Richardson hammered his off-spinners.

Matthews now resides in Sydney, and his forthright television coverage of the 2005 Ashes series in England was enjoyed by many viewers.

**It was "Mo" who clinched a historic tie for Australia at Madras, trapping the Indian tail-ender Maninder Singh lbw when the scores were locked together.**

## 323. SMITH, S.B. (Stephen) : 1961—.
Tests (3)
41 runs at 8.20

A dashing NSW opening batsman who failed in the only three Tests he played on the 1984 Caribbean tour.

## 324. JONES, D. J. (Dean "Deano") : 1961—.
Tests (52)
3,631 runs at 46.55
I wicket at 64.00

An impetuous and abrasive personality who played a Test innings of amazing heroism in the stifling heat of Madras, and who was regarded as being the premier one day player in the world during his long career.

Dean Jones first appeared for Victoria in 1981–82 and he scored 48 on a difficult wet wicket in his Test debut at Trinidad during the 1984 tour of the Caribbean. Jones played another test against the West Indies in that series, but he was then left out of Australia's Test team for over two years.

Consistent scoring at state level gained him selection on the 1986 tour of India, and it was there that Dean Jones became a hero of the game. While the temperature hovered constantly on 45 degrees C. and humidity stayed on 60%, Jones batted for 503 minutes to score 210.

The Indian captain Sunil Gavaskar and other players implored "Deano" to retire hurt when he suffered stomach cramps and vomiting attacks at the crease. After the dehydrated, exhausted and hallucinating Jones was finally dismissed, he was rushed to the nearest hospital and placed on a saline drip. Jones lost seven kilograms during his life-threatening stay at the crease, and the Australian coach Bob Simpson later summed up the emotions of all cricket followers when he said, "I doubt if there has ever been a more courageous Test innings."[49]

Jones carried his world class form back to Australia scoring an undefeated 184 in the only Test that Australia won in the 1986–87 Ashes series. The swing and guile of Richard Hadlee caused a hiccough in "Deano's" progress in Tests against New Zealand, but he bounced back by amassing 216 against the 1988–89 touring West Indians.

On the 1989 tour of England Jones was a main force in Australia regaining the Ashes, scoring two centuries and averaging 70.75 in the Tests. Jones' nimble footwork at the crease, his dashing stroke-play, his brilliant running between wickets and his excellent fielding made him the premier one day player in the world. However after 1992 he found it difficult to gain Test selection.

Sheer weight of runs from the Victorian captain forced his inclusion into the 1993–94 Australian team which toured South Africa, but he was not chosen for Tests. Dean Jones retired from first class cricket at the end of the tour after scoring 11 Test centuries and representing Australia in 164 limited over matches. Jones later became a cricket commentator before he was removed from that role after allegedly making racist remarks on air in August 2006.

## 325. BOON, D.C. (David "Boonie") : 1960—.

49. Pollard, 1982, p531

## Tests (107)
### 7,422 runs at 43.66

Tasmania's most successful player who joined an elite Australian batting group when he passed the milestone of scoring 7,000 runs in Test cricket.

David Boon hails from Launceston, and he debuted for Tasmania as an 18 year old in the 1978–79 season. The stocky young man came to notice nationally when he scored a dashing 134 from 136 deliveries for the Prime Minister's X1 in 1983–84, and it was the Windies who were also his first Test opponents in 1984. Boon scored 51 in his Gabba debut, and in tours to the Caribbean that year, and to England in 1985, the developing middle-order batsman gradually found his feet in Test cricket.

It was when the national selectors turned to him as an opener that David Boon blossomed. He scored two centuries and averaged 64.60 against the 1985–86 Indian team in the new role, and he continued to plague the Indian attack by scoring 122 in the dramatic tied Test in Madras. Another century in Adelaide followed against England in a less successful series for Boon, but he was part of a successful Australian World Cup team in 1987.

By then Boon was an accomplished stroke-player on both sides of the wicket, and Test centuries continued to flow against New Zealand and England. The selection of Mark Taylor forced Boon to revert to number three in the order against the West Indies during the 1988–89 series, but his score of 149 at the SCG showed that he was an effective batsman anywhere in the top order.

David Boon registered three scores over 50 when Australia regained the Ashes in 1989, and he scored heavily against the visiting Englishmen when he totalled 530 runs in the 1990–91 series. He also started the closely fought 1991 series in the Caribbean with a three figure score, and in the following Australian summer he reeled off a further three centuries against the Indian team. The run glut continued on the victorious 1993 tour of England when the consistent Boon posted three more Test centuries.

In lead up Tests to the eagerly awaited 1994 series in the Caribbean, Boon registered centuries opposed to Pakistani and English teams in home series. When Australia finally won in the West Indies in 1994, Boon scored a valuable half-century in the Guyana Test match. Then, after more than a decade of Test cricket when he played in over 100 Tests, took nearly 100 catches and scored 100 or more on 21 occasions, David Boon retired at the end of the 1995–96 home series against Sri Lanka.

"Boonie" is currently an Australian selector, and he has become the face of many advertising campaigns for Tasmanian banks and beer companies.

**"Boonie" is currently an Australian selector, and he has become the face of many advertising campaigns for Tasmanian banks and beer company enterprises.**

### 326. HOLLAND, R.G. (Robert "Bob") : 1946—.
Tests (11)
35 runs at 3.18
34 wickets at 39.76

**He was a genuine tail-end batsman, and his record of scoring five successive ducks in Test cricket has yet to be bettered.**

A courteous and friendly slow bowler who was based in Newcastle for much of his career, and who was regarded as being a specialist on the spinner friendly SCG pitch. He was a genuine tail-end batsman, and his record of scoring five successive ducks in Test cricket has yet to be bettered.

Bob Holland was an irregular selection in NSW teams for five years after he first played Shield cricket in 1978–79, but it was the 38 year old leg spinner that the Australian selectors turned to for the final Test of the 1984–85 series against the West Indies.

Holland justified the selection gamble, capturing the match winning figures of 10/144 at the SCG in his second Test of the summer. A year later he bowled "the baggy greens" to another stirring victory at Lords when he snared 5/68. This was the only success that he enjoyed in the four Tests he played on the 1985 tour of England.

### 327. BENNETT, M. J. (Murray) : 1956—.
#### Tests (3)
#### 71 runs at 23.67
#### 6 wickets at 54.17

A gangly, bespectacled left arm-orthodox spinner who played a crucial support role to Bob Holland when Australia defeated the West Indies at the SCG, but had little impact in his other two Test matches.

Murray Bennett  began in Shield cricket in 1982–83, and the accurate spinner was the perfect foil for the match-winning Holland when he played in his second Test of the 1984–85 series against the West Indies. Bennett bowled 65.5 overs in that New Year match at the SCG, and returned the economical match figures of 5/124.

Murray Bennett also toured England in 1985, but failed to impress in his only Test match.

## 328. MCDERMOTT, C.J. (Craig "Billy") : 1965—.
### Tests (71)
### 940 runs at 12.21
### 291 wickets at 28.63

**A Queensland and Australian fast bowler who gained his first Test wicket with a wild full-toss, lost his way for a time in the game during his "wild" days of youth, but who then matured to become of the best pace bowlers to ever wear "the baggy green".**

A Queensland and Australian fast bowler who gained his first Test wicket with a wild full-toss, lost his way for a time in the game during his "wild" days of youth, but who then matured to become of the best pace bowlers to ever wear "the baggy green".

Craig McDermott was born in Ipswich, and the strongly built red-head only had one season of apprenticeship in state cricket before he debuted for Australia at the age of 19 against the mighty West Indians. His first wicket came when he bowled Richie Richardson with a wayward full toss, which was one of six wickets he obtained in the MCG Boxing Day Test. His tally of ten wickets from two Tests was a promising start for young "Billy' (nicknamed after the wild west legend Billy the Kid).

At the end of that summer Craig McDermott packed his bags for an Ashes tour, and he enjoyed an outstanding 1985 series in England, capturing 30 Test wickets at 30.03. Hauls of 6/70 at Lords and 8/141 at Old Trafford were included in his statistics. Even before he turned 21 Australia's new young fast bowling sensation had captured 40 wickets in his first eight Tests.

However for the next five seasons Craig McDermott was in and out of the Australian side. His 17 wickets against New Zealand in 1987–88 was one rainbow amid the gloom, but knee and back injuries restricted

McDermott's effectiveness. "Billy" himself believed in retrospect that his early success came too easily, and that he was too immature to fulfil the role of being the main strike bowler for "the baggy greens".

McDermott took stock of his situation. Unwanted kilograms were shed in gruelling training sessions with the Australian ironman champion Trevor Hendy, and the re-married speedster again became a regular wicket-taker in Shield ranks. His recall to Test duties came in the Fourth Test of the 1990–91 home series against England, and "Billy" did not waste his new opportunity. In the first innings of that Ashes' clash in Adelaide, he collected 5/97, and in the final match of the series at the WACA, Craig McDermott returned the superb figures of 8/97 from 24.4 overs.

The born-again speedster continued his fine form. McDermott was the leading wicket-taker in both the Caribbean and a home series against India in 1991–92. Unfortunately he was forced to return home early because of illness early in the 1993 Ashes tour, but "Billy" had his revenge on the English team when he captured 32 wickets in the 1994–95 series.

Bad luck again intervened when McDermott tore his ankle ligaments while jogging in Guyana before the victorious 1995 series in the Caribbean had begun. However, when the toll of injuries finally forced him to retire in January 1997 McDermott was second only to Dennis Lillee in Australia's list of fast bowling wicket-takers.

Craig McDermott, together with his wife and four children, now reside on Queensland's Gold Coast, where he has become a wealthy building and property developer.

### 329. O'DONNELL, S.P. (Simon) : 1963—.
Tests (6)
206 runs at 29.43
6 wickets at 84.00

A hard hitting middle- order batsman and medium pace bowler from Victoria who proved to be more effective in the limited overs form of the game.

Simon O'Donnell was born in the NSW town of Deniliquin, but was educated in Victoria and debuted for that state in 1983–84. Encouraging all-round performances gained him selection for the 1985 Ashes tour, and the strongly built handsome novice played in five of the six Tests against England. He scored 48 in the Lords Test, and had the honour of scoring the winning runs at the famous ground.

O'Donnell played in one further Test against New Zealand in the following home series, and he was a member of Australia's winning World Cup team in 1987 on the subcontinent. He was a highly valued one day player, and won a  WSC Player of the Season award. He captained Victoria to a Sheffield shield title in 1990–91, and in his younger days O'Donnell briefly played Australian football with the St. Kilda club.

He required chemotherapy in his battle against lymphatic cancer shortly after the World Cup success, but appears to have made a full recovery from the illness. Simon O'Donnell is now employed by Channel Nine on their "Wide World of Sports" summer program.

## 330. GILBERT, D. R. (David) : 1960—.

Tests (9)
57 runs at 7.13
16 wickets at 52.69

A hardworking fast-medium bowler who represented Australia during the 1980s and has become a prominent administrator in the game.

Dave Gilbert first played for NSW in 1983–84, and he captured eight wickets against New Zealand in his Test debut series two seasons later. His figures of 3/48 at the WACA in the Third Test became his best result at this level. At the end of the summer he played one Test in New Zealand, he was chosen in two fixtures in the home series against India, and he again opposed India in Tests on the 1986–87 tour.

Gilbert was employed as a cricket administrator in England after he retired from playing, and he now occupies similar positions of responsibility with the NSWCA.

## 331. KERR, R. B. (Robert) : 1961—.

Tests (2)
31 runs at 7.75

A Queensland opening batsman who forced his way into the Australian Test team with large Sheffield Shield scores, but who was discarded from national duties after only two Tests.

Robbie Kerr played two Tests against the visiting New Zealand team in 1985–86, but was found wanting against the new ball skills of Hadlee and Chatfield. His top score in his only Test series was 17.

### 332. HUGHES, M. G. (Mervyn "Big Merv") : 1961—.
Tests (53)
2,649 runs at 16.65
212 wickets at 28.38



When he was orchestrating callisthenic sessions with spectators in Bay 13, or tweaking his outlandish moustache, it was tempting to dismiss Merv Hughes as one of the buffoons of the game. However he became a tireless warrior for the "baggy greens", and a quality cricketer who joined an elite group of less than ten Australians, when he reached the notable double of scoring over 1,000 runs and capturing over 200 wickets in Test match cricket.

Mervyn Hughes debuted for Victoria in 1981–82, and in 1985–86 he made an inauspicious Test debut against the visiting Indians. Sporadic appearances for Australia continued for two seasons, but "Big Merv" was then too wayward in his line and length to consistently trouble quality batsmen.

A back injury forced Hughes to shorten his run up, and this change seemed to provide more accuracy in his bowling. This improvement, combined with clever changes of pace and added variety, gradually improved his performances. The rewards from his new skills first came in December 1988 when he was chosen to play in the Second Test against the all-conquering 1988–89 West Indian team.

The WACA contest became very tense after the Australian tail-ender Geoff Lawson had his jaw broken from a vicious Curtly Ambrose delivery. An angry Merv Hughes then dismissed Ambrose and Patrick Patterson with successive deliveries to close the West Indies' first innings. The visitors were over

200 runs ahead when they commenced their second innings, but "Big Merv" remained undaunted. He rapped opener Gordon Greenidge on the pads with a searing first delivery, and when the lbw appeal was upheld, Mervyn Hughes had collected a Test hat trick!

Hughes came of age in that Test and his pace and fire yielded him the superb figures of 8/87 from 37 overs. The ungainly lion-hearted giant also obtained 5/130 from 36.1 overs in the Windies first innings. He also scored a brave, undefeated 72 against Viv Richard's team in Adelaide. These stirring performances at last cemented Hughes a regular place in Australia's team.

The big man continued to perform well for 'the baggy greens." In the 1989 winning Ashes team Hughes' 19 Test wickets provided valuable back-up support for McDermott and Lawson in Australia's attack, and he scored a cavalier 71 at Headingley. At home in the following summer he was the leading Test wicket-taker against Pakistan, and he was a consistent performer in further series against England and India at home, and the 1991 West Indians in the Caribbean. The 1993 Ashes series was dominated by Shane Warne's wonderful bowling. However Hughes, who by then was the spearhead of Australia's opening attack, helped to pave the way for the spinner's success by claiming 21 wickets for the series.

The false moustaches that his fans wore at the games disappeared after 1995, and his teammates no longer had to endure Big Merv's kisses after the fall of an opposition wicket. In that year the extroverted giant announced his retirement from first class cricket. Merv Hughes has since become an Australian selector, and he still enjoys the spotlight in his many media appearances.

He rapped opener Gordon Greenidge on the pads with a searing first delivery, and when the lbw appeal was upheld, Mervyn Hughes had collected a Test hat trick!

The false moustaches that his fans wore at the games disappeared after 1995, and his teammates no longer had to endure Big Merv's kisses after the fall of an opposition wicket, for in that year the extroverted giant announced his retirement from first class cricket.

### 333. MARSH, G.R. (Geoffrey "Swampy") : 1958—.
Tests (50)
2,854 runs at 33.19

A Western Australian farmer who served an eight-season apprenticeship in state cricket, but who became a reliable Test opening batsman once he was given the opportunity to wear the "baggy green".

Geoff Marsh came from Wandering near Perth, and he scored 58 on his 19th birthday when he debuted for W.A. He previously toured in a Young Australian team with his good friend David Boon, but had to wait until the 1985–86 season before he and the chunky Tasmanian played together in Test cricket. The new opening pair of Boon and Marsh shared an excellent first wicket partnership of 217 against India at the SCG, and Marsh contributed a fine 92.

Marsh registered his first Test century in that same season at Auckland in New Zealand, and he then scored 101 in the final Test of the 1986 Indian tour. The dependable opener also contributed 110 in the First Test at the Gabba against England in 1986–87. He then followed up with two half-centuries in Pakistan and another score over 50 in the 1988–89 series against the West Indies.

Geoff Marsh was vice-captain to Border when Australia regained the Ashes in 1989, and he scored 138 and shared a mammoth opening stand of 329 with Mark Taylor in the Fifth Test at Trent Bridge. He then missed selection in the Test side the following season, but regained his openers' post against the visiting English team in 1990–91, after scoring a massive 355 not out in just over ten hours against South Australia at the WACA. In the Ashes Test series Geoff Marsh averaged a useful 44.86 in five Tests.

In the Caribbean in 1991 Marsh scored 69 and 94 in the first two Tests against the fearsome West Indian fast bowlers, but at the end of the following Australian summer he was dropped for the final match against India after averaging a disappointing 26.43 in the first four Tests. This signalled the end of the gritty opener's Test career, but since then Geoff Marsh has become a respected coach. He has already coached "the baggy greens', and he has also coached in Africa and Asia.

## 334. REID, B. A. (Bruce) : 1963—.

Tests (27)
93 runs at 4.65
113 wickets at 24.64

A tall, slender left-handed opening bowler of the highest class, whose career was constantly thwarted by recurring back injuries.

Bruce Reid first played for W.A. in 1984–85, and in his second season of first class cricket the lanky new ball bowler was wearing the baggy green cap. He made a promising Test season debut against India, claiming 11 wickets at 29.55 in his three Tests, and at the end of that summer he was Australia's leading wicket taker in Tests on the New Zealand tour.

Reid struggled with injury in 1986–87, but he was equal leading wicket taker along with Tim May on Australia's testing tour of Pakistan at the start of the following season. Back injuries then sidelined the injury prone Perth player for two seasons, before he returned in triumph against the 1990–91 visiting English team.

Bruce Reid commenced that Ashes series in promising form when he captured 4/53 in the Gabba Test. He then destroyed the MCC batting line-up in the MCG Test when he returned the outstanding match figures of 13/154. The English batsmen could not cope with the steep bounce that a fit Bruce Reid obtained from good length deliveries, and he finished his most successful series with the enviable figures of 27 wickets at an average of 16.00.

Reid was predictably sidelined by injury for all but one Test when he toured the West Indies in 1991, but two fine international performances yielded 19 wickets in the next two injury-riddled seasons. Sadly, when Reid was in his 30th year, his interrupted cricket career was cruelly over, shortly after he had claimed 100 wickets in Test cricket.

Reid is still strongly involved in the game, and his expertise about new ball bowling is much respected in the cricket world.

## 335. WAUGH, S. R. (Stephen "Tugger") : 1965—.
Tests (168)
10,927 runs at 51.06
92 wickets at 37.45

A player who first wore the "baggy green" when Australia was at low ebb, after losing successive series to the West Indies, England and New Zealand. However he helped Australia gradually become the strongest cricket country in the world with his gritty and inspirational performances.

Stephen Waugh scored only 13 and 5 in the MCG Boxing Day Test when he made his debut at the age of 20 against the touring 1985–86 Indian team, and his early Test performances continued to be modest.

However in his 27th Test in 1989 he registered his first Test century, scoring a commanding 177 not out at Headingley, and in the next Test at Lords he compiled an unbeaten 152. A further score of 92 in the Old Trafford Test enabled Steve Waugh to finish with the formidable aggregate of 506 runs in the six Test series.

But soon the run flow slowed again to a trickle, and he contributed only 176 runs in his next ten Test innings. Consequently, when his 26 year old twin brother Mark was called into Australia's team for the Fourth Test against England at the Adelaide Oval in the 1990–91 series, it was Steve Waugh who was replaced in the "baggy green" squad. He did not regain his place in Australia's Test side until the Third Test of the 1991 series in the Caribbean.

The two brothers became the first twins to play Test cricket together when they took the field at Port of Spain in Trinidad, but Steve was again dropped from the team for the Fifth and final Test. He did not gain selection when India toured in 1991–92, but played in all home Tests against the West Indies in the following summer, and scored 100 at the SCG.

By then Steve Waugh was at the crossroads of his Test career, as his 52 Test batting average was only in the mid-30s. However the 1993 Ashes tour removed all doubts about the fine qualities of this fiercely focussed player.

Steve Waugh scored 157 not out in the Fourth Test at Headingley and his impressive batting average of 83.20 was the best of a star-studded Australian batting line-up that registered ten Test centuries in their triumphant series. Success continued for Waugh when

**The two brothers became the first twins to play Test cricket together when they took the field at Port of Spain in Trinidad.**

South Africa returned to the international arena, as he scored 164 against the visitors at the Adelaide Oval in 1993–94. Three years later in South Africa at Port Elizabeth in March 1997 Steve and Mark Waugh represented Australia together for the 45th time in Test cricket. This eclipsed the previous record of appearances for Australian brothers that had been set by Ian and Greg Chappell.

Much interest centred on the Caribbean when Mark Taylor led the Australian team there in 1995, as the "baggy greens" had not won the Sir Frank Worrell trophy since 1973. Fortune ebbed and flowed in the fiercely contested series, and Steve Waugh took a defiant stand against his intimidating and brilliant opponents with his strong performances.

In the final Test at Sabina Park in Kingston Jamaica, the Waugh battle was finally won. The outcome of the series hinged on this match, and the twins came together when Australia was a shaky 3/73, but their superb 231 fourth wicket partnership turned the tide towards the "baggy greens". Mark departed for 126, but his brother determinedly batted for 555 minutes to register a match-winning 200 (seventeen 4s and a 6) which became his highest Test score.

Steve Waugh finished the series with the outstanding Test batting average of 107.25, while Mark averaged 40. The importance of the Waugh twins' contributions in Australia's memorable victory is clearly shown by the statistics for the series, as the next best Australian batting average was 26.

"Tugger" (his nickname for constantly pulling at the brim of his beloved baggy green cap) continued his avalanche of Test runs. On the 1997 winning Ashes tour the new vice-captain Steve Waugh scored 108 in the first

innings and 116 in the second innings of the Old Trafford Test.

Waugh became captain of Australia's one day team in 1997–98. He averaged a less than impressive 38.00 when Australia's 29 year nightmare of series' defeats continued in India, but he scored two further centuries in the 1998–99 home Ashes series.

Following Mark Taylor's retirement at the end of that series, Steve Waugh was appointed as Australia's captain, and he led his "baggy green" team in an engrossing drawn series in the Caribbean in 1999. Leadership certainly did not adversely affect his batting as he scored 199 in the Barbados Test and averaged 58.43 for the series.

Despite suffering a broken jaw in an on-field accident in Sri Lanka, S.R. Waugh's impressive batting success continued in home series against Pakistan and the West Indies, before he again suffered disappointment in India in 2001. Once again his form in England was superb in the 2001 Ashes Tests in which he scored two additional centuries.

By now Steve Waugh was a legend to the Australian sporting public, and when he scored 102 in the last session of the 2002–03 Sydney Test against England, an estimated crowd of over 2,000,000 people witnessed his exciting innings on television. His century as stumps drew near was achieved with his trademark back-foot drive through the off-side, and his famous slog sweep was also well to the fore.

Steve Waugh retired at the end of that series after reaching three figures against all the major cricketing countries, and scoring even more Test hundreds than Bradman, though admittedly he played in far more matches. To many he remains an enigma, a man who wrote comprehensive and thoughtful published

**By now Steve Waugh was a legend to the Australian sporting public, and when he scored 102 in the last session of the 2002–03 Sydney Test against England, an estimated crowd of over 2,000,000 people witnessed his exciting innings on television.**

diaries, a man who greatly respected the historical traditions of the game, a philanthropist who still works tirelessly for an Indian rehabilitation centre, but who was also one of the most merciless "sledgers" the game has ever known.

Many criticised him for his caustic on-field remarks or "tactics of mental disintegration" during his successful Test career, but the Sydneysider's fighting qualities are much admired. Most Australians know that if you ever needed a player to bat for your life, you would be saved if you put your faith in the unflinching hands of Stephen Rodger Waugh.

## 336. DAVIS, S.P. (Simon) : 1959—.
Tests (1)
0 runs
0 wickets

A Victorian medium pace bowler whose extreme accuracy was valued in limited overs matches with Australia, but who lacked the penetration to trouble good Test batsmen.

Simon Davis toured New Zealand in 1985–86 and in his only Test at Wellington's Basin Reserve he returned the figures of 0/70 from 25 overs.

## 337. ZOEHRER, T. J. (Timothy) : 1961—.
Tests (10)
246 runs at 20.50
19 dismissals (18 catches, 1 stumping)

A talented but volatile WA and Australian wicket-keeper who dropped out of the Test scene after clashes with the games' officials.

Tim Zoehrer made a promising debut with Australia on the 1985–86 New Zealand tour accepting four catches and a stumping in the three Test series. Along with other Australian players he was involved in disputes with umpires in the heated First Test at Madras on the 1986–87 Indian tour. However his keeping was tidy throughout the series and Tim Zoehrer scored a valuable 52 not out in the Second Test in Delhi.

In his final Test series against the 1986–87 English team  Zoehrer accepted ten catches in the four Tests he played. He was understudy to Ian Healy on the 1989 tour of England, but did not play in any Tests.

## 338. MATTHEWS, C. D. (Christopher) : 1962—.
### Tests (3)
### 54 runs at 10.80
### 6 wickets at 52.17

A talented but wayward W.A. left-hand fast-medium bowler who only appeared briefly in Test match cricket.

Chris Matthews had the ability to cut a swathe through any opposition team when he controlled his swing and accuracy, but when he lost line and length in his bowling he became a captain's nightmare.

He first appeared for W.A. in 1984–85, and two seasons later he was picked to play his first Test at the Gabba against England. He bowled with moderate success but was dropped after two Tests.

Matthews then played both state and Lancashire League cricket before he was given another chance at Test level against the 1988–89 West Indians. His lead-up form to this Gabba fixture had been excellent, but his "radar" was seriously astray in this vital match.

A series of wides and match figures of 0/80 off 24.5 overs, resulted in the burly Western Australian being banished from the Test team for the rest of his first class career.

## 339. DYER, G. C. (Gregory) : 1959—.
### Tests (6)
### 131 runs at 21.83
### dismissals 24 (catches 22, stumpings 2)

A neat keeper and competent batsman from NSW who started promisingly in international cricket, but who lost his place in Australian teams after he was involved in a controversial dismissal

Greg Dyer first represented NSW in the 1983–84 season, and he was selected for one Test against the touring English team in 1986–87. He was the wicket keeper in Australia's victorious 1987 World Cup team in India, and his place in the Test team seemed safe after he scored a valuable 60 at the Adelaide Oval against New Zealand in the Second Test of the 1987–88 home series.

However Dyer's reputation was tarnished when he failed to notify the umpire in the Boxing Day Test at the MCG, that he had not gloved a catch from the Kiwi's Andrew Jones after that batsman had been given out. In a previous Test that summer New Zealand's Jeff Crowe had told the umpire that he had not caught Allan Border, so when television replays clearly showed the ball spilling out of Dyer's gloves, there was much criticism of his sportsmanship.

Greg Dyer appeared in two further Test matches that summer, but he was replaced by Queensland's Ian Healy for the 1988–89 tour of Pakistan.

## 340. TAYLOR, P. L. (Peter) : 1956—.
Tests (13)
431 runs at 26.94
27 wickets at 39.56

When this NSW off-spinner with only six first class games' experience was chosen to represent Australia against England in the Fifth Test of the 1986–87 series, many members of the media believed that "Taylor of NSW" was in fact Mark Taylor, a promising NSW opening batsman who later captained Australia.

Australian selector Lawrie Sawle vehemently denied that the wrong player was selected, and if it was a case of mistaken identity when the 30 year old novice was chosen, it proved to be a fortunate choice.

Peter Taylor enjoyed an excellent debut snaring 6/78 from 26 overs in England's first innings and 2/76 when England batted again. He also scored 42 vital runs in Australia's second innings, so he was a key factor in Australia's only success for the series.

The studious looking off-spinner then tasted World Cup success in India in 1987, and he captured 4/84 in the drawn Bicentennial Test against England at the SCG in 1988. He toured Pakistan later that year, but after he performed without success against the visiting West Indians in 1988–89, he was left out of the 1989 Ashes series in England.

Peter Taylor resurfaced in Test cricket against Pakistan at home in 1989–90, in one 1991 Test against the West Indies in the Caribbean, and two further home Tests against India in 1991–92. His final international appearances were in the 1992 World Cup that was staged in Australia and New Zealand.

**If it was a case of mistaken identity when the 30 year old novice was chosen, it proved to be a fortunate choice.**

## 341. VELETTA, M.R.J. (Michael) : 1963—.
Tests (8)
207 runs at 18.82

A versatile WA batsman who was a handy performer for Australia but who remained a fringe Test player during his first class career.

Mike Veletta accumulated large scores as an opening batsman in his three season apprenticeship of state cricket before performing well in the 1987 World Cup final in India. This gained him Test selection in the 1987–88 series against New Zealand. He scored 84 runs in four innings, and was recalled to Australia's team for two Tests against the 1988–89 West Indian tourists.

Veletta toured England in 1989 but failed to play in the victorious Ashes Test teams, and he only featured in one match for "the baggy greens" against Pakistan in 1989–90. On the 1991 West Indies tour this enthusiastic back-up player was the reserve wicket-keeper, but he did not appear in any of the Caribbean Test matches.

Mike Veletta coached the ACT team in Canberra after he retired from first class cricket, and after returning to Perth he became W.A's coach.

## 342. MAY, T.B.A. (Timothy) : 1962—.
Tests (24)
225 runs at 14.06
75 wickets at 34.75

A South Australian off-spinner with a fine action who was in and out of Australian Test teams, but became a force to be reckoned with on the 1993 Ashes tour.

Tim May played three seasons of state cricket before he made his Test debut on his home pitch in Adelaide against the 1987–88 New Zealand team. May then enjoyed a fruitful tour of Pakistan where his 14 wickets in three Tests made him the equal leading Australian wicket taker of the series. He toured England in 1989 without participating in the Test series, and three seasons elapsed before he rejoined the national team in Adelaide for the Fourth Test against the visiting West Indies.

It was a sensational match for May. In the Windies second innings he put Australia back in the game when he captured the remarkable figures of 5/9 off 6.5 overs. Then, in a nail biting finish, May and fellow tail-ender Craig McDermott added an invaluable 40 runs for the last wicket before McDermott fell for 18 which saw the Windies win in a thrilling finish. The battered and bruised Tim May remained 42 not out.

The off-spinner's most successful tour was the Ashes campaign of 1993, when he and Shane Warne became the most successful Australian spin bowling duo ever. The pair captured 55 Test wickets, with Warne claiming 34 victims while May snared 21. The South Australian's best Test figures were achieved at Edgbaston, where he captured 5/89.

On the 1994–95 tour of Pakistan the two Australian spinners were reportedly offered bribes to perform poorly in the Test series by the host captain, Salim Malik. Both May and Warne confirmed that offers of money were made, but a Pakistani judge cleared Malik of bribery charges. Later that season May played his last Test match in Australia against the touring 1994–95 English team.

In later years Tim May became a valued

advocate for the Players' Association. He recently moved to USA, but still represents players' interests in their dealings with various cricket authorities.

## 343. DODEMAIDE, A.T.C. (Anthony) : 1963—.

Tests (10)
202 runs at 22.44
34 wickets at 28.03

A tireless Victorian medium pace bowler and useful batsman who produced some sterling performances for his state and country before he suddenly lost form.

Tony Dodemaide served Victorian cricket well for three seasons before he was called into the 1987–88 Australian team for the final Test against New Zealand at the WACA. He scored an excellent 50 batting at number nine, and collected the exceptional bowling figures of 6/58 in the Kiwis second innings. Later that summer Dodemaide also played in one-off Tests against both England and Sri Lanka.

The strongly built bowler then collected nine wickets in his three Tests on the 1988–89 tour of Pakistan. However his bowling was harshly treated by the West Indian batsman when he opposed them in two Tests at home later that season. This caused him to be overlooked for the 1989 Ashes tour, and Tony Dodemaide did not re-appear gain in Test cricket.

## 344. HEALY, I. A. (Ian "Heals") : 1964—.

Tests (119)
4,356 runs at 27.40
395 dismissals (366 catches, 29 stumpings)

A chirpy, Queensland red-haired wicket-keeper batsman who was plucked from obscurity to tour Pakistan in 1988. Twelve years later he was chosen by a panel of experts in Australia's prestigious "team of the century", ahead of such great keepers as Bert Oldfield, Rod Marsh, Don Tallon and Wally Grout.

It was Greg Chappell who pushed strongly for Ian Healy's inclusion in the Australian team after only a few state games with Queensland, and the young gloveman performed well in trying conditions on the sub-continent. He scored 26 and a top score of 21 in Australia's miserable second innings of 116 on a diabolical Test pitch at the National Stadium in Karachi, and he maintained his position as Australia's first choice wicket keeper for the next 12 years.

Multiple tours of England, India, Pakistan, the West Indies, New Zealand and Sri Lanka followed, as well as other campaigns in Zimbabwe and South Africa. His preparation for games was always professional, he kept brilliantly to the great spinner Shane Warne and a multitude of fast bowlers, and he had a huge influence in Australia's ascendancy to become a top Test cricket nation.

Healy was also a competent and determined batsman who scored four Test centuries and averaged nearly 30 with the bat. Today he is well known as a cricket commentator on Channel Nine's Wide World of Sport.

A chirpy, Queensland red-haired wicket-keeper batsman who was plucked from obscurity to tour Pakistan in 1988. Twelve years later he was chosen by a panel of experts in Australia's prestigious "team of the century", ahead of such great keepers as Bert Oldfield, Rod Marsh, Don Tallon and Wally Grout.

### 345. HOHNS, T.V. (Trevor) : 1954—.

Tests (7)

136 runs at 22.67

17 wickets at 34.12

A tidy leg spin bowler and useful left-handed batsman, who was a stalwart of Queensland cricket.

Trevor Hohns represented Queensland for 16 years before he was called into the Australian team at the age of 34. He debuted in the Fourth Test at the SCG against the West Indies and captured match figures of 4/118. This earned the Queenslander a berth in the final Test at the Adelaide Oval, and Hohns was also chosen to tour England with the 1989 tourists.

He played five Tests in that winning series, and his crucial dismissals of both Gower and Botham in the Fifth Test at Trent Bridge helped deliver the Ashes to "the baggy greens." Hohns captured 11 wickets at 27.27 in the series, and he also scored a timely 40 in the third Test at Edgbaston.

Trevor Hohns was later Chairman of the Australian Selection Panel, before he stepped down from that position shortly after the completion of the 2005 Ashes series.

# TURNING TO TAYLOR AND WAUGH

Mark Taylor assumed the captaincy from Allan Border with strong credentials. He had captained NSW with success, he had totalled over 4,000 Test runs and scored centuries against seven countries, and he was liked and respected by his teammates.

Despite this impressive criteria Taylor endured a nightmare debut as the leader of "the baggy greens." He became the only player to score a pair of ducks in his first Test as captain, and Australia lost the series in Pakistan 1:0. However it was only a temporary hiccough as Taylor became one of the country's greatest captains.

Mark Taylor's 1995 team won the Sir Frank Worrell trophy in the Caribbean for the first time in 22 years, and his leadership of the team group was challenged before the series even started  Only hours before the First Test began in Guyana, Taylor's main strike bowler Craig McDermott tore his ankle ligaments. A shoulder injury to another key bowler in Damien Fleming also put him out action for the Test series.

Taylor was forced to rely on relatively untried members of his team such as Glenn McGrath, Paul Reiffel and Brendon Julien to share the new-ball responsibilities, and the trio responded magnificently to Taylor's calm, positive leadership style .

Taylor's 1997–98 team also broke a 40 year old drought when they won a series in South Africa, and in 1998 they tasted success in Pakistan for the first time in 29 years.

Taylor also retained the Ashes against England and the Sir Frank Worrell trophy against West Indian teams. He captained "the baggy greens" on 54 occasions, and his only series' failure against the major Test-playing nations occurred on the 1998 Indian tour.

# THE SUCCESSFUL WAUGH ZONE

Steve Waugh inherited a strong side in 1999 when he first led Australia in Test matches and statistics indicate that under "Tugger" the "baggy greens" became even stronger.

He skippered Australia on 57 occasions for 41 wins, nine losses and seven draws, and his success rate of 71.93% is second only to Warwick Armstrong on the list of long serving captains. Under Waugh the powerful Australian team was more ruthless than their previous counterparts, as they won all home Test matches against Sri Lanka, India, Pakistan, South Africa and the West Indies. Waugh's touring teams also enjoyed "clean sweeps" in New Zealand, Pakistan, Zimbabwe and England. The 1999 "baggy greens' did lose in Sri Lanka, and Waugh's driving ambition to win in India became derailed in 2001, but his overall success rate was very impressive. His own batting form remained consistently high.

The Taylor–Waugh captaincy years were very fruitful for Australia, and the present skipper Ricky Ponting now faces the significant challenge of maintaining the supremacy of "the baggy greens."

# PLAYERS OF THE ERA

## 346. TAYLOR, M. A. (Mark "Tubby") : 1964—.
Tests (104)
7,525 runs at 43.50
I wicket at 26.00

Mark Taylor scored 937 runs in his 1985–86 debut season for NSW, and the consistent left-hand opener first played for Australia in the Fourth Test of the 1988–89 series against the West Indies. He made a poor start to his Test career, but emphatically showed that he was a world class opener on the 1989 Ashes tour.

Taylor finished the Test series in England with the superb average of 83.90, a performance that has only been bettered by Bradman. Scores of 219 and 136 were included in his prodigious run scoring feats, and Mark Taylor was named as one of "Wisden's" Five Cricketers of the Year at the end of the tour.

His form then faltered a little, but when he returned for another successful Ashes' quest in 1993, Taylor scored centuries in the first two Tests. However, while the solidly built man from country NSW continued to captain the team successfully, his own batting form became disappointing. When he finally registered another century in the opening Test of the 1997 Ashes series, it was "Tubby" Taylor's first score over 50 in his past 20 Test innings.

But on the 1998 tour of Pakistan, Mark Taylor created history when he batted for 938 minutes in the Test match at Peshawar to score 334 not out and 92 in two mammoth innings.

**Mark Taylor was named as one of "Wisden's" Five Cricketers of the Year at the end of the tour.**

Taylor showed his unselfishness and team focus when he elected to pursue victory rather than personal glory, by declaring Australia's innings closed after equalling Sir Donald Bradman's highest Test score in Australia's first innings.

Mark Taylor retired from Test cricket after leading Australia to a 3:1 Ashes victory at home. His batting and captaincy record were both impressive, and "Tubby" Taylor was also highly respected for his excellent fielding in the slips area where he accepted 157 catches in his 104 Tests. Today his cheerful personality is popular with many viewers who follow the television coverage of international cricket matches in Australia.

## 347. CAMPBELL, G.D. (Gregory) : 1964—.
### Tests (40)
### 10 runs at 2.50
### 13 wickets at 38.69

A Tasmanian swing bowler who was a shock selection for the 1989 Ashes' tour, where his most memorable feat was to propose to his future wife on television.

Like David Boon, Greg Campbell was raised in the northern Tasmanian town of Launceston, and he debuted for his island state during the 1986–87 season. Useful performances at state level convinced the Australian selection panel that his swing bowling would be ideally suited to English conditions, and the strongly built blonde headed bowler was chosen for "the baggy greens" tour of England in 1989.

The experiment was not a success as Campbell was frequently injured and only

His most memorable feat was to propose to his future wife on television.

played in one Test match. He later appeared in two Tests against New Zealand and one against Sri Lanka.

The most vivid image of Greg Campbell's 1989 tour of England occurred when he appeared on the players' balcony in front of the TV cameras at a Test venue, and held up a sign which proposed marriage to his Australian sweetheart.

Campbell's intended was the sister of the present Australian captain Ricky Ponting. The Campbell family have since settled on Queensland's Gold Coast where he became involved in cricket coaching.

## 348. MOODY, T. M. (Thomas "Long Tom") : 1965—.
Tests (8)
456 runs at 32.57
2 wickets at 73.50

A capable all-rounder from W.A. who was highly valued in limited overs cricket, but who struggled to cement a Test spot in strong Australian teams.

Tom Moody debuted for Western Australia in 1985–86 after performing well in Australian junior teams. He scored an excellent 106 against Sri Lanka at the Gabba in his 1989–90 Test debut, but only played three further matches in "the baggy green" cap until the final Test at the WACA ground in the 1991–92 season.

In his home city of Perth, the tall handsome all-rounder scored 50 and 101 against India. In the following season on the Australian tour of Sri Lanka, coach Bob Simpson selected "Long Tom" as an opener in all three Tests. He scored 54 in the opening match of the series, but after only averaging 11.83 runs in six innings, he disappeared from the Test scene.

Tom Moody enjoyed many successful seasons of English county cricket with Worcestershire, whom he captained towards the end of his playing days. He is now coach of the Sri Lankan national team.

## 349. WAUGH, M.E. (Mark "Junior", "Afghanistan") : 1965—.
### Tests (128)
### 8,029 runs at 41.82
### 59 wickets at 41.17

A graceful batsman who scored runs with a seemingly languid ease. He was a useful change bowler, and one of the greatest fieldsman of all time. At his best Mark Waugh was the complete package – "The Rolls Royce" of Australian cricket.

Mark Waugh, who was dubbed "Junior" because he was born four minutes after his twin brother Steve, virtually became a run machine before he was finally presented with "a baggy green" cap at he age of 25 in the 1990–91 Fourth Test against England. During the 1989–90 season he averaged 80.58 for NSW, he scored over 2,000 runs for Essex in the 1990 English county season, and five weeks before gaining Test selection he plundered 219 for NSW against the WA attack in Perth. Little wonder that some wag nicknamed him "Afghanistan" (the forgotten Waugh)!

Mark Waugh captivated the Adelaide crowd in his first Test match with "an innings that was as lovely as the ground itself". He came to the wicket when Australia was struggling at 4/104, and scored a superb 138 from just 186 balls, with his first 95 runs coming in

**At his best Mark Waugh was the complete package – "The Rolls Royce" of Australian cricket.**

**Mark Waugh captivated the Adelaide crowd in his first Test match with "an innings that was as lovely as the ground itself".**

just one session of play. His twin brother Steve was the player he replaced in the Australian team, and Mark Waugh later admitted that he had "mixed feelings" about his debut success because of his sibling's omission.

The younger twin could be a frustrating player to some critics who resented his casual style, especially when he failed to score runs. However Mark Waugh's record in crucial Tests was outstanding. On the 1993 tour of England he scored 137 at Edgbaston and 99 at Lords before averaging an impressive 61.1 for the series, and in the victorious 1995 series in the Caribbean he was second in the Test averages to his twin brother Steve. In India when "the baggy greens" suffered defeat in 1998, Mark Waugh scored a brilliant 153 not out at Bangalore and averaged 70.00 for the series. He also scored heavily against strong sides from South Africa and Pakistan, and registered at least one century on each of the six Australian Test grounds. This proud record compensated greatly for the two dismal tours he endured in Sri Lanka.

Mark Waugh retired from Test cricket after being dropped from the Australian team for the opening Test of the 2002–03 Ashes series. He recently married, and both his wife and he are strongly involved in the horse racing industry.

### 350. WARNE, S.K. (Shane "Warney") : 1969—.

Tests (140)
2,958 runs at 16.61
685 wickets at 25.25

Regarded by many as being the most talented cricketer of his generation as well as the best leg-spinner of all time. Shane Warne's world record tally of over 650 wickets is significantly better than his nearest rival, he remains a very handy late order batsman, and he is one of the safest slips catches in international cricket.

Warne represented Victoria with modest success in four first class games before he was fast-forwarded into the Australian Test team for the 1992 Sydney fixture against India. Ravi Shastri scored a commanding century against "the baggy greens" in that match, and the less-than-trim 22 year old with peroxide blonde hair returned the embarrassing figures of 1/150 from 45 overs.

However during the following winter months Warne shed 14 kilograms in weight, and his fitness campaign bore fruit when his 3/11 off 5.1 overs delivered an unexpected Test victory for Australia on their 1992 tour of Sri Lanka. He then toured England with Allan Border's 1993 team, and with his very first delivery in an Ashes Test Shane Warne sent shock waves through the opposition camp when he bowled "the ball of the century" to England's Mike Gatting.

Warne's first ball curved inwards in flight before pitching about 10 centimetres outside leg stump. As Gatting came forward to play the delivery on the on side, it spun back so viciously that it clipped the off bail. Warne continued to spin a web of mystery around the baffled home side for the rest of the series, capturing 34 Test wickets and winning "Wisden's" Cricketer of the Year award.

The "Sultan of Spin" quickly became the idol of many young, aspiring slow bowlers, and Warne continued to develop more tricks in his bowling repertoire. He used both side spin and overspin in his variations of leg break bowling,

**The most talented cricketer of his generation as well as the best leg-spinner of all time.**

**With his very first delivery in an Ashes Test Shane Warne sent shock waves through the opposition camp when he bowled "the ball of the century" to England's Mike Gatting.**

he used his wrong'un and top spin cleverly, he obtained considerable bounce with his deadly accurate deliveries, and his faster "flipper" delivery caught many batsman unawares. No wonder Richie Benaud described him as "the best young leg-spinner I have ever seen."

"Warney's" rise to fame continued in spectacular fashion. Forty-seven Test wickets fell to him in the 1993–94 season, and he snared another 45 victims in  1994–95. A MCG hat trick against England was included in his 1994 haul, before a finger injury temporarily halted his impressive progress. By 1997 he was near his best again, taking 24 wickets at 24.04 on an Ashes tour, and the only sobering note to his superb strike rate was the 1998 tour of India where he had limited success. An operation to his injured shoulder further stalled his Test match appearances.

Warne's recuperation from this injury was slower than expected, and indifferent form saw him dropped from Australia's team for the final Test of the 1999 series in the Caribbean. By then Warne, with some poor on-field behaviour in South Africa and some well publicised off-field infidelities in various parts of the world, was constantly being featured in the tabloid press. His most damaging misdemeanour occurred just before the commencement of the 2003 World Cup in South Africa.

Shane Warne was sent home in disgrace after testing positive to diuretic, a prohibited weight reducing substance, and he was banned for playing first class cricket for a year. To many players this would have been a career ending blow, but Warne displayed amazing resilience. He surged past the leading wicket taking tally of 519 wickets after he returned to Test action, and he also performed well against India when Ponting's team finally won a series there in 2004.

Early signs of success for the 2005 Ashes campaign in England were promising, but after the media highlighted the collapse of his marriage many feared that his off-field pressures would reduce his on-field effectiveness.

However Warne yet again put the turmoil of his private life aside, and showed once more that he is a magnificent competitor. In a superb display he took 40 series wickets for less than 20 runs, he scored two vital 40s in Australia's late order. When his fellow strike bowler McGrath was absent because of injury, Shane Warne captured 18 wickets to keep the hopes of "the baggy greens" alive in the closely fought series.

Shane Warne has since performed well against other Test playing nations, and in this coming 2006–07 season, the talent, mental strength, ability under pressure, showmanship and guile of Shane Warne will be priceless assets for Australia in the battle for Ashes' supremacy.

**The talent, mental strength, ability under pressure, showmanship and guile of Shane Warne will be priceless assets for Australia in the battle for Ashes' supremacy.**

## 351. PHILLIPS, W. N. (Wayne) : 1962—.

### Tests (1)
### 22 runs at 11.00

Wayne Phillips was a solid Victorian opening batsman who averaged 38.39 in 60 first class matches.

After scoring 205 in a 1991–92 Sheffield shield game, Phillips replaced Geoff Marsh later that season in the Fifth Test against India at the WACA ground. The Geelong born player only managed scores of eight and 14 on debut, and failed to gain selection again in Australian Test teams.

### 352. REIFFEL, P.R. (Paul "Pistol") : 1966—.

Tests (35)
955 runs at 26.53
104 wickets at 26.96

A consistent seam bowler who was a reliable performer for both Victoria and Australia.

Paul Reiffel debuted for Australia against India in 1991–92 after three seasons of state cricket, but he failed to make an impact at this level until he replaced an injured Craig McDermott on the 1993 Ashes tour. In England he claimed 19 Test wickets after gaining selection for the final three Tests, and his two five wicket hauls at Headingley and Manchester were crucial performances in Australia's victory in the series.

He again rose to the occasion when injury threatened to derail Mark Taylor's quest to capture the Sir Frank Worrell trophy in the 1995 Caribbean series. Reiffel's accurate seam bowling to the many left-handers in the West Indies feared batting line-up proved very effective, and his dismissal of Brian Lara for a duck in the final Test was crucial to Australia's ultimate success.

Paul Reiffel has now turned his attention to umpiring, and he was recently added to Australia's first class panel.

### 353. MARTYN, D.R. (Damien) : 1971—.

| Tests (65) | ODIs (200) |
|---|---|
| 4361 runs at 47.40 | 5030 runs at 40.24 |
| 2 wickets at 84.00 | 12 wickets at 58.66 |

The current phoenix of Australian cricket, who rose to the position of being a world class batsman from the ashes of a five season rejection, and now needs to repeat the transformation.

There were few signs that Damien Martyn would endure a roller-coaster ride in Test cricket when he made his debut against the 1992–93 West Indian team at the Gabba. The stylish Western Australian averaged a promising 28.17 in four Tests that summer, with his top score being 67 in the MCG Boxing Day match.

However it was difficult to cement a spot in Australia's formidable batting line-up. Martyn was not called into the Test team when he toured England in 1993, and when he was selected against the 1993–94 touring South Africans the young man felt the selectors' wrath after he failed in the tense Sydney Test.

Martyn was discarded from the national team for five seasons. At first the despairing 24 year old performed poorly, but he then adopted a disciplined life-style, tightened his batting technique, and began the huge task of clawing his way back to international cricket.

Selection in the 2001 Ashes' touring team was Martyn's reward for consistent run making, and the classy WA batsman became a revelation in England that summer. He scored his first Test century at Edgbaston, added another at Headingley, and averaged an excellent 76.40 for the series. One observer called him "the best kept secret in the Australian team", and the Australian writer Gideon Haigh provided this generous accolade about the elegance and power of Martyn's batting.

"To say he is a textbook batsman is not to flatter him: it is to flatter the text book."[50]

Damien Martyn's run avalanche continued. In 2001–02 he scored two centuries at

50. Haigh, 2004, p651

home against South Africa, and added a third at the Wanderers in Johannesburg when the Aussies played there. His success continued against Sri Lankan and Pakistani teams. A hand injury outed him from the 2003 tour of the Caribbean, but when he averaged 55.00 and was named the Player of the Series against India in 2004, it seemed as if he was a permanent fixture in "baggy green" teams.

However his progress stuttered again on the 2005 Ashes tour. Some dubious umpiring decisions went against him in early Tests, and Martyn's disappointing series' batting average of 19.78 resulted in him being omitted for all home Tests in the 2005–06 season.

Martyn has since "risen from the ashes" again after scoring his 13th Test hundred in South Africa. His series average there of 56.25 returns the recently married Damien Martyn into calculations for Ashes selection against the old foe for the 2006–07 series.

## 354. LANGER, J. L. (Justin) : 1970—.
Tests (100)
7,393 runs at 45.35

A true warrior of Australian cricket who was full of brave enthusiasm when he faced the fearsome West Indian bowlers on debut at Adelaide in 1992–93, and remains just as committed in the Test match arena 13 seasons later.

The diminutive Western Australian survived for over four hours against the Caribbean speedsters in the second innings of that Test, and his gritty innings of 54 nearly clinched a victory for the Australian team.

Justin Langer then had a long apprenticeship in international cricket, being often a tourist but seldom a Test player in the seasons between 1993–97. His first Test century in Pakistan at Peshawar in 1998 cemented a place in the national team against England for the following Australian summer, and he celebrated his return to the Test team by scoring an unbeaten 179.

Langer then registered another century in Antigua on the 1999 tour of the Caribbean, but Australia's number three batsman then began to struggle. He failed in Sri Lanka in 2001–02 before a match winning partnership with Adam Gilchrist against Pakistan in Hobart restored him to favour. However two disappointing series against the visiting West Indians and India on the sub-continent was not an ideal preparation for the 2001 Ashes tour.

Early indications were that his days of wearing the "baggy green" were coming rapidly to an end, as he endured a nightmare tour until he was thrust into the opener's role for the final Test at The Oval. There the determined martial arts expert scored 102 not out before retiring hurt, and since then Justin Langer and his close friend Matthew Hayden have established one of Australia's best ever opening partnerships.

In the opening role Langer has become a more attacking player with an almost insatiable appetite for runs. He scored 250 against the 2002 03 English team at the MCG, while a further seven centuries have been registered against New Zealand, South African, West Indian, Indian and Sri Lankan teams. In the most recent Ashes' series the focussed opener scored 105 in The Oval Test, and he topped the Australian Test batting averages.

Since then Langer has suffered another blow on the head, after he was felled in South Africa by the Proteas's speedster Ntini, and he

**In the opening role Langer has become a more attacking player with an almost insatiable appetite for runs.**

has since recuperated at his home in Perth with his wife and growing family. There is some doubt that the little Aussie battler will receive medical clearance to oppose the English team for the next Ashes' series contest in 2006–07, but the Australian cricket public will be hoping that the combative Justin Langer will be opening up against the old foe.

## 355. ANGEL, J.P. (Jo) : 1968—.
Tests (4)
35 runs at 5.83
10 wickets at 46.30

A tall, durable opening bowler who was a tireless performer for WA, but fell short of being Test class.

Jo Angel played in two home Tests against the West Indies and England between 1993 and 1995, and in two Tests in Pakistan in 1994. On the tour he took 3/54 from 13 overs at Karachi, which were his best Test match figures.

## 356. JULIAN, B.P. (Brendon) : 1970—.
Tests (7)
128 runs at 16.00
15 wickets at 39.33

A tall left-arm opening bowler and right-hand late order batsman from WA who failed to achieve his true potential.

Julian played in two Tests on the 1993 tour of England and scored a valuable 56 not out in the Trent Bridge fixture. The handsome all-rounder later replaced an injured Damien Fleming on the 1995 Caribbean tour, and captured 4/36 on the opening day of the first Test in Bridgetown, Barbados. Julian's last Test appearance was against Sri Lanka on his home ground in Perth in December 1995, and in 2001 he retired from first class cricket at the age of 30.

Since then Brendon Julian has been a reporter on the popular TV travel show "Getaway". He is now employed by both Fox Sports and Channel Nine in their Sports News presentations.

## 357. SLATER, M.J. (Michael) : 1970—.
Tests (74)
5,372 runs at 42.84
1 wicket at 10.00

A dashing opening batsman whose unabashed passion for "the baggy green" cause was unquestioned, but whose off-field problems finally impinged on his ability to perform consistently at Test level.

Michael Slater made a memorable start to his Test career on the 1993 English tour. He scored 58 and 70 on debut at Old Trafford, and then blazed a magnificent 152 in his second Test at Lords. The memory of the exuberant 23 year old joyously kissing the Australian emblem on his helmet after he reached his maiden Test century, is still a vivid image for many fans of the game.

Slater continued his fine form in series against Pakistan and Sri Lanka, and in the 1994–95 Ashes series in Australia, he scored another three dashing centuries. The cricket world appeared to be at the hypo-active young man's feet, but a series of disappointing scores saw him dropped for the opening Test of the 1996–97 Test against the West Indies.

Slater's form continued to fluctuate, with memorable centuries being followed by a series

A dashing opening batsman whose unabashed passion for "the baggy green" cause was unquestioned, but whose off-field problems finally impinged on his ability to consistently perform at Test level.

of low scores. He scored three "tons" in a superb home series against England in 1998–99, and he also registered Test centuries on tours of Pakistan, Sri Lanka and the West Indies.

However the young NSW player from Wagga Wagga was gaining the reputation of being "a loose cannon". On his disappointing 2001 tour of India Slater engaged in an unnecessary and acrimonious dispute with the star opposition batsman Rahul Dravid. His commitment was so poor later that year on the English Ashes tour, that he was dropped for the final Test after only contributing 93 runs in his previous six innings.

Slater's marriage broke up shortly after, and he later revealed that he was prone to panic attacks that were triggered from his bi-polar condition. Since he retired from first class cricket Michael Slater has become a cricket commentator.

### 358. McGRATH, G.D. (Glenn "Pigeon") : 1970—.

| Tests (119) | ODIs (220) |
|---|---|
| 631 runs at 7.51 | 104 runs at 3.85 |
| 542 wckts at 21.55 | 330 wckts at 22.38 |

When did the pendulum swing decisively towards England in the closely contested 2005 Ashes' series? Some observers believe that the host team became a "shoe-in" to regain the coveted trophy, after Glenn McGrath badly twisted his ankle when he trod on a cricket ball and became a much less potent force in the Test matches.

This opinion demonstrates the importance of McGrath's influence in Australia's fast bowling attack, as the tall Narromine farmer has become a wicket taking machine for "the

**Some observers believe that the host team became a "shoe-in" to regain the coveted trophy, after Glenn McGrath badly twisted his ankle when he trod on a cricket ball and became a much less potent force in the Test matches.**

baggy greens" over the past decade.

The defining moment came for "Pigeon" McGrath early in the successful 1995 tour of the Caribbean. At that stage the 25 year old opening bowler had only played in a handful of Tests, but when Craig McDermott and Damien Fleming were sidelined with injury, it was McGrath who became Australia's strike bowler. The aggressive NSW bowler was not afraid to bowl bouncers at his Caribbean counterparts, and he claimed 17 wickets at the economical rate of 21.71 in the four Test series.

McGrath enjoyed a superb first Ashes tour in 1997, claiming 36 wickets at 19.47 in the Test series. His proudest moment came at the home of cricket, where he collected his best ever Test match figures of 8/38 from 20.3 overs in the Lords Test.

Before long the microscopic accuracy of McGrath's probing seam bowling made him the world's premier fast bowler. He has been a model of consistency in series both at home and overseas, and he enjoys a similarly successful strike rate in all countries. On the dry dusty pitches of Asia Glenn McGrath has claimed 72 wickets at 23 in 19 Tests while on the fast bowler-friendly Australian surfaces he has captured 247 victims at 21.4.

Problems have surfaced for Glenn McGrath in the veteran's highly successful career. He missed the 2003–04 series against India and Sri Lanka because of ankle surgery, and another ankle injury inconvenienced him on the 2005 Ashes' tour. He has also missed Tests because of his wife's ongoing battle with cancer, and he remains in doubt for the 2006–07 home series against England if Jane McGrath's health does not improve.

### 359. HAYDEN, M.L. (Matthew) : 1971—.

Tests (84)                    ODIs (119)
7326 runs at 53.08   4137 runs at 40.11

Australian captain Steve Waugh surprised the cricket media when he predicted that Matthew Hayden would go on to double his modest Test average of 20.33 after he scored only two in his comeback game in New Zealand. However Waugh's opinion was clearly wide of the mark as the powerful Queenslander has since nearly trebled his year 2000 average.

Matthew Hayden was a prolific run scorer for his state before he made his Test debut in Johannesburg, but it took many years before the left-handed opener produced that form on the international stage. He failed in that first encounter against South Africa, and continued to struggle in the seven Test appearances he made between 1994 and 1997.

Hayden did register his maiden Test century against the West Indians at the Adelaide Oval in 1996–97, but he was still a "baggy green" fringe player who had made little impact in Tests until he suddenly exploded into form on the 2001 tour of India.

Hayden had a superb series against the strong home side scoring 549 runs at an average of 109.80. His run feast in the Tests included innings of 119, 97 and 203, and the powerful stroke-player continued his breakthrough to greatness against other countries. Six centuries were blazed from his bat in seven Tests in 2000–01, and the run orgy culminated with his mammoth score of 380 against Zimbabwe at the WACA in 2003.

Thirty-eight 4s and eleven 6s were smashed from the visitor's bowling attack, and Hayden briefly held the world record for the most runs in a Test innings. The cricket media was impressed by Hayden's dominance, especially.

Peter Roebuck was convinced that Hayden deserved comparison with  the greats of the game. "None of them hit the ball as hard or straighter… none was as strong, none was as blessed with greater stamina, none was as full of desire in the middle years of their careers. He is a batsman of beautiful brutality."[51]

There seemed to be no end to the constant flow of centuries as the big opener peeled of three figure scores against the various Test playing nations, before clever tactical planning by the English attack reduced Hayden's effectiveness in the 2005 Ashes series. Hayden did score 138 in the final Test of that series, but his overall Test batting average of 35.33 was well below his recent best.

In the 2006 series in South Africa Hayden continued his gradual climb back to form, and the 35 year old Queenslander will be determined to make a significant impact in the 2006–07 home series against England.

## 360. BEVAN, M. G. (Michael) : 1970—.

| Tests (18) | ODIs (232) |
| --- | --- |
| 785 runs at 29.07 | 6912 runs at 53.58 |
| 29 wickets at 24.24 | 36 wickets at 45.97 |

An attacking left-handed batsman, an occasional match-winning googly bowler, and a brilliant fieldsman. In his prime Michael Bevan was the world's premier one day cricketer, yet he only appeared in 18 Test matches for his country.

Bevan was raised in Canberra, and after

51. Haigh, 2004, p671

he finished a program with the Adelaide Cricket Academy the impressive young player performed well in state games for South Australia and then NSW.

He averaged an excellent 60.75 in his first Test series in Pakistan, but the English fast bowlers exploited his perceived weakness to short pitched bowling. Michael Bevan only averaged a disappointing 13.50 runs per innings in three Tests during the 1994–95 Ashes series.

The NSW player was then out of favour with the Test selectors until the 1996–97 series against the West Indians, when his all-round skills came to the fore. In four Tests that summer Bevan averaged 55.00 with the bat, and he snared 15 wickets at 17.67 with his left-arm unorthodox deliveries. The highlight performance came in the Fourth Test at the Adelaide Oval where Bevan scored a patient 85 not out and returned the superb match figures of 10/123 off 32.1 overs.

However the taciturn all-rounder refused to take his bowling seriously, and after two disappointing series against South Africa and England he disappeared from the Test scene. Many observers still wonder how this talented player who performed so brilliantly in international one day matches, inter-state fixtures and English county cricket, played so few Tests.

In recent seasons Bevan has captained Tasmania, and his prolific run scoring has continued with the island state.

## 361. FLEMING, D.W. (Damien) : 1970—.

| Tests (20) | ODIs (88) |
|---|---|
| 305 runs at 19.06 | 152 runs at 11.69 |
| 75 wickets at 25.89 | 134 wickets at 25.39 |

A Victorian and Australian swing bowler who nearly gained the unique double of gaining a second Test hat trick in the 2000 fixture against India at the Adelaide Oval. He missed out on a place in history when the usually dependable Shane Warne muffed a regulation slips catch on the hat trick delivery.

Six years later the personable Fleming remains philosophical about the disappointing outcome. "Absolutely no regrets about that moment at all," was his emphatic statement. "'Warney's' increasing the longevity of my public speaking career… As long as he stays famous I'm sitting on a gold mine!"[52]

In more than a decade of successful first class cricket, Damien Fleming has produced a compelling ability to swing the ball late at a zippy pace. He also has an equally consistent tendency to miss vital games through injury. In 1994 Fleming captured a Test hat trick at Rawapindi against Pakistan in his Test series' debut, and he subsequently performed well against England and India in home series. In international limited overs games it was Damien Fleming who was skipper Steve Waugh's "go to" bowler in moments of crisis.

But Fleming also suffered a frustrating run of injuries. A knee operation, three shoulder reconstructions, and a series of torn muscle and tendon injuries resulted in the talented new ball bowler only enjoying one injury free season in first class cricket. He was never passed fit to complete tours in either England or the West Indies.

In retirement Damien Fleming first coached at Brisbane's Centre of Excellence, but he recently returned to Melbourne where he is popular on the public speaking circuit. He also commentates on sport with Foxtell, the ABC and "Inside Cricket".

52. Inside Cricket, 2004, p64

**'Warney's' increasing the longevity of my public speaking career… As long as he stays famous I'm sitting on a gold mine!**

### 362. EMERY, P.A. (Phillip) : 1964—.
Tests (1)
8 runs n.a.
6 dismissals (5 catches and 1 stumping)

A long-serving NSW wicketkeeper and captain who was called into action in Pakistan when Ian Healy's broken thumb made him unavailable for the Third Test at Lahore. Emery performed well in his only Test, taking five catches and a stumping in the home side's second innings.

### 363. BLEWETT, G. S. (Gregory).
| Tests (46) | ODIs (32) |
|---|---|
| 2,552 runs at 34.03 | 551 runs at 20.41 |
| 14 wickets at 51.43 | 14 wickets at 46.14 |

A stylish and capable player, especially when matched against fast bowlers. Greg Blewett enjoyed some fine moments in Test cricket, but he suffered from being constantly shuffled around the top six batting positions.

The tall opening batsman, whose father Bob Blewett previously captained South Australia, pressed for Test selection in the early 1990s when he scored a mammoth 268 against Victoria at the MCG. He later rewrote the cricket history books with his brilliant start for the "baggy greens."

In the 1994–95 season Greg Blewett scored a fine 102 in his first Test on his home ground in Adelaide. He added another century in the Test that followed at the WACA, and when he scored 125 at Edgbaston on the 1997 tour of England, he became the first Australian to score centuries in his first three Ashes Tests. Blewett averaged a solid 38.10 for

He became the first Australian to score centuries in his first three Ashes Tests.

that 1997 series against England, and earlier that year in South Africa he notched his highest Test score – an excellent 214 at the Wanderers ground in Johannesburg.

Blewett was a match winner that day in his long batting partnerships with the Waugh twins, but he was soon experiencing lean times as he began to be moved around the batting order. In the 1997–98 home series against South Africa Blewett only averaged 21.40 with the bat, and followed up with a miserable average of 8.00 against skilled spin bowling in the 2001 series against India.

After spending time out of the national team, Greg Blewett batted with some success at number six on his second visit to the Caribbean in 1999, and in September of that year he opened the batting in Sri Lanka. However after averaging only 12.50 in the opening two Tests of the 2000 tour of New Zealand Greg Blewett was omitted from Australia's Test team again, and he has not been chosen to wear "the baggy green" since. He is still a valuable all-rounder for South Australia, but will probably not be called up for the 2006–07 Ashes series.

## 364. McINTYRE, P.E. (Peter) : 1966—.

Tests (2)

16 runs at 7.32

5 wickets at 38.80

A tidy leg-spinner who debuted alongside Shane Warne at the Adelaide Oval in the Fourth Test of the 1994–95 Ashes series. His only other Test appearance came on the 1996 tour of India.

Peter McIntyre began his first class career with Victoria in 1988–89, but he soon moved to South Australia where he became a valuable state player.

## 365. LAW, S.G. (Stuart) : 1968—.
Tests (1)
54 runs, n.a.

An accomplished all-rounder and captain for Queensland, who was unlucky to play only one Test for Australia.

Stuart Law scored an unbeaten 54 at the WACA against Sri Lanka, but was dropped from "the baggy green" line-up for the next Test when an injured Steve Waugh returned to the Australian team. He never played Test cricket again, but his accomplished batting and useful slow-medium bowling were much valued on the 54 occasions he played ODIs for his country.

After being a driving force behind Queensland's resurgence in the Pura cup competition, Stuart Law moved his cricket career to Lancashire where he still resides with his English wife.

# PONTING POINTS THE WAY

**366. PONTING, R.T. (Ricky "Punter") : 1974—.**

Tests (105)  ODIs (251)
8792 runs at 58.22  9095 runs at 42.10
5 wickets at 46.20  3 wickets at 34.66

A dashing Tasmanian batsman who was once described by Rod Marsh as being "the best teenage batsman I've ever seen", and has since become arguably the best batsman in the world.



In his early years the talented lad from Launceston had a somewhat erratic career. He scored 96 in his Test debut against Sri Lanka at the WACA in 1995–96, played three Ashes fixtures in 1997 which included his first Test century at Headingley, but then became unpredictable both with his match performances and off-field social life.

Ponting's career reached its lowest ebb on the 2001 series in India, when the champion off-spinner Harbajan Singh reduced his series' average to an embarrassing 3.40. Captain Steve Waugh demonstrated his confidence in Ponting's potential by elevating him to number three in Australia's batting order for the 2001 Ashes series in England, but failure continued to dog the man that his teammates called "Punter". Waugh's gamble appeared to have failed when the besieged Tasmanian took guard against the English attack at Headingley, as he had not scored a Test century in 19 months of cricket.

He snicked the third ball he faced into the

slips region, but the confident appeal for a catch was rejected by the umpire. "Punter" took full advantage of his change of luck as he went on to score an excellent 144 , with twenty 4s and three 6s being included in his attacking innings.

Since then Ricky Ponting has raced past the great Sir Vivian Richards on the all-time number of Test centuries, and in 2003 he scored an imposing 1503 Test runs at an average of 100.20.  A happy marriage and the responsibility of captaincy appear to have stabilized him, and he has become the premier number three batsman in the world in both forms of the game. Ponting possesses a wonderful array of attacking strokes, his technique is sound, and the only apparent weakness for his opponents to probe is a tendency to make shaky starts to his innings.

On the 2003 tour of the Caribbean Ponting registered centuries in each of the three Tests he played, and his current tally of 25 Test centuries includes scores of 254 and 242 in the home series Tests against India in 2003–04. In the 2005 Ashes series Ponting's useful average of 39.89 placed him second in Australia's Test batting averages, and his memorable innings of 156 at Old Trafford enabled his "baggy greens" to salvage a draw

Following the narrow defeat in the 2005 Ashes' Tests, which the experienced Richie Benaud described as being "the best series he has ever seen", Ponting has continued his rich vein of form, scoring recent centuries against both South Africa and Bangladesh. The determined captain of the "baggy greens" will now seek to wrest back the legendary Ashes trophy from England's grasp in the eagerly anticipated 2006–07 series in Australia.

### 367. HOGG, G.B. (Bradley) : 1971—.

| Tests (4) | ODIs (85) |
|---|---|
| 38 runs at 9.50 | 560 runs at 20.74 |
| 9 wickets at 50.22 | 107 wickets at 27.73 |

A chirpy Western Australian left-arm spinner, handy late order batsman and excellent fieldsman who has only represented the "baggy greens four times in Test matches, but has played in over 70 ODIs.

Brad Hogg played three seasons with WA before he gained selection with Australia in a one-off Test at Dehli in the 1996–97 season. The persistent and ever-cheerful spinner then waited another seven years before he next donned the cherished green cap in Tests in the Caribbean on the 2003 tour. Again he only performed with modest success, though he did dismiss the West Indian champion batsman Brian Lara twice in the Test series.

### 368. ELLIOTT, M.T.G. (Matthew) : 1971—.

| Tests (21) | ODIs (1) |
|---|---|
| 1,172 runs at 33.48 | 1 run at 1.0 |

An enigma of Australian cricket, who nine seasons ago was rated among the world's best batsmen, but who now seems to have disappeared from the international scene.

Matthew Elliott looked to be the complete package when he debuted for Australia against the 1996–97 West Indian team. His defence was sound and his driving and powerful pull shots produced impressive scores. Elliot averaged 42 .67 in his two Tests that summer, and he also produced sound performances in three Tests in South Africa.

It was on the 1997 Ashes tour that Matthew Elliott really blossomed. He scored 112 at Lords, a magnificent 199 at Headingley, and his tally of 556 series' runs at 55.60 gave every indication that a long and successful Test career awaited him. Elliott's first Test century on home soil, which was scored against New Zealand at Hobart, was further confirmation that Australia had found an opening batsman of world class.

But Matthew Elliott's pleasing progress grinded to an abrupt halt. He was dropped from the national team after only averaging 10.20 in three Tests in South Africa in 1997–98, and he did not wear "the baggy green" again until he toured the Caribbean in 1999 with Steve Waugh's Australian team. However Elliott failed against the West Indian pace attack, averaging only 11.50 in three Tests.

He still amassed large scores in both state and English county cricket, and after he plundered a record 1381 runs against other states when Victoria won the 2003–04 Pura Cup, Matthew Elliott was selected again for Australia in the winter Test against Sri Lanka in Darwin. The visitor's fine swing bowler, Chaminda Vaas, dismissed the tall Victorian left-hander for 1 and 0, and since then Matthew Elliott has not been chosen in Australian Test teams.

Why did this obviously talented opener disappear so quickly from Test cricket? Matthew Elliott has struggled with knee injuries since he collided with Mark Waugh in a Sydney Test, and on the 1999 tour of the Caribbean his team spirit was questioned by some elements in the media. Since 2005–06 he has shifted his state cricket allegiance to South Australia, a move that Matthew Elliott hopes will rejuvenate his career.

# 369. KASPROWICZ, M.S. (Michael) : 1972—.

| Tests (38) | ODIs (43) |
|---|---|
| 445 runs at 10.59 | 74 runs at 18.50 |
| 113 wckts at 32.88 | 67 wckts at 24.98 |

A durable hard working swing and seam bowler who has been an outstanding performer for Queensland and is also highly rated in Australia's attack.

Michael Kasprowicz debuted for his state in his teenage years, but six seasons elapsed before he was called up for duty with the national team. His first Test match was on his home Gabba ground against New Zealand. Kasprowicz struggled to make an impact at this level initially, but he produced his best current figures in the final Test of the 1997 Ashes tour when he captured 7/36 from 15.5 overs at The Oval in a superb spell of bowling.

A year later he toiled for 116 overs in the sweltering Test series in India, which prompted the genial fast bowler to describe himself as "the fashionable bowler for unfashionable tours". The lion-hearted Queenslander was a match winner in the final Test at Bangalore taking 5/28.[53]

**"the fashionable bowler for unfashionable tours"**

Despite his sterling service on the sub-continent Kasprowicz only gained selection in four Tests over the next six years, even though he produced outstanding performances in the Pura Cup competition. However between 2003 and 2005 Kasprowicz was often preferred to the NSW speedster Brett Lee as Australia's number three pace bowler, and he responded with some excellent performances, especially his 7/39 against Sri Lanka in the 2004 winter Test in Darwin.

In the engrossing 2005 Ashes series in

53. Inside Cricket, 2004, p760

England Kasprowicz suffered no ball problems, and his disappointing Test bowling statistics of four wickets at an average of 62.50 saw him omitted again from "the baggy green" line-up for the following Australian summer. By the end of the season, however, the persistent Queenslander was recalled to the Test team, and after producing some creditable performances in recent overseas tours Michael Kasprowicz remains well in contention for selection in the coming 2006–07 Ashe series.

## 370. GILLESPIE, J.G. (Jason "Dizzy") : 1975—.

| Tests (71) | ODIs (97) |
|---|---|
| 1,218 runs at 18.73 | 289 runs at 12.56 |
| 259 wckts at 26.13 | 142 wckts at 25.42 |

**On the strength of just one memorable score of 201 not out, the tall, ungainly late order batsman with the mullet style haircut, has become a batting cult figure, following the innings he played for Australia against Bangladesh at Chittagong in 2006.**

Jason Gillespie has captured over 250 Test wickets but averages less than 20 with the bat in over 70 Test matches. One would expect, therefore, that he will be best remembered for his excellent bowling performances when his career in international cricket ends. However this may not be the case, for on the strength of just one memorable score of 201 not out, the tall, ungainly late order batsman with the mullet style haircut, has become a batting cult figure, following the innings he played for Australia against Bangladesh at Chittagong in 2006.

Jason Gillespie has now joined the great Pakistani all-rounder Wasim Akram in the record books for being the only players in Test cricket to bag more than 250 wickets and score a double ton. Gillespie turned 31 during his marathon spell of over nine hours at the batting crease, and the man they call "Dizzy" (after "Dizzy" Gillespie, the famous American jazz musician), was still lost in the music of the moment after he became the first night-watchman to register a double century in Test match cricket.

"It's unbelievable," commented a dazed Gillespie when he later reflected on his historic achievement. "It's a fairytale really. Hansel and Gretel and Dizzy's double hundred. It's one and the same. Absolute fairytale."[54]

The tall South Australian has often frustrated previous international opponents with his solid defence, and after he scored his maiden Test half-century against New Zealand in 2004 he reacted joyfully by "riding" his bat down the wicket. However Jason Gillspie would have been entitled to parade around the Chittagong ground on an elephant to celebrate his unforgettable double hundred performance.

Gillespie's dream innings was a welcome relief from the cricket nightmare that he endured over the previous year. On the 2005 Ashes tour the high achieving fast bowler was dropped from the Australian Test team after only capturing three wickets in three Tests, and he languished in the state cricket competition when the West Indies and South African teams toured Australia during the following summer. "Dizzy's" Test cricket career appeared to be spinning into oblivion before injury opened up another opportunity in Bangladesh for Australia's long serving pace-man.

On the sub-continent Gillespie performed creditably with the new ball, and the big man remains in the selection frame for "the baggy greens" when England defends its Ashes' trophy in Australia in 2006–07.

It is hard to comprehend why Jason Gillespie's place in the Australian Test team is

**Jason Gillspie would have been entitled to parade around the Chittagong ground on an elephant to celebrate his unforgettable double hundred performance.**

54. Age newspaper, 2006

under threat when his record is examined, as he has consistently produced brilliant bowling performances since his Test match debut in 1996–97. On the 1997 Ashes tour he collected his current best figures when he took 7/37 in the Fourth Test at Headingley, and he has bagged two other five wicket hauls against English teams. Gillespie also cut a swathe through the West Indian team in 2000–01 when he took 5/84 in Adelaide and 6/40 at the MCG, and he performed admirably for six years with "baggy green" teams before his form fell away on the last English tour.

With Jason Gillespie one should always expect the unexpected. In 1993 he reportedly bet his third grade Adelaide club teammates that he would be playing for Australia within five years. "Dizzy's prediction was incorrect as it took him only three years to be awarded a "baggy green".

A man with such vision, self-belief and a proud record should not be prematurely ruled out of selection consideration.

## 371. BICHEL, A.J. (Andrew) : 1970—.

| Tests (19) | ODIs (47) |
|---|---|
| 355 runs at 16.90 | 471 runs at 20.48 |
| 58 wickets at 32.24 | 78 wickets at 31.59 |

A durable and reliable Queensland fast bowler whose enthusiasm and commitment have been highly valued in Australian teams.

At the 1992 National Country Championships in South Australia's Riverland area, 21 year old Andy Bickel was the fourth ranked fast bowler in the Queensland Country team. At the start of the following season Bichel's net form impressed the state coach Jeff Thomson so much that he was soon playing Pura Cup cricket with Queensland.

This anecdote equates well with Bichel's future Test career, as despite being often underrated he persevered until success came his way. In an Australian X1/ West Indian fixture in Hobart some years ago, the great Brian Lara contemptuously dispatched every ball of an Andy Bichel over to the boundary fence. However on the 2003 Caribbean tour Bichel dismissed the master batsman five times in the Test series, which prompted the "Prince of Trinidad" to present the affable Queenslander with his West Indian cap on which he had written:

"You are inspirational. Keep it up."[55]

Bichel obtained his best bowling figures against the Windies with his 5/60 at the MCG Boxing Day Test in 2000, and he also played in Tests against Pakistan, India, England and Zimbabwe. He is an inspirational figure to his teammates with his enthusiastic commitment, but has struggled to gain selection in consecutive Tests throughout his international career.

In recent years Andy Bichel has performed well with Worcestershire in English county cricket. If he is called into the Test match arena again in the coming 2006–07 Ashes series he is certain to give his all for the cause of "the baggy greens."

## 372. YOUNG, S. (Shaun) : 1970—.

Tests (1)<br>4 runs at 4.00

A Tasmanian all-rounder who was called in to action from the Gloucestershire county team for just one appearance with "the baggy greens", after Jason Gillespie was injured before The Oval Test began in 1997.

55. Inside Cricket, 2004, p80

His capable batting and accurate medium-pace bowling was well regarded during his many years of state cricket with "the apple isle."

## 373. COOK, S.H. (Simon) : 1972—.
Tests (2)
3 runs, n.a.
7 wickets at 20.29

A Victorian and NSW fast bowler who suffered shocking injuries during his much interrupted first class career – two broken ankles, an ongoing back problem, and then four broken ribs and severe muscle and tissue damage when he was caught under a Sydney council steamroller in 1998.

Simon Cook enjoyed a spectacular Test debut at the WACA in 1997 when he took a career best 5/39 against New Zealand after he replaced an injured Glenn McGrath. The horrific Sydney work accident ended his injury prone career a season later.

## 374. MACGILL, S.C.G. (Stuart) : 1971—.

| Tests (40) | ODIs (3) |
|---|---|
| 347 runs at 10.20 | 1 run at 1.00 |
| 198 wickets at 27.20 | 6 wickets at 17.50 |

It is fitting that Stuart MacGill has the initials "S.C.G" because he is commonly regarded as a Sydney ground specialist, though the accomplished leg spinner questions the assumption that he is "ä one track pony".

Statistics provide inconclusive supporting evidence about this notion. Some of MacGill's finest moments have unquestionably been at the SCG. It was there against England in the

1998–99 Ashes series that the Perth born slow bowler snared the superb match figures of 12/101, and he has also collected bags of seven wickets against South African and West Indian teams at his adopted home ground.

However it was in Adelaide where Stuart MacGill captured five wickets on debut, and when the attacking leg spinner obtained 16 wickets against the 2000–01 West Indians, and 14 wickets against India in 2003–04, only two of MacGill's 30 wickets were obtained at the SCG.

The biggest impediment to Stuart MacGill's career has been the giant shadow cast by Shane Warne, the greatest leg spinner the game has known. The reluctance of national selectors to choose both champion leg spinners in the same team group, has resulted in MacGill being overlooked for three tours of India, and he was also a surprise omission for overseas series in Pakistan, South Africa and England. On the most recent Ashes tour McGill was selected in the team, but he was overlooked for all Tests when many observers believed that he could have formed a match winning combination with Shane Warne.

When Warne was missing from the "baggy green" team which toured the Caribbean in 2003, Stuart MacGill captured an impressive 9/182 in Barbados. It is hoped that the Australian selectors will remember the match winning talents of S.C.G. MacGill when the 2006–07 Ashes series commence.

## 375. ROBERTSON, G.R. (Gavin) : 1966—.

### Tests (4)
140 runs at 20.00
13 wickets at 39.62

A journeyman off-spinner who represented both NSW and Tasmania in state cricket, and whose haul of 12 wickets in the 1998 Test series in India elevated him to being Australia's leading wicket-taker in the three Tests.

Gavin Robertson took 4/72 from 29 overs in the First Test at Chennai, and his fourth and final Test appearance occurred in that same year when he opposed Pakistan at the National Stadium in Karachi.

## 376. WILSON, P. (Paul) : 1972—.
Tests (1)
 0  runs and 0 wickets

A bulky NSW born opening bowler who played successfully for South Australia and also represented WA..

His sole Test match was played at Eden Gardens in Calcutta where the Indian team won easily after compiling a massive 5/663 before a declaration ended the run orgy.

In recent times Paul Wilson has coached the WA women's' cricket team.

## 377. DALE, A.C. (Adam) : 1968—.
Tests (2)
6 runs at 2.00
6 wickets at 31.17

A Victorian born swing bowler who starred for Queensland after he was transferred in his work.

Adam Dale debuted in Test cricket at Bangalore against India in 1998, and he also opposed the West Indians in Antigua in 1999. The accurate new ball bowler did not play a significant role in either game, but he was a part of a winning team in both Tests.

## 378. LEHMANN, D.S. (Darren "Boof") : 1970—.

Tests (27)                ODIs (117)
1798 runs at 44.95   3078 runs at 38.96
15 wickets at  27.47 52 wickets at 27.78

A cavalier South Australian, Victorian, Australian and Yorkshire left-handed batsman who was named 12th man in a national team at the age of 19, but who then waited another 13 years  before he cemented a spot with the "baggy green" team.

Darren Lehmann amassed large scores in entertaining style from the time he first played for South Australia at the age of 17, but he was not chosen in a Test X1 until the 1998 tour of India when he scored 52 and took 1/27 with his orthodox left arm spinners in the Bangalore Test. A score of 98 at Rawalpindi against Pakistan in the same year further boosted his reputation, but after he failed in two Tests against the touring English team in 1998–99, "Boof" Lehmann was banished from Australian teams for the next ten Test series.

The stocky South Australian achieved moderate success when he was re-instated for three Ashes fixtures in 2002–03, and the explosive batting talents of Lehmann finally blossomed on the 2003 tour of the Caribbean. He amassed 353 runs in the four Tests at an average of 58.83, and Darren Lehmann achieved the milestone of scoring a Test century when he blazed 160 at Port of Spain in Trinidad.

Lehmann's quest for large scores continued. He scored successive centuries against Bangladesh at Darwin and Cairns in the winter of 2003, and on the 2004 tour of Sri Lanka the often unorthodox South Australian

A cavalier South Australian, Victorian, Australian and Yorkshire left-handed batsman who was named 12th man in a national team at the age of 19, but who then waited another 13 years  before he cemented a spot with the "baggy green" team.

smashed 129 at Galle and 153 at Colombo, where he also took 6/92 with his tidy spinners.

By then Lehmann was playing the game continuously, and the popular international cricketer  helped guide Yorkshire to their first county championship in 32 years. However his heavy commitments resulted in Achilles tendon and shoulder injuries, which made it difficult for the aging cricket warrior to remain in national teams.

Darren Lehmann's on-field advice was greatly valued by Ricky Ponting when he succeeded to the captaincy in 2002, and there may well be a future position of importance for him  in Australian cricket when he relinquishes his captaincy role with South Australia.

## 379. MILLER, C.R. (Colin "Funky") : 1964—.
Tests (18)
174 runs at 8.28
69 wickets at 26.16

A cricket nomad who played for Victoria, South Australia and Tasmania, and participated in cricket outpost competitions in the Netherlands, Thailand and USA, before he re-invented himself as an off-spinner and debuted for Australia at the age of 34.

Colin Miller was raised in Melbourne's western suburbs, and he was a handy medium pace bowler before he started bowling off-spinners for the Hobart club where he was a professional player. His reincarnation was a great success, and Miller took an impressive 63 wickets for Tasmania in the 1997–98 Pura Cup competition. This superb performance resulted in Colin Miller being chosen in the1998

Australian team which toured Pakistan, 13 years after he began his first class career.

On the sub-continent, Miller's success continued as he captured the prized wicket of Salim Malik with the fifth delivery he bowled in Test cricket. He went on to play in a series against England at home, and Miller also toured New Zealand, India and the West Indies with " baggy green" teams. His highlight period was in 2000–01, for in that season Colin Miller captured match figures of 10/113 against the Windies in Adelaide. His reward for claiming 35 Test wickets in three series that year came when he gained the 2001 Test Cricketer of the Year award.

"Funky" Miller had his hair dyed purple when he received his prestigious award at the Allan Border Medal presentation dinner, and the zany, knockabout character also appeared in international matches that summer with bright blue and fire engine red hair. Now the globe–trotting Colin Miller is an umpires' selector for Cricket Australia, and he also participates regularly in public speaking engagements.

## 380. NICHOLSON, M.J (Matthew) : 1974—.

### Tests (1)
### 14 runs at 7.00
### 4 wickets at 28.75

A NSW and WA fast bowler who overcame a severe bout of Chronic Fatigue Syndrome to play one Test for Australia, which was the Boxing Day fixture of the 1998–99 season,

Matthew Nicholson took 3/56 in England's first innings, and he twice gained the prized wicket of Nasser Hussain in his debut match. However he was overlooked for the next Test in Sydney, and the 32 year old Nicholson has now returned from Perth to NSW to continue his first class career.

### 381. GILCHRIST, A.C. (Adam "Gillie") : 1971—.

| Tests (85) | ODIs (241) |
|---|---|
| 5124 runs at 48.80 | 8209 runs at 36.48 |
| 355 dismissals | 391 dismissals |
| (320 c, 35 st) | (344 c, 47 st) |



Very few cricketers change the game, both tactically and as a spectator sport, Bradman was one, Warne is another, and Adam Gilchrist is very much in the same mould. Before the advent of this tall wicket-keeper into Test cricket, a batting average of about 25 was expected from a team's gloveman. Gilchrist's Test average hovers consistently around 50, and his international opponents are now insisting that their wicketkeepers must be recognized batsmen, as well as being competent behind the stumps.

England's Les Ames and Alan Knott were reasonable batsmen, Australia's Rod Marsh and Ian Healy both scored Test centuries, and Dennis Lindsay briefly plundered international attacks before South Africa was banned for years from Test cricket. However none of these champion performers had the same impact that Adam Gilchrist currently enjoys. Both Knott and Healy were more skilled behind the stumps, but no previous wicket keeper holds a candle to Adam Gilchrist's all-round skills; he is the best wicketkeeper-batsman the game has known.

Adam Gilchrist first moved to Sydney

from the Lismore area on the NSW coast to break into big cricket, but found that Phil Emery was entrenched as the Blues wicket keeper. Consequently, after playing a few games with the state as a batsman, the young man moved west where he soon was standing behind the stumps for WA in Pura Cup games. Gilchrist first established him self in limited overs cricket with the national team, and when Australia's long serving Test keeper Ian Healy hung up his gloves at the end of the 1998–99 season, Gilchrist gained his first "baggy green" cap.

The left-handed middle order batsman score a breezy 81 in his Test debut at the Gabba against Pakistan, and he then became an integral part of one of Australia most stirring victories at Hobart's Bellerive Oval.

When Gilchrist joined his WA team mate Justin Langer at the crease in Australia's second innings, the home side was facing almost certain defeat. The Aussies were five wickets down and over 300 runs behind the confident visitor's tally, but Langer and Gilchrist safely saw out the last session of play.

Next day, after the pair was associated in a mammoth 238 run partnership for the sixth wicket. They carried the "baggy greens" within sight of an unlikely victory before Langer departed after scoring 127, and when Gilchrist scored the winning run he remained undefeated on 149. His maiden century came from only 108 deliveries, and he clouted five boundaries from just one over from the hapless Pakistani spinner, Mushtaq Ahmed.

This high scoring rate is typical of most Gilchrist innings, as he has an incredible eye, he times the ball sweetly, and he has an amazing ability to choose the right ball to dispatch with his powerful array of strokes. In England at Edgbaston on the 2001 Ashes tour, Gilchrist carried his score from 100 to 152 from only 25 balls during his 50 run partnership with McGrath for the last wicket. McGrath's contribution to this explosive stand was an undefeated 0.

Another Adam Gilchrist epic Test innings was witnessed on the 2002 tour of South Africa. Gilchrist shrugged aside some baseless off-field rumours about his personal life, and blazed a brilliant 204 not out against the Proteas at the Wanderers ground in Johannesburg. He raced to his unbeaten double century from only 213 deliveries, and his memorable innings included an amazing 19 fours and 8 sixes. The world's cricket media almost queued up to acclaim the great player's performance.

"...an innings that mixed savage power with delicate artistry.. Adam Gilchrist reached the holy grail for which every batsman has been aspiring for more than 100 years," enthused the late Peter McFarline. Gilchrist also scored 91 in the Kingsmead Test at Durban, and 138 at Newlands in Cape Town, before finishing the series with the superb batting average on 171.50.[56]

However the man who has transformed cricket in both forms of the game has also endured lean periods in his brilliant career. After blazing 122 in the first Test of the 2001 series in India, Gilchrist struggled in the remaining games to combat the wiles of the champion off-spinner Harbajan Singh. The reverse swing obtained by the English fast bowling attack on the Ashes tour of 2005 also found him wanting in a Test series. Failure also dogged Adam Gilchrist on the 2006 tour of South Africa, and it will be interesting to see how this personable wicket keeper-batsman

56. Haigh, 2004, p658

performs against the strong visiting English team in 2006–07.

## 382. MULLER, S.A. (Scott) : 1971—.

Tests (2)

6 runs, n.a.

7 wickets at 36.86

A strongly built Queensland fast bowler who captured over 100 wickets for his state, but faded out of Test cricket quickly after he became embroiled in an on-field controversy.

The fair-headed Muller debuted for Australia at the Gabba in 1999 against Pakistan, and he took 3/68 in the visitor's first innings of the Second Test in Hobart. In that game, after Muller fired a wayward throw from the outfield to the bowler's end, an audible remark of "Can't bowl, can't throw," was uttered and brought to the attention of a television station commentator. In the minor furore that followed this incident, the finger of blame was first pointed at Shane Warne, but a television camera man at the ground later confessed that he was the culprit.

**"Can't bowl, can't throw"**

A distressed Muller was clearly unhappy about the whole incident, and he did not play Test cricket again. He now works as a sales representative with a brewery company and resides on the Gold Coast. Recently Scott Muller became involved in a coaching role with the Beenleigh-Logan Cricket Club.

## 383. LEE, B. (Brett "Binga") : 1976—.

| Tests (54) | ODIs (135) |
|---|---|
| 1033 runs at 21.08 | 694 runs at 19.27 |
| 211 wckts at 31.45 | 237 wckts at 22.84 |

A NSW and Australian player who is

**Arguably the fastest bowler on the planet.**

arguably the fastest bowler on the planet. Brett Lee is regarded by many as being the premier limited overs fast bowler on the international scene, and he is fast becoming a Test player of world class.

The blonde headed younger brother of Shane Lee, a useful all-rounder for both NSW and Australian limited overs teams, made an impressive Test debut against India at the MCG in 1999, claiming 5/47 from 18 overs. He continued his impressive wicket taking form in the following series against New Zealand, and he also revealed his batting credentials when he scored an unbeaten 62 against the Kiwis in Perth.

The tearaway fast bowler then struggled to maintain a consistent line and length at Test match level, and he was also plagued by no ball problems. By 2004–05 he was squeezed out of the Australian Test team, but in recent times the super-fit speedster, who regularly bowls at speeds of around 150 kilos per hour, has become a significant strike weapon for the "baggy greens".

Brett Lee topped the Australian bowling averages in the recent Ashes series in England, and he also captured an impressive 17 wickets at 19.52 on the 2006 tour of South Africa. In both these series he also averaged close to 30 as an attacking late order batsman, and the recently married Brett Lee could be a potent force in the Australian team which contests the next Ashes series in 2006–07.

**384. KATICH, S.M. (Simon) : 1975—.**
Tests (23)                          ODIs (41)
1260 runs at 36.00    1232 runs at 37.33
12 wickets at 33.83

A neat left handed batsman who has a calm temperament and is capable of batting competently in any of top order Australian batting positions.

Simon Katich was selected for the 2001 Ashes tour after accumulating large scores for WA, and he scored 15 in his debut Test at Headingley when he replaced an injured Steve Waugh. He then was forced to wait another two years before he once again donned "the baggy green" cap, and was finally selected in successive Tests against the 2003–04 Indian touring team. Katich scored 125 at the SCG when Steve Waugh played his last Test match, and an undefeated 77 in the second innings seemingly cemented his spot in the Australian team.

However in the same season Simon Katich was not selected for the first two Tests in Sri Lanka. He fittingly showed the tour selectors his worth by scoring 86 in the final match of the series, but Katich continues to endure a unpredictable ride in international cricket. He did play in all five Test against England in 2005 where he achieved the moderate batting series average of 27.56, and at times his batting appeared to pose a threat to the home side.

In 2006–07 the newly married Simon Katich will start his fourth season with NSW, a team he has often captained in Pura Cup games. Katich is also a handy left-arm spin bowler, and his versatility will be borne in mind when top order batting places  are allocated in the Australian team.

## 385. LOVE, M.L. (Martin) : 1974—.

Tests (5)

223 runs at 46.60

A stylish batsman who has accumulated huge scores in Australian domestic and English county cricket, but appears to have been overtaken by other candidates for "baggy green" selection, despite scoring 100 not out in the last of his five current Tests.

Martin Love started his Test career after crashing two double centuries early in the 2002–03 against the English touring team. He then scored 62 not out against the visitors in the Boxing Day Test at the MCG in 2002, when he replaced an ill Darren Lehmann. After failing at the SCG in the final fixture of the series, Love played one Test on the Caribbean tour of 2003, and he then represented Australia in two Tests against Bangladesh that winter.

He scored an undefeated 100 at Cairns, but was dropped when Damien Martyn returned from injury. The elegant top order batsman has now played over 130 games of first class cricket, and Martin Love achieved the dubious distinction of becoming only the fifth player to be dropped from an Australian team after notching a century. He continues to represent Queensland with distinction.

**Martin Love achieved the dubious distinction of becoming only the fifth player to be dropped from an Australian team after notching a century.**

## 386. WILLIAMS, B.A. (Bradley) : 1974—.

| Tests (4) | ODIs (25) |
|---|---|
| 23 runs at 7.67 | 27 runs at 13.50 |
| 9 wickets at 45.11 | 35 wickets at 23.25 |

A fiery fast bowler who battled back and shoulder injuries for much of his career with Victoria, WA and Australia.

Williams debuted for Australia against Zimbabwe in 2003–04,  he played another two home Tests opposed to India, and finally the last Test of the 2005 series in Sri Lanka. His best figures were 4/53 in the second innings of the 2003 Boxing Day Test in Melbourne, but he then made way for Jason Gillespie for the following Sydney fixture.

Brad Williams fell out with WA cricket authorities in the 2005–06 season, and he is now reportedly living and working on Queensland's Gold Coast.

### 387. BRACKEN, N.W. (Nathan) : 1977—.

Tests (5)                         ODIs (38)
70 runs at 17.50          84 runs at 21.00
12 wickets at 42.08   65 wickets at 21,18

A consistent performer in ODIs and a fringe player in the Australian Test squad

Nathan Bracken was a potent force for NSW when it defeated Queensland in a recent Pura Cup final at the Gabba, and when conditions suit his left-arm swinging deliveries the tall new ball bowler from the Blue Mountains area can be a match-winner against the strongest opposition.

His progress has been thwarted by injuries, but the window of opportunity is still there for the tall new-ball bowler, especially if he bowls with more venom than he showed against the West Indies in 2004–05.

### 388. SYMONDS, A. (Andrew) : 1975—.

Tests (10)                         ODIs (146)
286 runs at 19.06   3,697 runs at 39.32
9 wickets at 45.44   114 wickets at 36.38

The smear of white zinc cream on the lower lip has been regularly applied by

The smear of white zinc cream on the lower lip has been regularly applied by Andrew Symonds in nearly 150 ODIs, but the big Queensland all-rounder has rarely needed to be "sun-smart" in the Test match arena.

Andrew Symonds in nearly 150 ODIs, but the big Queensland all-rounder has rarely needed to be "sun-smart" in the Test match arena.

However this scenario may still change, as the national selectors have recently given Andrew Symonds every opportunity to become the all-rounder that Australians crave. He was tried without success in two Tests on the 2005 tour of Sri Lanka, he was marginally more successful against the Windies and the Proteas at home in 2005–06, and he was again chosen for overseas Test series against South Africa and Bangladesh in the early months of 2006.

It is easy to see why the selectors have been patient with Symonds as he has the potential to be a match winner with "the baggy greens." His aggressive batting can turn the course of a game, he can bowl either medium pace swing or accurate off-spin deliveries, and he is one of the most brilliant fieldsmen in world cricket.

All these qualities have frequently been displayed in many ODI games. If Andrew Symonds can replicate these skills in the coming Australia/England Test series, it will greatly improve Australia's chances of regaining the Ashes.

## 389. CLARKE, M.J. (Michael "Pup") : 1981—.

| Tests (22) | ODIs (82) |
|---|---|
| 1123 runs at 36.22 | 2393 runs at 44.31 |
| 8 wickets at 9.37 | 25 wickets at 36.40 |

An exciting young cricketer who possesses the rare ability to change the course of a game with a burst of inspired play.

This "X factor' was evident when the lad they call "Pup" scored an exuberant century at

Bangalore in his debut Test match on the 2004 tour of India. Clarke's excellent contribution of 151 against the wiles of the Indian spinners was widely acclaimed by the cricket media, especially David Sygall who declared that it was "an innings that Hans Christian Andersen would have had trouble fantasising about."[57]

Clarke's fairytale introduction to Test cricket continued on a mine field of a wicket at Mumbai where he snared astonishing an 6/9 with his orthodox left-arm spinners. Then after he blazed an exhiliarating 148 in his home debut Test against the Kiwis, the cheerful NSW youngster appeared to be destined for greatness. His dream run culminated with the awarding of the prestigious Allan Border Medal at the end of the 2004–05 season.

Since those heady days the dream has soured somewhat. Clarke only averaged a moderate 37.22 in the five Ashes Tests on the 2005 tour of England, where he was troubled at times with a back injury. His form on the last tour of New Zealand was indifferent, and further failures in the 2005–06 home series against the West Indies resulted in him being dropped from the Australian team.

Clarke returned to Test action on the 2006 tour of Bangladesh, and the selectors must be tempted to persevere with his adventurous talent. England's gamble with the similarly aggressive Kevin Pietersen was hugely successful in the last Ashes series, and the "X-factor" of a player like Michael Clarke may be the extra ingredient that is needed for "the baggy greens' to regain the Ashes.

### 390. HAURITZ, N.M. (Nathan) : 1981—.

57. Inside Cricket, 2004, p106

Tests (1)            ODIs (8)
15 runs at 7.50      35 runs at 35.00
5 wickets at 20.60    9 wickets at 34.22

A Queensland off-spinner who replaced an injured Shane Warne for the Mumbai Test of the 2005 Indian tour, and captured 3/16.

The poor quality of that wicket makes it difficult to judge the potential of the young spinner, but he has since struggled to maintain his position in the Queensland state team. He may now have been overtaken by South Australia's Daniel Cullen in the contest to become Australia's next off-spinner.

Nathan Hauritz is likely to re-locate to Sydney for the 2006–07 season in an attempt to rejuvenate his faltering career.

## 391. WATSON, S.R. (Shane) : 1981—.

Tests (3)            ODIs (43)
81 runs at 20.25     507 runs at 31.68
2 wickets at 61.50    37 wickets at 37.18

The strongly built blonde-headed all-rounder would be the Australian selectors' first choice as the "baggy green's" all-rounder, if he could only stay on the field long enough. Shane Watson suffered three stress fractures to the back by the time he was 16, and had to withdraw from the 2003 World Cup squad when he suffered his fourth worrying spinal injury. Recently a dislocated shoulder added to the injury woes of this dedicated player.

Dennis Lillee has since helped Watson remodel his bowling action following a long period of recuperation, and the strongly motivated all-rounder is confident that the worst is over. He has now returned to Queensland after a successful stint with Tasmania in the

Pura Cup competition, and the ever-enthusiastic Shane Watson hopes to vindicate the selector's faith in him in the 2006–07 Ashes series in Australia.

## 392. TAIT, S.W. (Shaun) : 1983—.

Tests (2)<br>8 runs at 8.00<br>5 wickets at 42.00

A fast-medium bowler with a slinging action who has suffered a succession of recent injuries. When fit this South Australian strike bowler can bowl an almost unplayable delivery, such as the late moving in-swinger that comprehensively bowled English opener Marcus Trescothic in the 2005 Ashes series.

Shaun Tate gained selection for that 2005 English tour after taking a record breaking 65 Pura Cup wickets in the 2004–05 season. He appears best suited to short bursts of bowling, and the reverse swing that he gains from the old ball makes him a potent wicket-taking force for the duration of an innings.

An injury-free Shaun Tate could be Australia's saviour in the 2006–07 Ashes series.

## 393. HUSSEY, M.E.K. (Michael) : 1975—.

| Tests (11) | ODIs (40) |
| --- | --- |
| 1139 runs at 75.93 | 1156 runs at 77.06 |

A prolific run maker as an opening batsman for WA, Northamptonshire and Durham for over a decade, who blossomed into a world class middle-order batsman once he was belatedly selected for "the baggy greens in 2005–06.

Mike Hussey showed his class as a number five batsman during the 2005 ODIs in England, and in the following Australian summer he replaced an injured Justin Langer at the head of the order in his first Test at the Gabba against the West Indies.

Hussey registered a century in the second fixture of that series, and he has now notched an impressive four centuries and four 50s in his 11 Tests against the Windies, South Africa and Bangladesh. The left-handed Perth school teacher has emphatically cemented a middle order batting position for the 2006–07 Ashes series, and on current form he could be one of the star players of the summer.

## 394. HODGE, B.J. (Bradley) : 1974—.

| Tests (5) | ODIs (5) |
|---|---|
| 409 runs at 58.52 | 79 runs at 15.80 |

A small talented batsman who scored an avalanche of runs for Victoria, Leicestershire and Lancashire for more than ten years, before he finally gained Test selection against South Africa in 2005–06. During his long apprenticeship the quiet achiever visited India, New Zealand and England with Australian touring teams, and  Brad Hodge scored an excellent 203 not out against the Proteas in Perth after he finally donned "the baggy green" cap.

A Test tour of South Africa and Bangladesh seemed almost inevitable, but some injudicious shots in the next Test, and poor form in state games, resulted in Hodge being unexpectedly dropped from the Australian squad.

Since then the determined top order batsman has scored a century in the last Pura Cup final, and Brad Hodge will be pressing strongly to bat at number four again for his country during the 2006–07 Ashes series.

## 395. JAQUES, P.A. (Phillip) : 1979—.

Tests (2)                    ODIs (2)
96 runs at 32.00       94 runs at 47.00

An English born NSW left-handed opening batsman who has been a prolific run scorer for the Blues, Worcestershire and Australia A in recent seasons. Phil Jaques was called into action for the 2005 Boxing Day Test against South Africa, and he also replaced an injured player during the 2006 Test series in Bangladesh.

Some doubts have been raised about Jaques' batting technique and fielding ability, but the big NSW player has a keen eye, and his ability to provide a good start to his teams' innings will keep him in the selectors' sights when the Australians oppose England in 2006–07.

## 396. CLARK, S.R. (Stuart "Sarfraz") : 1975—.

Tests (4)                    ODIs (15)
31 runs at 10.33       33 runs at 33.00
21 wickets at 18.76  23 wickets at 29.91

A late maturing NSW new ball bowler who has a similar bowling approach to the former Pakistani paceman Sarfraz Narwaz. Stuart Clark has recently played ODIs with Australia, and he was nearly called into a 2005 Ashes team when the original squad was beset with injuries.

Stuart Clark bowls long, accurate spells of seam bowling in similar vein to Glenn McGrath, and when that great fast bowler was forced to withdraw from the 2006 tour of South Africa and Bangladesh, it was his tall Blues' teammate who took his place.

Clark was a revelation in South Africa. He was named "man of the match" after taking 5/58 in the first innings of his first Test in Johannesburg, and his series statistics of 20 wickets at 15.85 topped the Australian Test bowling averages.

This fine performance has strengthened Australia's fast bowling resources, and Stuart Clark now has strong credentials to play against England in the 2006–07 Ashes series.

## 397. CULLEN, D.J. (Daniel) : 1985—.
Tests (1)
0 runs, n. a.
1 wicket at 54.00

A young, competitive South Australian off-spinner who has impressed respected judges with his bowling potential.

Dan Cullen collected a wicket in his first Test match in Bangladesh, and during the 2006 off-season he played county cricket in England. This developmental bowler is very much a player of the future, but Dan Cullen is not likely to gain Test selection for the 2006–07 Ashes series.

# BIBLIOGRAPHY


AGE newspaper, Melbourne, Victoria (April, 2006).

BARDWIN, Mark "The Ashes Strangest Moments" Robson Books, The Crystalis Building, London (2005).

BEECHER, Eric "The Cricket Revolution" Newspress Pty Ltd. Melbourne, Victoria (1978).

CHAPPELL, Ian "Passing Tests" Lynton Publications Pty. Ltd Coramendal Valley, South Australia. (1973).

CLARK, Manning "A Short History of Australia. The New American Library, New York and Toronto, North America. (1963).

Cricinfoaustralia the home of www.baggygreen.com.au

FERGUSON, Ian "Cricket's Far Horizons", Rex Thompson and Family Pty Ltd (1996)

HAIGH, Gideon (afterword) "200 Years of Australian Cricket 1804–2004, Pan McMillan Australia Pty Ltd, (2004.)

"INSIDE CRICKET" magazine Souvenir Edition "a Decade of Champions 1995–2005, Sydney, NSW (2005)

McFARLINE, Peter "A Game Divided", Hutchinson Group (Australia) Pty Ltd, (1977)

POLLARD, Jack "Australian Cricket The Game and Its Players", Hodder and Stoughton (Australia) Pty Ltd, 1982.

PIESSE, Ken & FERGUSON, Ian "Bradman And The Bush" Newspress Pty Ltd, Melbourne Victoria. (1986)

PONTING, Ricky & MURGATROYD, Brian "Ashes Diary 2005." Harper Collins Australia (2005).

# Australia vs England Test Results

**Aust. vs England 1st Test: M.C.G. March 15th, 16th, 17th and 19th 1877**

Australia won the toss. Australia 1st Innings 245 (Bannerman 165) England 1st Innings 196 (Jupp 63, Midwinter 5/78) Australia 2nd Innings 104 (Shaw 5/38) England 2nd Innings 108 (Kendall 7/55) Australia won by 45 runs.

**Aust. vs England 2nd Test: M.C.G. March 31st, April 2nd, 3rd and 4th 1877**

Australia won the toss. Australia 1st Innings 122 England 1st Innings 261 Australia 2nd Innings 259 England 2nd Innings 6 for 122 (Ulyett 63) England won by 4 wickets.

**Only Test 1878–79 Australia vs England: M.C.G. January 2nd, 3rd, 4th 1879**

England won the toss. England 1st Innings 113 (Absolom 52 Spofforth 6/48) Australia 1st Innings 256 (Bannerman 73 Emmett 7/68) England 2nd Innings 160 (Spofforth 7/62) Australia 2nd Innings 0 for 19 Australia won by 10 wickets.

**Only Test 1880 England vs Australia: Kennington Oval LONDON September 6th, 7th and 8th 1880**

England won the toss. England 1st Inning 420 (Grace 152) Australia 1st Innings 149 (Morley 5/56) Australia 2nd Innings 327( Murdoch 153 N.O.) England 2nd Innings 5 for 57 England won by 5 wickets.

**First Test 1881–82 Australia vs England: M.C.G. Dec 31 1881 Jan 2nd, 3rd and 4th 1882**

England won the toss England 1st Innings 294 (Ulyett 87) Australia 1st Innings 320 (Horan 124) England 2nd Innings 308 (Cooper 6/120) Australia 2nd Innings 3 for 127 Match drawn

**Second Test 1881–82 Australia vs England: S.C.G. February 17th, 18th, 20th and 21st 1882**

England won the toss. England 1st Innings 133 (Palmer 7/68) Australia 1st Innings 197 England 2nd Innings 232 Australia 2nd Innings 5 for 169 Australia won by 5 wickets

**Third Test 1881–82 Australia vs England: S.C.G. March 3rd, 4th, 6th and 7th 1882**

England won the toss. England 1st Innings 188 (Shrewsbury 82 Palmer 5/46) Australia 1st Innings 262 (McDonnell 147 Peate 5/43) England 2nd Innings 134 (Garrett 6/78) Australia 2nd Innings 4 for 64 Australia won by 6 wickets

**Fourth Test 1881–82 Australia vs England: M.C.G. March 10th, 11th, 13th 14th (no play) 1882**

England won the toss. England 1st Innings 309 (Ulyett 149 Garrett 5/80) Australia 1st Innings 300 (Murdoch 85) England 2nd Innings 2 for 234 Match drawn.

**Only Test 1882 England vs Australia: Kennington Oval London august 28th, 29th 1882**

Australia won the toss. Australia 1st Innings 63 (Barlow 5/19) England 1st Innings 101 (Spofforth 7/46) Australia 2nd Innings 122 England 2nd Innings 77 (Spofforth 7/44) Australia won by 7 runs.

**First Test 1882–83 Australia vs England: M.C.G. December 30th 1882 Jan 1st 2nd 1883**

Australia won the toss. Australia 1st Innings 291 (Bonnor 85) England 1st Innings 177 (Palmer 7/65) England 2nd Innings 169 Australia 2nd Innings 1 for 58. Australia won by 9 wickets.

**Second Test 1882–83 Australia vs England: M.C.G. January 19th, 20th, 22nd 1883**

England won the toss. England 1st Innings 294 (Read 75 Palmer

5/103) Australia 1st Innings 114 (Bates 7/28) Australia 2nd Innings 153 (Bates 7/74) England won by an innings and 27 runs

## Third Test 1882–83 Australia vs England: S.C.G. January 26th, 27th, 29th, 30th 1883

England won the toss. England 1st Innings 247 Australia 1st Innings 218 (Bannerman 94) England 2nd Innings 123 (Spofforth 7/44) Australia 2nd Innings 83 (Barlow 7/40) England won by 69 runs.

## Fourth Test 1882–83 Australia vs England: S.C.G. February 17th, 19th, 20th, 21st 1883

England won the toss. England 1st Innings 263 (Steel N.O. 135) Australia 1st Innings 262 (Bonnor 87) England 2nd Innings 197 Australia 2nd Innings 6 for 199 Australia won by 4 wickets.

## First Test 1884 England vs Australia : Old Trafford, Manchester July 10 (no play) 11th, 12th 1884

Australia won the toss. England 1st Innings 95 (Boyle 6/42) Australia 1st Innings 182 England 2nd Innings 9 for 180 Match drawn

## Second Test 1884 England vs Australia: Lord's Cricket Ground London July 21st, 22nd, 23rd 1884

Australia won the toss. Australia 1st Innings 229 (Scott 75 Peate 6/85) England 1st Innings 379 (Steel 148 Palmer 6/111) Australia 2nd Innings 9 for 145 (Ulyett 7/36) England won by an innings and 5 runs

## Third Test 1884 England vs Australia: Kennington Oval London August 11th, 12th, 13th 1884

Australia won the toss. Australia 1st Innings 551 (Murdoch 211, McDonnell 103, Scott 102) England 1st Innings 346 (Read 117) England 2 for 85

Match drawn

## First Test 1884–85 Australia vs England: Adelaide Oval December 12th, 13th, 15th, 16th 1884

Australia won the toss. Australia 1st Innings 243 (McDonnell 124 Bates 5/31) England 1st Innings 369 (Barnes 134 Palmer 5/81) Australia 9 for 191 (McDonnell 83 Peel 51) England 2nd Innings 2 for

67 England won by 8 wickets.

## Second Test 1884–85 Australia vs England: M.C.G. Jan 1st, 2nd, 3rd and 5th 1885

England won the toss. England 1st Innings 401 (Briggs 121) Australia 1st Innings 279 (Jarvis 82) Australia 2nd Innings 126 (Barnes 6/31) England 2nd Innings 0 for 7 England won by 10 wickets.

## Third Tests 1884–85 Australia vs England: S.C.G Feb. 20th, 21st, 23rd and 24th 1885

Australia won the toss. Australia 1st Innings 181(Flowers 5/46) England 1st Innings 133 (Horan 6/40) Australia 2nd Innings 165 (Bates 5/24) England 2nd Innings 207(Spofforth 6/90) Australia won by 6 runs.

## Fourth Test 1884–85 Australia vs England: S.C.G. March 14th, 16th and 17th 1885

England won the toss. England 1st Innings 269 (Giffen 7/117) Australia 1st Innings 309 (Bonnor 128 ) England 2nd Innings 77 (Spofforth 5/30) Australia 2nd Innings 2 for 38  Australia won by 8 wickets.

## Fifth Test 1884–85 Australia vs England: M.C.G. March 21st, 23rd, 24th and 25th 1885

Australia won the toss. Australia 1st Innings 163 England 1st Innings 386 (Shrewsbury 105 n.o.) Australia 2nd Innings 125 England won by an innings and 98 runs.

## First Test 1886 England vs Australia: Old Trafford Manchester July 5th, 6th and 7th 1886

Australia won the toss. Australia 1st innings 205 (Jones 87) England 1st Innings 223 Australia 2nd Innings 123 (Barlow 7/ 44) England 2nd Innings 6 for 107 England won by 4 wickets.

## Second Test 1886 England vs Australia: Lord's Cricket Ground July 19th, 20th and 21st 1886

England won the toss. England 1st Innings 353 (Shrewsbury 164) Australia 1st Innings 121(Briggs 5/29) Australia 2nd Innings 126 (Briggs 6/45) England won by an innings and 106 runs.

## Third Test 1886 England vs Australia: Kennington Oval London August 12th, 13th and 14th 1886

England won the toss. England 1st Innings 434 (Grace 170 Read 94) Australia 1st Innings 68 (Lohmannn 7/36) Australia 2nd Innings 149 (Lohmann 5/68) England won by an innings and 217 runs.

## First Test 1886–87 Australia vs England: S.C.G. January 28th, 29th and 31st 1887

Australia won the toss. England 1st Innings 45 (Turner 6/15) Australia 1st Innings 119 England 2nd Innings 184 (Ferris 5/76) Australia 2nd Innings 97 (Barnes 6/28) England won by 13 runs.

## Second Test 1886–87 Australia vs England: S.C.G. February 25th, 26th, 28th March 1st 1887

England won the toss. England 1st Innings 151  (Ferris 5/71 Turner 5/41) Australia  1st Innings 84 (Lohmann 8/35) England 2nd Innings 154  Australia 2nd Innings 150 England won by 71 runs.

## Only Test 1887–88 Australia vs England: S.C.G. February 10th, 11th–13th (no play) 14th & 15th 1888

Australia won the toss. England 1st Innings 113 (Turner 5/44) Australia 1st Innings 42 (Lohmann 5/17 Peel 5/18) England 2nd Innings 137 Australia 2nd Innings 82 England won by 126 runs.

## First Test 1888 England vs Australia: Lord's London July 16th & 17th 1888

Australia won the toss. Australia 1st Innings 116  England 1st Innings 53 (Turner 5/27) Australia 2nd Innings 60 England 2nd Innings 62 (Turner 5/36 Ferris 5/26) Australia won by 61 runs.

## Second Test 1888 England vs Australia: Kennington oval London August 13th & 14th 1888

Australia won the toss. Australia 1st Innings 80 (Briggs 5/25) England 1st Innings 317 (Abel 70 Turner 6/112) Australia 2nd Innings 100 (Barnes 5/32) England won by an innings and 117 runs.

## Third Test 1888 England vs Australia: Old Trafford Manchester August 30th and 31st 1888.

England won the toss. England 1st Innings 172 (Turner 5/86) Australia 1st Innings 81 (Peel 7/31) Australia 2nd Innings 70 England won by an innings and 21 runs.

## First Test 1890 England vs Australia: Lord's London July 21st, 22nd & 23rd 1890

Australia won the toss. Australia 1st Innings 132 England 1st Innings 173 (Ulyett 74( Lyons 5/30) Australia 2nd Innings 176 (Barrett 67 n.o.) England 2nd Innings 3 for 137 (Grace 75 n.o.) England won by 7 wickets.

## Second Test 1890 England vs Australia: Kennington Oval London August 11th and 12th 1890

Australia won the toss. Australia 1st Innings 92  (Martin 6/50) England 1st Innings 100  Australia 2nd Innings 102 (Martin 6/52) England 2nd Innings 8 for 95 England won by 2 wickets.

## First Test 1891–92 Australia vs England: M.C.G. January 1st, 2nd, 4th, 5th and 6th 1892

Australia won the toss. Australia 1st Innings 240 (Sharpe 6/84) England 1st Innings 264 (McLeod 5/53) Australia 2nd Innings 236 England 2nd Innings 158 (Turner 5/51) Australia won by 54 runs.

## Second Test 1891–92 Australia vs England: S.C.G. January 29th, 30th Feb. 1st, 2nd & 3rd 1892

Australia won the toss. Australia 1st Innings 144 (Lohmann 8/58) England 1st Innings 307 (Abel 132 n.o.) Australia 2nd Innings 9 for 391 (Lyons 134 Bannerman 91 England 2nd Innings 156 (Giffen 6/72) Australia won by 72 runs.

## Third Test 1891–92 Australia vs England: Adelaide Oval March 24th, 25th, 26th & 28th 1892

England won the toss. England 1st Innings 499 (Stoddart 134) Australia 1st Innings 100 (Briggs 6/49) Australia 2nd Innings 169 (Briggs 6/87) England won by an innings and 230 runs.

## First Test 1893 England vs Australia : Lord's Cricket Ground London July 17th, 18th and 19th 1893

England won the toss. England 1st Innings 334 (Shrewsbury 106 Jackson 91 Turner 6/67) Australia 1st Innings 269 (Graham 107 Lockwood 6/101) England 2nd Innings 8 dec for 234 (Shrewsbury 81 Giffen 5/43) Match drawn.

**Second Test 1893 England vs Australia: Kennington Oval London August 14th, 15th and 16th 1893**

England won the toss. England 1st Innings 483 (Jackson 103 Giffen 7/128) Australia 1st Innings 91 (Briggs 5/34) Australia 2nd Innings 349 (Trott 92 Briggs 5/114) England won by an innings and 43 runs.

**Third Test 1893 England vs Australia: Old Trafford Manchester August 24th, 25th and 26th 1893**

Australia won the toss. Australia 1st Innings 204 (Richardson 5/49) England 1st Innings 243 (Gunn 102 n.o.) Australia 2nd Innings 236 (Richardson 5/107) England 2nd Innings 4/118 Match drawn

**First Test 1894–95 Australia vs England: S.C.G. December 14th, 15th, 17th, 18th, 19th & 20th 1894**

Australia won the toss. Australia 1st Innings 586 (Giffen 161 Gregory 201 Richardson 5/181) England 1st Innings 325 Australia 2nd Innings 166 (Peel 6/67) England 2nd Innings 437 (Ward 117) England won by 10 runs.

**Second Test 1894–95 Austrtalia vs England: M.C.G. December 29th, 31st 1894 January 1st, 2nd and 3rd 1895**

Australia won the toss. England 1st Innings 75 (Turner 5/32) Australia 1st Innings 123 (Richardson 5/57) England 2nd Innings 475 (Stoddart 173 Giffen 6/155) Australia 2nd Innings 333 (Trott 95) England won by 94 runs.

**Third Test 1894–95 Australia vs England: Adelaide Oval January 11th, 12th, 14th and 15th 1895**

Australia won the toss. Australia 1st Innings 238 (Richardson 5/75) England 1st Innings 124 (Giffen 5/76 Callaway 5/37) Australia 2nd Innings 411 (Iredale 140) England 2nd Innings 143 (Trott 8/43) Australia won by 382 runs.

**Fourth Test 1894–95 Australia vs England: S.C.G. February 1st, 2nd (no play) 4th 1895**

England won the toss. Australia 1st Innings 284 (Graham 105) England 1st Innings 9 for 65 England 2nd Innings 9 for 72 (Giffen 5/26) Australia won by an innings and 147 runs.

## Fifth test 1894–95 Australia vs England : M.C.G. March 1st, 2nd, 4th, 5th and 6th 1895

Australia won the toss. Australia 1st Innings 414 England 1st Innings 385 (Maclaren 120) Australia 2nd Innings 267 (Richardson 6/104) England 2nd Innings 4 for 298 (Brown 140) England won by 6 wickets.

## First Test 1896 England vs Australia: Lord's Cricket Ground London  June 22nd, 23rdand 24th 1896

Australia won the toss. Australia 1st innings 53 (Richardson 6/39) England 1st Innings 292 (Abel 94 ) Australia 2nd Innings 347 (Trott 143 Gregory 103 Richardson 5/134 Hearne 5/76) England 2nd Innings 4 for 111 England won by 6 wickets.

## Second Test 1896 England vs Australia: Old Trafford Manchester July 16th, 17th and 18th 1896

Australia won the toss. Australia !st Innings 412 (Iredale 108 Richardson 7/168) England 1st Innings 231 England 2nd Innings 305 (Ranjitsinhji 154 n.o. Australia 2nd Innings 7 for 125 (Richardson 6/76) Australia won by 3 wickets.

## Third Test 1896 England vs Australia: Kennington oval London August 10th, 11th & 12th 1896

England won the toss. England 1st Innings 145 (Trumble 6/59) Australia !st Innings 119 (Hearne 6/41) England 2nd Innings 84 (Trumble 6/30) Australia 2nd Innings 44 (Peel 6/23) England won by 66 runs.

## First Test Australia vs England 1897–98: S.C.G. December 13th, 14th, 15th, 16th & 17th !897

England won the toss. England 1st Innings 551 (Maclaren 109 Ranjitsinhji 175 Australia 1st Innings 237 (Hearne 5/42) Australia 2nd Innings 408 (Darling 101 Hill 96) England 2nd Innings 1 for 96 England won  by 9 wickets.

## Second Test 1897–98 Australia vs England: M.C.G. January 1st, 3rd, 4th & 5th 1898

Australia won the toss. Australia 1st Innings 520 (McLeod 112) England 1st Innings 315 England 2nd Innings 150 (Noble 6/49) Australia won by an innings and 55 runs.

### Third Test 1897–98 Australia vs England: Adelaide oval January 14th, 15th, 17th, 18th & 19th 1898

Australia won the toss. Australia 1st Innings 573 (Darling 178) England 1st Innings 278 England 2nd Innings 282 (MacLaren 124 Noble 5/84 McLeod 5/65) Australia won by an innings and 13 runs.

### Fourth Test 1897–98 Australia vs England: M.C.G. Jan 29th, 31st Feb 1st & 2nd 1898

Australia won the toss. Australia 1st Innings 323 (Hill 188 Hearne 6/98) England 1st Innings 174  England 2nd Innings 263 Australia 2nd Innings 2 for 115 Australia won by 8 wickets.

### Fifth Test 1897–98 Australia vs England: S.C.G. February 26th, 28th, March 1st & 2nd 1898

England won the toss. England 1st Innings 335 (Jones 6/82) Australia 1st Innings 239 (Richardson 8/94) England 2nd Innings 178 Australia 2nd Innings 4 for 276 (Darling 160) Australia won by 6 wickets.

### First Test 1899 England vs Australia: Trent Bridge, Nottingham June 1st, 2nd and 3rd 1899

Australia won the toss. Australia 1st Innings 252 England 1st innings 193 (Jones 5/88) Australia 2nd innings 8 dec for 230 (Hill 80 ) England 2nd Innings 7 for 155 Match drawn.

### Second Test 1899 England vs Australia: Lord's Cricket Ground London June 15th, 16th and 17th 1899

England won the toss. England 1st Innings 206 (Jones 7/88) Australia 1st Innings 421 (Hill 135 Trumper n.o. 135 England 2nd Innings 240  (MacLaren n.o. 88) Australia 2nd Innings 0 for 28 Australia won by 10 wickets.

### Third Test 1899 England vs Australia: Headingly, Leeds June 29th, 30th, July 1st (no play) 1899

Australia won the toss. Australia 1st Innings 172  England 1st Innings 9 for 220 (Trumble 5/60) Australia 2nd Innings 224 England 2nd Innings 0 for 19 Match drawn.

### Fourth Test 1899 England vs Australia: Old Trafford Manchester

**July 17th, 18th & 19th 1899**

England won the toss. England 1st Innings 372 (Hayward 130) Australia 1st Innings 196 (Bradley 5/ 67) Australia 2nd Innings 7 dec for 346 (Noble 89 ) England 2nd Innings 3 for 94 Match drawn.

**Fifth test 1899 England vs Australia: Kennington oval London August 14th, 15th & 16th 1899**

England won the toss. England 1st Innings 576 (Jackson 118 Hayward 137) Australia !st innings 352 (Gregory 117 Lockwood 7/71) Australia 2nd Innings 5 for 254 Match drawn.

# Australia v England Test Results No.2

**First Test 1901–02 Australia v England: S.C.G. December 13th, 14th & 16th 1901**

England won the toss. England 1st Innings 464 (MacLaren 116) Australia 1st Innings 168 (Barnes 5/65) Australia 2nd Innings 172 (Braund 5/61) England won by an innings and 124 runs.

**Second Test 1901–02 Australia v England: M.C.G. January 1st, 2nd, 3rd and 4th 1902**

England won the toss. Australia 1st Innings 112  (Barnes 6/42) England 1st Innings 61 (Noble 7/17) Australia 2nd Innings 353 (Duff 104 Barnes 7/121) England 2nd Innings 175 (Noble 6/60) Australia won by 229 runs.

**Third test 1901–02 Australia v England: Adelaide Oval January 17th, 18th, 20th, 21st, 22nd & 23rd 1902**

England won the toss. England 1st Innings 388 (Braund n.o. 103 Hayward 90) Australia 1st Innings 321 (Hill 98 Gunn 5/76) England 2nd Innings 9 for 247 (Trumble 6/74) Australia 2nd Innings 6 for 315 (Hill 97) Australia won by 4 wickets.

**Fourth Test 1901–02 Australia v England: S.C.G. February 14th, 15th, 17th &18th 1902**

England won the toss. England 1st Innings 317 (MacLaren 92) Australia 1st Innings 299 England 2nd Innings 99 (Saunders 5/43 Noble 5/54) Australia 2nd Innings 3 for 121 Australia won by 7 wickets.

**Fifth Test 1901–02 Australia v England: M.C.G. Feb. 28th March 1st, 3rd & 4th 1902**

Australia won the toss. Australia 1st Innings 144 England 1st Innings 189 (Trumble 5/62) Australia 2nd Innings 255 (Hill 87 Braund 5/95) England 2nd Innings 178 (Noble 6/98) Australia won by 32 runs.

**First Test 1902 England v Australia: Edgbaston Birmingham May 29th, 30th & 31st 1902**

England won the toss. England 1st innings 9 dec for 376 (Tyldesley 138 Australia 1st Innings 36 (Rhodes 7/17) Australia 2nd Innings 2 for 46 Match drawn.

**Second Test 1902 England v Australia: Lord's C.G. London June 12th, 13th (no play) 14th (no play) 1902**

England won the toss. England 1st Innings 2 for 102. Match drawn.

**Third Test 1902 England v Australia: Bramall Lane Sheffield July 3rd, 4th & 5th 1902**

Australia won the toss. Australia 1st Innings 194 (Barnes 6/49) England 1st Innings 145 (Saunders 5/50 Noble 5/51) Australia 2nd Innings 289 (Hill 119 Rhodes 5/63) England 2nd Innings 195 (Noble 6/52) Australia won by 143 runs.

**Fourth Test 1902 England v Australia: Old Trafford Manchester July 24th, 25th & 26th 1902**

Australia won the toss. Australia 1st Innings 299 (Trumper 104 Lockwood 6/48) England 1st Innings 262 (Jackson 128 ) Australia 2nd Innings 86 (Lockwood 5/28) England 2nd Innings 120 (Trumble 6/53) Australia won by 3 runs.

**Fifth Test 1902 England v Australia: Kennington Oval London August 11th, 12th & 13th 1902**

Australia won the toss. Australia 1st innings 324 (Hirst 5/77) England 1st Innings 183 (Trumble 8/65) Australia 2nd Innings 121 (Lockwood 5/45) England 2nd Innings 9 for 263 (Jessop 104) England won by 1 wicket.

**First Test 1903–04 Australia v England: S.C.G. December 11th, 12th, 14th, 15th, 16th & 17th 1903**

Australia won the toss. Australia 1st Innings 285 (Noble 133 ) England 1st Innings 577 (Foster 287 Braund 102 ) Australia 2nd innings 485 Trumper n.o. 185 Rhodes 5/94) England 2nd Innings 5 for 194 (Hayward 91 ) England won by 5 wickets.

**Second Test 1903–04 Australia v England:  M.C.G. January 1st, 2nd, 4th & 5th 1904**

England won the toss. England 1st innings 9 for 315 (Tyldesley 97) Australia 1st Innings 122 (Rhodes 7/56) England 2nd Innings 9 for 103 (Trumble 5/34) Australia 2nd Innings 111 (Rhodes 8/68) England won by 185 runs.

**Third Test 1903–04 Australia v England: Adelaide Oval January 15th, 16th, 18th, 19th and 20th 1904**

Australia won the toss. Australia !st Innings 388 (Trumper 113 England 1st Innings 245 Australia 2nd Innings 351 (Gregory 112 ) England 2nd Innings 278  Australia won by 216 runs.

**Fourth Test 1903–04 Australia v England: S.C.G. February 26th, 27th, 29th (no play) March 1st, 2nd & 3rd 1904**

England won the toss. England 1st innings 249 (Noble 7/100) Australia 1st Innings 131 England 2nd Innings 210 Australia 2nd Innings 171 (Bosanquet 6/51) England won by 157 runs.

**Fifth Test 1903–04 Australia v England: M.C.G. March 5th, 7th & 8th 1904**

Australia won the toss. Australia 1st Innings 247 (Trumper 88Braund 8/81) England 1st Innings 61 (Cotter 6/40) Australia 2nd Innings 133 (Hirst 5/48) England 2nd Innings 9 for 101 (Trumble 7/28) Australia won by 218 runs.

**First Test 1905 England v Australia: Trent Bridge Nottingham May 29th, 30th & 31st 1905**

England won the toss. England 1st Innings 196 ( Laver 7/64) Australia 1st Innings 9 for 221  (Jackson 5/52) England 2nd Innings 5 dec 426 (MacLaren 140 Australia 2nd Innings 188 (Bosanquet 8/107) England won by 213 runs.

**Second Test 1905 England v Australia: Lord's C.G. London June 15th, 16th & 17th (no play) 1905**

England won the toss. England 1st Innings 282 Australia 1st Innings 181 England 2nd Innings 5 for 151 Match drawn.

### Third Test 1905 England v Australia: Headingley Leeds July 3rd, 4th & 5th 1905

England won the toss. England 1st Innings 301 (Jackson n.o.144 Australia 1st Innings 195 (Warren 5/57) England 2nd Innings 5 dec 295 (Tyldesley 100 Armstrong 5/122) Australia 2nd Innings 7 for 224 Match drawn.

### Fourth Test 1905 England v Australia: Old Trafford Manchester July 24th, 25th & 26th 1905

England won the toss. England 1st Innings 446 (Jackson 113 McLeod 5/125) Australia 1st Innings 197 Australia 2nd Innings 169 England won by an innings and 80 runs.

### Fifth Test 1905 England v Australia: Kennington Oval London August 14th, 15th & 16th 1905

England won the toss. England 1st Innings 430 (Fry144Cotter 7/148) Australia 1st Innings 363 (Duff 146 Brearley 5/110) England 2nd Innings 6 dec for 261 (Tyldesley n.o.112)  Australia 2nd Innings 4 for 124 Match drawn.

### First Test 1907–08 Australia v England: S.C.G. December 13th, 14th, 16th, 17th, 18th (no Play) 19th 1907

England won the toss. England 1st Innings 273 (Gunn 119 Cotter 6/101) Australia 1st Innings 300 (Hill 87 Fielder 6/82) England 2nd Innings 300  Australia 2nd Innings 8 for 275 Australai won by 2 wickets.

### Second Test 1907–08 Australia v England: M.C.G. January 1st, 2nd, 3rd, 4th, 6th & 7th 1908

Australia won the toss. Australia 1st Innings 266 (Crawford 5/79) England 1st Innings 382 (Hutchings 126 Cotter 5/142) Australia 2nd Innings 397 (Barnes 5/72) England 2nd Innings 9 for 282 England won by 1 wicket.

### Third Test 1907–08 Australia v England: Adelaide Oval January 10th, 11th, 13th, 14th, 15th, 16th 1908

Australia won the toss. Australia 1st Innings 285 England 1st Innings 363 Australia 2nd Innings 506 (Hill 160 Hartigan 116

England 2nd Innings 183 O'Connor 5/40 Saunders 5/65) Australia won by 245 runs.

**Fourth Test 1907–08 Australia v England: M.C.G. February 7th, 8th, 10th& 11th 1908**

Australia won the toss. Australia 1st Innings 214 (Crawford 5/48) England 1st Innings 105 (Saunders 5/28) Australia 2nd Innings 385 (Armstrong n.o. 133 England 2nd Innings 186 Australia won by 308 runs.

**Fifth Test 1907–08 Australia v England:  S.C.G. February 21st, 22nd, 24th, 25th, 26th & 27th 1908**

England won the toss. Australia 1st Innings 137 (Barnes 7/60) England 1st Innings 281 (Gunn n.o. 122) England 2nd Innings 229 (Saunders 5/82) Australia won by 49 runs.

**First Test 1909 England v Australia: Edgbaston Birmingham May 27th, 28th & 29th 1909**

Australia won the toss. Australia 1st Innings 74 (Blythe 6/44) England 1st Innings 121 (Armstrong 5/27 Australia 2nd Innings 151 (Hirst 5/58 Blythe 5/58) England 2nd Innings 0 for 105 England won by 10 wickets.

**Second Test 1909 England v Australia: Lord's C.G. London June 14th, 15th & 16th 1909**

Australia won the toss. England 1st Innings 269  Australia 1st Innings 350 (Ransford n.o. 143 Relf 5/85) England 2nd innings 121 (Armstrong 6/35) Australia 2nd Innings 1 for 41 Australia won by 9 wickets.

**Third Test 1909 England v Australia: Headingley Leeds July 1st, 2nd & 3rd 1909**

Australia won the toss. Australia 1st Innings 188 England 1st Innings 9 for 182 (Macartney 7/58) Australia 2nd innings 207(Barnes 6/63) England 2nd Innings 9 for 87 (Cotter 5/38) Australia won by 126 runs.

**Fourth Test 1909 England v Australia: Old Trafford Manchester July 26th, 27th & 28th 1909**

Australia won the toss. Australia 1st Innings 147 (Barnes 5/56

Blythe 5/63) England 1st Innings 119 (Laver 8/31) Australia 2nd Innings 9 dec for 279 (Rhodes 5/83) England 2nd Innings 3 for 108 Match drawn.

## Fifth Test 1909 England v Australia: Kennington Oval London August 9th, 10th & 11th 1909

Australia won the toss. Australia 1st Innings 325 (Bardsley 136 Carr 5/146) England 1st Innings 352 (Sharp 105 Cotter 6/95) Australia 2nd Innings 5 dec for 339 (Bardsley 130 England 2nd Innings 3 for 104 Match drawn.

## First test 1911–12 Australia v England: S.C.G. December 15th, 16th, 18th, 19th, 20th & 21st 1911

Australia won the toss. Australia 1st Innings 447 (Trumper 113 Minnett 90) England 1st Innings 318 (Hordern 5/85) Australia 2nd Innings 308 (Foster 5/92) England 2nd Innings 291 (Hordern 7/90) Australia won by 146 runs

## Second Test 1911–12 Australia v England: M.C.G. December 30th 1911 January 1st, 2nd & 3rd 1912

Australia won the toss. Australia 1st Innings 184 (Barnes 5/34) England 1st Innings 265 (Hearne 114) Australia 2nd Innings 299 (Armstrong 90  Foster 6/91) England 2nd Innings 2 for 219 England won by 8 wickets.

## Third test 1911–12 Australia v England: Adelaide Oval January 12th, 13th, 15th, 16th, 17th 1912

Australia won the toss. Australia 1st Innings 133 (Foster 5/36) England 1st Innings 501 (Hobbs 187) Australia 2nd Innings 476 (Hill 98 Barnes 5/105) England 2nd Innings 3 for 112 England won by 7 wickets.

## Fourth Test 1911–12 Australia v England: M.C.G. February 9th, 10th, 12th, 13th 1912

England won the toss. Australia 1st Innings 191 (Barnes 5/74) England 1st Innings 589 (Hobbs 178 Rhodes 179) Australia 2nd Innings 173 (Douglas 5/ 46) England won by an innings and 225 runs.

## Fifth Test 1911–12 Australia v England: S.C.G. February 23rd, 24th 26th (no play) March 1st 1912

England won the toss. England 1st Innings 324 ( Woolley n.o. 133Hordern 5/95) Australia 1st Innings 176 England 2nd Innings 214 (Hordern 5/66) Australia 2nd Innings 292 England won by 70 runs.

### First Test 1912 England v Australia: Lord's C.G. London June 24th, 25th & 26th 1912

England won the toss. England 1st Innings 7 dec for 310 (Hobbs 107 ) Australia 1st Innings 7 for 282 (Macartney 99) Match drawn.

### Second Test 1912 England v Australia: Old Trafford Manchester July 29th, 30th, 31st (no play) 1912

England won the toss. England 1st Innings 203 (Rhodes 92 ) Australia 1st Innings 0 for 14 Match drawn.

### Third Test 1912 England v Australia: Kennington Oval London August 19th, 20th, 21st & 22nd 1912

England won the toss. England 1st Innings 245 Australia 1st Innings 111 (Barnes 5/30 Woolley 5/39) England 2nd Innings 175 (Fry 79 Hazlitt 7/25) Australia 2nd Innings 65 (Woolley 5/20) England won by 244 runs.

### First Test 1920–21 Australia v England: S.C.G. December 17th, 18th, 20th, 21st & 22nd 1920

Australia won the toss. Australia 1st Innings 267 England 1st Innings  190 Australia 2nd Innings 581 (Collins 104 Armstrong 158 England 2nd Innings 281 Australia won by 377 runs.

### Second Test 1920–21 Australia v England: M.C.G. January 1st, 3rd & 4th 1921

Australia won the toss. Australia 1st Innings 499 (Pellew 116 Gregory 100 England 1st Innings 9 for 251 (Hobbs 122 Gregory 7/69) England 2nd Innings 9 for 157 Australia won by an innings and 91 runs.

### Third Test 1920–21 Australia v England: Adelaide Oval January 14th, 15th, 17th, 18th, 19th & 20th 1921

Australia won the toss. Australia !st Innings 354 (Collins 162 Parkin5/60) England 1st Innings 447 (Russell n.o. 135Mailey 5/160) Australia 2nd Innings 582 (Kelleway 147 Armstrong 121 Pellew 104 England 2nd Innings 370 (Hobbs 123 Mailey 5/142) Australia won by

119 runs.

## Fourth Test 1920–21 Australia v England: M.C.G. February 11th, 12th, 14th, 15th, 16th 1921

England won the toss. England 1st Innings 284 (Makepeace 117) Australia 1st Innings 389 (Armstrong n.o. 123 Fender 5/122) England 2nd Innings 315 (Mailey 9/121) Australia 2nd Innings 2 for 211 Australia won by 8 wickets.

## Fifth Test 1920–21 Australia v England: S.C.G. February 225th, 26th 28th March 1st 1921

England won the toss. England 1st Innings 204 Australia 1st Innings 392 (Macartney 170 Fender 5/90) England 2nd Innings 280(Mailey 5/119) Australia 2nd Innings 1 for 93 Australia won by 9 wickets.

## First Test 1921 England v Australia: Trent Bridge Nottingham May 28th & 30th 1921

England won the toss. England 1st Innings 112 (Gregory 6/58) Australia 1st Innings 232 England 2nd Innings 147 (McDonald 5/32 Australia 2nd Innings 0 for 30 Australia won by 10 wickets.

## Second Test 1921 England v Australia: Lord's C.G. London June 11th, 13th & 14th 1921

England won the toss. England 1st Innings 187 (Woolley 95) Australia 1st Innings 342 (Bardsley 88) England 2nd Innings 283 (Woolley 93 ) Australia 2nd Innings 2 for 131 Australia won by 8 wickets.

## Third Test 1921 England v Australia: Headingly Leeds July 2nd, 4th & 5th 1921

Australia won the toss. Australia 1st Innings 407 (Macartney 115 England 1st Innings 9 for 259 Australia 2nd Innings 7 dec for 273 (Andrews 92) England 2nd Innings 9 for 202 Australia won by 219 runs.

## Fourth Test 1921 England v Australia: Old Trafford Manchester July 23rd (no play) 25th & 26th 1921

England won the toss. England 1st Innings 4 dec for 362 (Russell 101) Australia !st Innings 175 (Parkin 5/38) England 2nd Innings 1 for

44 Match drawn.

**Fifth Test 1921 England v Australia: Kennington Oval London August 13th, 15th & 16th 1921**

England won the toss. England 1st Innings 8 dec for 403 (Mead n.o. 182 McDonald 5/143) Australia 1st Innings 389 (Andrews 94 ) England 2nd Innings 2 for 244 (Russell n.o. 102 Brown 84) Match drawn.

**First Test 1924–25 Australia v England: S.C.G. December 19th, 20th, 22nd, 23rd, 24th, 26th & 27th 1924**

Australia won the toss. Australia 1st Innings 450 (Collins 114 Ponsford 110 Tate 6/130) England 1st Innings 298 (Hobbs 115 Gregory 5/111) Australia 2nd Innings 452 (Taylor 108 Tate 5/98) England 2nd Innings 411 (Sutcliffe 115 Woolley 123 Australia won by 193 runs.

**Second Test 1924–25 Australia v England:  M.C.G. January 1st, 2nd, 3rd, 5th, 6th, 7th & 8th 1925**

Australia won the toss. Australia 1st Innings 600 (Ponsford 128 Richardson 138 Tate 6/130) England 1st Innings 479 (Hobbs 154 Sutcliffe 176 ) Australia 2nd Innings 250 (Taylor 90 Tate 6/99) England 2nd Innings 290 (Sutcliffe 127 Mailey 5/92) Australia won by 81 runs.

**Third Test 1924–25 Australia v England: Adelaide Oval January 16th, 17th, 19th, 20th, 21st, 22nd & 23rd 1925.**

Australia won the toss. Australia 1st Innings 489 (Ryder n.o. 201) England 1st Innings 365 (Hobbs 119 Hendren 92 ) Australia 2nd Innings 250 (Ryder 88 )

England 2nd Innings 363 Australia won by 11 runs.

**Fourth Test 1924–25 Australia v England:  M.C.G. February 13th, 14th, 16th, 17th & 18th 1925**

England won the toss. England 1st Innings 548 (Sutcliffe 143) Australia 1st Innings 269 Australia 2nd Innings 250 ( Tate 5/75) England won by an innings and 29 runs.

**Fifth Test 1924–25 Australia v England: S.C.G. February 27th, 28th, March 2nd, 3rd & 4th 1925**

Australia won the toss. Australia 1st Innings 295 (Ponsford 80) England 1st Innings 167 (Grimmett 5/45) Australia 2nd Innings 325 (Andrews 80 Tate 5/115) England 2nd Innings 146 (Grimmett 6/37) Australia won by 307 runs.

**First Test 1926 England v Australia: Trent Bridge Nottingham June 12th, 14th (no play) 15th (no play) 1926.**

England won the toss. England 1st Innings 0 for 32 Match drawn.

**Second Test 1926 England v Australia: Lord's C.G. London June 26th, 28th & 29th 1926**

Australia won the toss. Australia 1st Innings 383 (Bardsley 193) England 1st Innings 3 dec for 475 ( Hobbs 119 Hendren n.o. 127) Australia 2nd Innings 5 for 194 (Macartney 133) Match drawn.

**Third Test 1926 England v Australia: Headingley Leeds July 10th, 12th & 13th 1926**

England won the toss. Australia 1st Innings 494 (Woodfull 141 Macartney 151 Richardson 100) England 1st Innings 294 (Grimmett 5/88) England 2nd Innings 3 for 254 (Hobbs 88 Sutcliffe 94) Match drawn

**Fourth Test 1926 England v Australia: Old Trafford Manchester July 24th, 26th & 27th 1926**

Australia won the toss. Australia 1st Innings 335 (Woodfull 117 Macartney 109) England 5 for 305 Match drawn.

**Fifth Test 1926 England v Australia: Kennington oval London August 14th, 16th, 17th & 18th 1926**

England won the toss. England 1st Innings 280 (Mailey 6/138) Australia 1st Innings 302 England 2nd Innings 436 (Hobbs 100 Sutcliffe 161 Australia 2nd Innings 125 England won by 289 runs.

# Australia v England Test results No. 3

**First Test 1928–29 Australia v England: Exhibition Ground Brisbane November 30th, Dec. 1st, 3rd, 4th & 5th 1928**

England won the toss. England 1st Innings 521 (Hendren 169) Australia 1st Innings 9 for 122 (Larwood 6/32) England 2nd Innings 8 dec for 342 (Grimmett 6/131) Australia 2nd Innings 8 for 66 England won by 675 runs.

**Second Test 1928–29 Australia v England: S.C.G. December 14th, 15th, 17th, 18th, 19th & 20th 1928**

Australia won the toss. Australia 1st Innings 9 for 253 (Geary 5/35) England 1st Innings 636 (Hammond 251 ) Australia 2nd Innings 9 for 397 (Hendry 112) England 2nd Innings 2 for 16 England won by 8 wickets.

**Third test 1928–29 Australia v England: M.C.G. Dec. 29th, 31st 1928 Jan. 1st, 2nd, 3rd, 4th & 5th 1929**

Australia won the toss. Australia 1st Innings 397 (Kippax 100 Ryder 112 ) England 1st Innings 417 (Hammond 200 Blackie 6/94) Australia 2nd Innings 351 (Woodfull 107 Bradman 112 White 5/107) England 2nd Innings 7 for 332 (Sutcliffe 135 ) England won by 3 wickets.

**Fourth Test 1928–29 Australia v England: Adelaide Oval February 1st, 2nd, 4th, 5th, 6th, 7th & 8th 1929**

England won the toss. England 1st Innings 334 (Hammond n.o.119 Grimmett 5/102) Australia 1st Innings 369 (Jackson 164 White 5/130) England 2nd Innings 383 (Hammond 177 Jardine 98) Australia 2nd Innings 336 (White 8/126) England won by 12 runs.

**Fifth Test 1928–29 Australia v England: M.C.G. March 8th, 9th, 11th, 12th, 13th, 14th, 15th, 16th 1929**

England won the toss. England 1st Innings 519 (Hobbs 142 Hendren 95 Leyland 137 Australia 1st Innings 491 (Woodfull 102 Bradman 123 Geary 5/105) England 2nd Innings 257 (Wall 5/66) Australia 2nd Innings 5 for 287 Australia won by 5 wickets.

**First Test 1930 England v Australia: Trent Bridge Nottingham July 13th, 14th, 16th & 17th 1930**

England won the toss. England 1st Innings 270 (Grimmett 5/107) Australia 1st Innings 144  England 2nd Innings 9 for 302 (Grimmett 5/94) Australia 2nd Innings 335 (Bradman 131) England won by 93 runs.

**Second Test 1930 England v Australia: Lord's C.G. London June 27th, 28th, 30th July 1st 1930**

England won the toss. England 1st Innings 425 (Duleepsinhji 173) Australia 1st Innings 6 dec for 729 (Woodfull 155 Bradman 254 England 2nd Innings 375 (Chapman 121 Grimmett 6/167) Australia 2nd Innings 3 for 72 Australia won by 7 wickets.

### Third Test 1930 England v Australia: Headingley Leeds July 11th, 12th, 14th & 15th

Australia won the toss. Australia 1st Innings 566 (Bradman 334 Tate 5/124) England 1st Innings 391 (Hammond 113 Grimmett 5/135) England 2nd Innings 3 for 95 Match drawn.

### Fourth Test 1930 England v Australia: Old Trafford Manchester July 25th, 26th, 28th, 29th (no play) 1930

Australia won the toss. Australia 1st Innings 345 England 1st Innings 8 for 251 Match drawn.

### Fifth Test 1930 England v Australia: Kennington Oval London August 16th, 18th, 19th, 20th (no play) 22nd 1930

England won the toss. England 1st Innings 405 (Sutcliffe 181) Australia 1st Innings 695 (Ponsford 110 Bradman 232 Peebles 6/204) England 2nd Innings 251 (Hornibrook 7/92) Australia won by an innings and 39 runs.

### First Test 1932–33 Australia v England: S.C.G. December 2nd, 3rd, 5th, 6th & 7th 1932

Australia won the toss. Australia 1st Innings (McCabe n.o. 187 Larwood 5/96) England 1st Innings 524 (Sutcliffe 194 Hammond 112 Nawab of Pataudi 102) Australia 2nd Innings 164 (Larwood 5/28) England 2nd Innings 0 for 1 England won by 10 wickets.

### Second Test 1932–33 Australia v England: M.C.G. Dec. 30th, 31st, Jan. 2nd and 3rd 1933

Australia won the toss. Australia 1st Innings 228 England 1st Innings 169 (O'Reilly 5/63) Australia 2nd Innings 191 (Bradman n.o. 103) England 2nd Innings 139 (O'Reilly 5/66) Australia won by 111 runs.

### Third Test 1932–33 Australia v England: Adelaide Oval January 13th, 14th, 16th, 17th, 18th & 19th 1933

England won the toss. England 1st Innings 341 (Wall 5/72)

Australia 1st Innings 9 for 222 England 2nd Innings 412 Australia 2nd Innings for 193  England won by 338 runs.

**Fourth Test 1932–33 Australia v England: Brisbane C.G. February 10th, 11th, 13th, 14th, 15th & 16th 1933**

Australia won the toss. Australia 1st Innings 340 England 1st Innings 356 Australia 2nd Innings 175  England 2nd Innings 4 for 162 England won by 6 wickets.

**Fifth Test 1932–33 Australia v England: S.C.G. February 23rd, 24th, 25th, 27th & 28th 1933**

Australia won the toss. Australia 1st Innings 435 England 1st Innings 454 (Hammond 101 Larwood 98 Australia 2nd Innings 182 (Verity 5/33) England 2nd Innings 2 for 168 England won by 8 wickets.

**First test 1934 England v Australia: Trent Bridge Nottingham June 8th, 9th, 11th & 12th 1934**

Australia won the toss. Australia 1st Innings 374 (Chipperfield 99 Farnes 5/102) England 1st Innings 268 (Grimmett 5/81) Australia 2nd Innings 8 dec for 273 (Farnes 5/77) England 2nd Innings 141 (O'Reilly 7/54) Australia won by 238 runs.

**Second Test 1934 England v Australia: Lord's C.G. London June 22nd, 23rd & 25th 1934**

England won the toss. England 1st Innings 440 (Leyland 109 Ames 120 Australia 1st Innings 284 (Brown 105 Verity 7/61) Australia 2nd Innings 118 (Verity 8/43) England won by an innings and 38 runs.

**Third Test 1934 England v Australia: Old Trafford Manchester July 6th, 7th, 9th & 10th 1934**

England won the toss. England 1st Innings 9 dec 627 (Hendren 132 Leyland 153 O"Reilly 7/189) Australia 491 (McCabe 137) England 2nd Innings 0 dec for 123 Australia 2nd Innings 1 for 66 Match drawn.

**Fourth Test 1934 England v Australia: Headingley Leeds July 20th, 21st, 23rd, 24th 1934**

England won the toss. England 1st Innings 200 Australia 1st

Innings 584 (Ponsford 181 Bradman 304) England 2nd Innings 6 for 229 Match drawn.

**Fifth Test 1934 England v Australia: Kennington Oval London August 18th, 20th, 21st & 22nd 1934**

Australia won the toss. Australia 1st Innings 701 (Ponsford 266 Bradman 244) England 1st Innings 8 for 321 (Leyland 101) Australia 2nd Innings 327 (Clark 5/95) England 2nd Innings 9 for 145 (Grimmett 5/64) Australia won by 562 runs.

**First Test 1936–37 Australia v England: Brisbane C.G. December 4th, 5th, 7th, 8th & 9th 1936**

England won the toss. England 1st Innings 358 (Leyland 126 O"Reilly 5/102) Australia 1st Innings 234 (Fingleton 100 Voce 6/41) England 2nd Innings 256 (Ward 6/102) Australia 2nd Innings 9 for 58 (Allen 5/36) England won by 322 runs.

**Second Test 1936–37 Australia v England: S.C.G. December 18th, 19th, 21st & 22nd 1936**

England won the toss. England 1st Innings 6 dec for 426 (Hammond n.o. 231) Australia 1st Innings 9 for 80 Australia 2nd Innings 324 England won by an innings and 22 runs.

**Third Test 1936–37 Australia v England: M.C.G. January 1st, 2nd, 4th, 5th, 6th & 7th 1937**

Australia won the toss. Australia 1st Innings 9 dec for 200 England 1st Innings 9 dec for 76 (Sievers 5/21) Australia 2nd Innings 564 (Fingleton 136 Bradman 270) England 2nd Innings 323 (Leyland n.o. 111 (Fleetwood–Smith 5/124) Australia won by 365 runs.

**Fourth Test 1936–37 Australia v England: Adelaide Oval January 29th, 30th, Feb. 1st, 2nd, 3rd & 4th 1937**

Australia won the toss. Australia 1st Innings 288 (McCabe 88) England 1st Innings 330 (Barnett 129) Australia 2nd Innings 433 (Bradman 212 Hammond 5/57) England 2nd Innings 243 (Fleetwood–Smith 6/110) Australia won by 148 runs.

**Fifth Test 1936–37 Australia v England: M.C.G. February 26th, 27th, March 1st, 2nd & 3rd 1937**

Australia won the toss. Australia 1st Innings 604 (Bradman 169

McCabe 112 Badcock 118 Farnes 6/96) England 1st Innings 239 (O'Reilly 5/51) England 2nd Innings 165 Australia won by an innings and 200 runs.

**First Test 1938 England v Australia: Trent Bridge Nottingham June 10th, 11th, 13th & 14th 1938**

England won the toss. England 1st Innings 8 dec for 658 (Barnett 126 Hutton 100 Paynter n.o. 216 Compton 102) Australia 1st Innings 411 (McCabe 232) Australia 2nd Innings 6 for 427 (Brown 133 Bradman n.o. 144) Match drawn.

**Second Test 1938 England v Australia: Lord's C.G. London June 24th, 25th, 27th & 28th 1938**

England won the toss. England 1st Innings 494 (Hammond 240 Paynter 99) Australia 1st Innings 422 (Brown n.o. 206) England 2nd Innings 8 for 242 Australia 2nd Innings 6 for 204 (Bradman n.o. 102) Match drawn.

**Third Test 1938 England v Australia: Headingley Leeds July 22nd, 23rd, 25th 1938**

England won the toss. England 1st Innings 223 (O'Reilly 5/66) Australia 1st Innings 242 (Bradman 103)  England 2nd Innings 123 (O'Reilly 5/56) Australia 2nd Innings 5 for 107 Australia won by 5 wickets.

**Fourth Test 1938 England v Australia:  Kennington Oval London August 20th, 22nd, 23rd & 24th 1938**

England won the toss. England 1st Innings 7 dec for 903 (Hutton 364 Leyland 187 Hardstaff jr n.o. 169 Australia 1st Innings 8 for 201 (Bowes 5/49) Australia 2nd Innings 8 for 123 England won by an innings and 579 runs.

**First test 1946–47 Australia v England:  Brisbane C.G. November 29th, 30th Dec. 2nd, 3rd & 4th 1946**

Australia won the toss. Australia 1st Innings 645 (Bradman 187 Hassett 128 McCool 98 Wright 5/167) England 1st Innings 141 (Miller 7/60) England 2nd Innings 172 (Toshack 6/82) Australia won by an innings and 332 runs.

**Second Test 1946–47 Australia v England: S.C.G. December**

**13th, 14th, 16th, 17th, 18th & 19th 1946**

England won the toss. England 1st Innings 255 (Johnson 6/42) Australia 1st Innings 8 dec for 659 (Barnes 234 Bradman 234) England 2nd Innings 371 (Edrich 119 (McCool 5/109) Australia won by an innings and 33 runs.

**Third Test 1946–47 Australia v England: M.C.G. Jan 1st, 2nd, 3rd, 4th, 6th & 7th 1947**

Australia won the toss. Australia 1st Innings 365 (McCool n.o. 104) England 1st Innings 351 (Edrich 89) Australia 2nd Innings 536 (Morris 155 Lindwall 100) England 2nd Innings 7 for 310 (Washbrook 112) Match drawn.

**Fourth Test 1946–47 Australia v England: Adelaide Oval January 31st, February 1st, 3rd, 4th, 5th & 6th 1947**

England won the toss. England 1st Innings 460 (Hutton 94 Compton 147) Australia 1st Innings 487 (Morris 122 Miller n.o. 141) England 2nd Innings 8 dec for 340 (Compton n.o. 103) Australia 2nd Innings 1 for 215 (Morris n.o. 124) Match drawn.

**Fifth Test 146–47 Australia v England: S.C.G. February 28th, March 1st (no play) 3rd, 4th & 5th 1947**

England won the toss. England 1st Innings 9 dec for 280 (Hutton retired hurt 122 Lindwall 7/63) Australia 1st Innings 253 (Wright 7/105) England 2nd Innings 9 dec for 186 (McCool 5/44) Australia 2nd Innings 5 for 214 Australia won by 5 wickets.

**First Test 1948 England v Australia: Trent Bridge Nottingham June 10th, 11th, 12th, 14th & 15th 1948**

England won the toss. England 1st Innings 165 (Johnston 5/36) Australia 1st Innings 509 (Bradman 138 Hassett 137) England 2nd Innings 441 (Compton 184 ) Australia 2nd Innings 2 for 98 Australia won by 8 wickets.

**Second Test 1948 England v Australia: Lord's C.G. London June 24th, 25th, 26th, 28th & 29th 1948**

Australia won the toss. Australia 1st Innings 350 (Morris 105) England 1st Innings 215 (Lindwall 5/70) Australia 7 dec for 460 (Barnes 141) England 2nd Innings 186 (Toshack 5/40) Australia won by 409 runs.

**Third Test 1948 England v Australia: Old Trafford Manchester July 8th, 9th, 10th, 12th (no play) 13th 1948**

England won the toss. England 1st Innings 363 (Compton n.o.145) Australia 1st Innings 9 dec for 221 England 2nd Innings 3 dec for 174 Australia 2nd Innings 1 for 92 Match drawn.

**Fourth Test 1948 England v Australia: Headingley Leeds July 22nd, 23rd, 24th 26th & 27th 1948**

England won the toss. England 1st Innings 496 (Washbrook 143 Edrich 111) Australia 1st Innings 458 (Harvey 112) England 2nd Innings 8 dec for 365 Australia 2nd Innings 3 for 404 (Morris 182 Bradman n.o. 173) Australia won by 7 wickets.

**Fifth Test 1948 England v Australia: Kennington Oval London August 14th, 16th, 17th & 18th 1948**

England won the toss. England 1st Innings 52 (Lindwall 6/20) Australia 1st Innings 399 (Morris 196 Hollies 5/131) England 2nd Innings 188 Australia won by an innings and 149 runs.

# Australia v England Test results No. 4

**First Test 1950–51 Australia v England: Brisbane C.G. December 1st, 2nd (no play) 4th & 5th 1950**

Australia won the toss. Australia 1st innings 228 England 1st Innings 7 dec for 68 (Johnston 5/35) Australia 2nd Innings 7 dec for 32 England 2nd Innings 122 (Hutton n.o. 62) Australia won by 70 runs.

**Second Test 1950–51 Australia v England:  M.C.G. December 22nd, 23rd, 26th & 27th 1950**

Australia won the toss. Australia 1st Innings 194 England 1st Innings 197 Australia 2nd Innings 181 England 2nd Innings 150 Australia won by 28 runs.

**Third Test 1950–51 Australia v England: S.C.G. January 5th, 6th, 8th & 9th 1951**

England won the toss. England 1st Innings 290 Australia 1st Innings 426 (Miller n.o. 145) England 2nd Innings 9 for 123 (Iverson

6/27) Australia won by an innings and 13 runs.

**Fourth Test 1950–51 Australia v England: Adelaide Oval February 2nd, 3rd, 5th, 6th, 7th & 8th 1951**

Australia won the toss. Australia 1st Innings 371 (Morris 206) England 1st Innings 272 (Hutton n.o. 156) Australia 2nd Innings 8 dec for 403 (Burke n.o. 101 England 2nd Innings 9 for 228 Australia won by 274 runs.

**Fifth Test 1950–51 Australia v England: M.C.G. February 23rd, 24th (no play) 26th, 27th & 28th 1951**

Australia won the toss. Australia 217 (Hassett 92 Bedser 5/46) England 1st Innings 320 (Simpson n.o. 156) Australia 2nd Innings 197 (Bedser 5/59) England 2nd Innings 2 for 95 England won by 8 wickets.

**First Test 1953 England v Australia: Trent Bridge Nottingham June 11th, 12th, 13th, 15th (no play) 16th 1953**

Australia won the toss. Australia 1st innings 249 (Hassett 115 Bedser 7/55) England 1st Innings 144 (Lindwall 5/57) Australia 2nd Innings 123 (Bedser 7/44) England 2nd Innings 1 for 120 Match drawn.

**Second Test 1953 England v Australia: Lord's C.G. London June 25th, 26th, 27th, 29th & 30th 1953**

Australia won the toss. Australia 1st Innings 346 (Hassett 104 Bedser 5/105) England 1st Innings 372 (Hutton 145 Lindwall 5/66) Australia 2nd Innings 368 (Miller 109 Morris 89) England 2nd Innings 7 for 282 (Watson 109) Match drawn.

**Third Test 1953 England v Australia: Old Trafford Manchester July 9th, 10th, 11th, 13th (no play) 14th 1953.**

Australia won the toss. Australia 1st Innings 318 (Harvey 122 Bedser 5/115) England 1st Innings 276 Australia 2nd Innings 8 for 35 Match drawn.

**Fourth Test 1953 England v Australia: Headingley Leeds July 23rd, 24th, 25th, 27th & 28th 1953**

Australia won the toss. England 1st innings 167 (Lindwall 5/54) Australia 1st Innings 266 (Bedser 6/95) England 2nd Innings 275

Australia 2nd Innings 4 for 147 Match drawn.

**Fifth Test 1953 England v Australia: Kennington Oval London August 15th, 17th, 18th & 19th 1953**

Australia won the toss. Australia 1st Innings 275 England 1st Innings 306 Australia 2nd Innings 162(Lock 5/45) England 2nd Innings 2 for 132 England won by 8 wickets.

**First Test 1954–55 Australia v England: Brisbane C.G. November 26th, 27th, 29th, 30th, Dec 1st 1954**

England won the toss. Australia 1st Innings 8 dec for 601 (Morris 153 Harvey 162 England 1st Innings 190 (Bailey 88) England 2nd Innings 257 (Edrich 88) Australia won by an innings and 154 runs.

**Second Test 1954–55 Australia v England: S.C.G. December 17th, 18th, 20th, 21st, 22nd 1954**

Australia won the toss. England 1st Innings 154 Australia 1st Innings 228 England 2nd Innings 296 (May 104) Australia 2nd Innings 184 (Harvey n.o. 92 Tyson 6/85) England won by 38 runs.

**Third Test 1954–55 Australia v England: M.C.G. Dec. 31st 1954 Jan 1st, 3rd, 4th & 5th 1955**

England won the toss. England 1st Innings 191 (Cowdrey 102) Australia 1st Innings 231 (Statham 5/60) England 2nd Innings 279 (May 91 Johnston 5/85) Australia 2nd Innings 111 (Tyson 7/27) England won by 128 runs.

**Fourth Test 1954–55 Australia v England: Adelaide Oval January 28th, 29th, 31st Feb. 1st & 2nd 1955**

Australia won the toss. Australia 1st Innings 323 England 1st Innings 341 Australia 2nd Innings 111 England 2nd Innings 5 for 97 England won by 5 wickets.

**Fifth test 1954–55 Australia v England: S.C.G. February 25th (no play) 28th (no play) March 1st, 2nd & 3rd 1955.**

Australia won the toss. England 1st Innings 7 for 371 (Graveney 111) Australia 1st Innings 221 (Wardle 5/79) Australia 2nd Innings 6 for 118 Match drawn.

**First Test 1956 England v Australia: Trent Bridge Nottingham**

**June 7th, 8th (no play) 9th, 11th & 12th 1956.**

England won the toss. England 1st Innings 8 dec for 217 Australia 1st Innings 9 dec for 148 England 2nd Innings 3 dec for 188 (Cowdrey 81) Australia 2nd Innings 3 for 120 Match drawn.

**Second Test 1956 England v Australia: Lord's C.G. London June 21st, 22nd, 23rd, 25th & 26th 1956**

Australia won the toss. Australia 1st Innings 285 England 1st Innings 171 (Miller 5/72) Australia 2nd Innings 257 (Benaud 97 Trueman 5/90) England 2nd Innings 186 (Miller 5/80) Australia won by 185 runs.

**Third Test 1956 England v Australia: Headingley Leeds July 12th, 13th 14th (no play) 16th & 17th 1956**

England won the toss. England 1st Innings 325 (May 101) Australia 1st Innings 143 (Laker 5/58) Australia 2nd Innings 140 (Laker 6/56) England won by an innings and 42 runs.

**Fourth Test 1956 England v Australia: Old Trafford Manchester July 26th, 27th, 28th, 30th & 31st 1956**

England won the toss. England 1st Innings 459 (Richardson 104 Sheppard 113) Australia 1st Innings 84 (Laker 9/37) Australia 2nd Innings 205 (McDonald 89 Laker 10/53) England won by an innings and 170 runs.

**Fifth Test 1956 England v Australia: Kennington Oval London August 23rd, 24th, 25th, 27th (no play) 28th 1956**

England won the toss. England 1st Innings 247 (Compton 94 R. Archer 5/53) Australia 1st Innings 202 England 2nd Innings 3 dec for 182 Australia 2nd Innings 5 for 27 Match drawn.

**First Test 1958–59 Australia v England: Brisbane C.G. December 5th, 6th, 8th, 9th & 10th 1958**

England won the toss. England 1st Innings 134 Australia 1st Innings 186 England 2nd Innings 198 Australia 2nd Innings 2/147 (O'Neill n.o. 71) Australia won by 8 wickets.

**Second Test 1958–59 Australia v England: M.C.G. Dec 31st 1958 January 1st, 2nd 3rd & 5th 1959**

England won the toss. England 1st Innings 259 (May 113

Davidson 6/64) Australia 1st Innings 308 (Harvey 167 Statham 7/57) England 2nd Innings 87 (Meckiff 6/38) Australia 2nd Innings 2 for 42 Australia won by 8 wickets.

**Third Test 1958–59 Australia v England: S.C.G. January 9th, 10th, 12th, 13th, 14th & 15th 1959**

England won the toss. England 1st Innings 219 (Benaud 5/83) Australia 1st Innings 357 (Laker 5/107) England 2nd Innings 7 dec for 287 (Cowdrey n.o. 100 May 92 Australia 2nd Innings 2 for 54 Match drawn.

**Fourth Test 1958–59 Australia v England: Adelaide Oval January 30th, 31st, Feb. 2nd, 3rd, 4th & 5th 1959**

England won the toss. Australia 1st Innings 476 (McDonald 170) England 1st Innings 240 (Cowdrey 84 Benaud 5/91) England 2nd Innings 270 Australia 2nd Innings 0 for 36 Australia won by 10 wickets.

**Fifth Test 1958–59 Australia v England: M.C.G. February 13th, 14th, 16th, 17th & 18th 1959**

Australia won the toss. England 1st Innings 205 Australia 1st Innings 351 (McDonald 133 Laker 5/107) England 2nd Innings 214 Australia 2nd Innings 1 for 69 Australia won by 9 wickets.

**First Test 1961 England v Australia: Edgbaston Birmingham June 8th, 9th, 10th, 12th & 13th 1961**

England won the toss. England 1st Innings 195 Australia 1st Innings 9 dec for 516 ((Harvey 114) England 2nd Innings 4 for 401 (Subba Row 112 Dexter 180) Match drawn.

**Second Test 1961 England v Australia: Lord's C.G. London June 22nd, 23r, 24th & 26th 1961**

England won the toss/ England 1st Innings 206 (Davidson 5/42) Australia 1st Innings 340 (Lawry 130) England 2nd Innings 202 (McKenzie 5/37) Australia 2nd Innings 5 for 71 Australia won by 5 wickets.

**Third Test 1961 England v Australia: Headingley Leeds July 6th, 7th & 8th 1961**

Australia won the toss. Australia 1st Innings 237 (Trueman 5/58) England 1st Innings 299 (Cowdrey 93 Davidson 5/63) Australia 2nd

Innings 120 (Trueman 6/30) England 2nd Innings 2 for 62 England won by 8 wickets.

**Fourth Test 1961 England v Australia: Old Trafford Manchester July 27th, 28th 29th, 31st August 1st 1961**

Australia won the toss. Australia 1st innings 190 (Statham 5/53) England 1st Innings 367 (May 95) Australia 2nd Innings 432 (Lawry 102) England 2nd Innings 201 (Benaud 6/70) Australia won by 54 runs.

**Fifth Test. 1961 England v Australia: Kennington Oval London august 17th, 18th, 19th, 21st & 22nd 1961**

England won the toss. England 1st Innings 256 Australia 1st Innings 494 (O'Neill 117 Burge 181) England 2nd Innings 8 for 370 (Subba Row 137 Mackay 5/121) Match drawn.

**First Test 1962–63 Australia v England: Brisbane C.G. November 30th, Dec. 1st, 3rd, 4th & 5th 1962**

Australia won the toss. Australia 1st Innings 404 (Booth 112) England 1st Innings 389 (Benaud 6/115) Australia 2nd Innings 4 dec for 362 (Lawry 98) England 2nd Innings 6 for 278 Match drawn.

**Second Test 1962–63 Australia v England: M.C.G. December 29th, 31st January 1st, 2nd & 3rd 1963**

Australia won the toss. Australia 1st Innings 316 England 1st Innings 331 (Cowdrey 113 Dexter 93 Davidson 6/75) Australia 2nd Innings 248 (Booth 103 Trueman 5/62) England 2nd Innings 3 for 237 (Sheppard 113) England won by 7 wickets.

**Third Test 1962–63 Australia v England: S.C.G. January 11th, 12th, 14th & 15th 1963**

England won the toss. England 1st Innings 279 (Simpson 5/57) Australia 1st Innings 319 (Simpson 91 Titmus 7/79) England 2nd innings 104 (Davidson 5/25) Australia 2nd Innings 2 for 67 Australia won by 8 wickets.

**Fourth Test 1962–63 Australia v England: Adelaide Oval January 25th, 26th, 28th, 29th & 30th 1963**

Australia won the toss. Australia 1st Innings 393 (Harvey 154 O'Neill 100) England 1st Innings 331 (McKenzie 5/89) Australia 2nd

Innings 293 England 2nd Innings 4 for 223 (Barrington n.o. 132) Match drawn.

**Fifth Test 1962–63 Australia v England: S.C.G. February 15th, 16th, 18th, 19th & 20th 1963**

England won the toss. England 1st Innings 321 (Barrington 101 ) Australia 1st Innings 349 (Burge 103 Titmus 5/103) England 2nd Innings 8 dec for 268 (Barrington 94 ) Australia 2nd Innings 4 for 152 Match drawn.

**First Test 1964 England v Australia: Trent Bridge Nottingham June 4th, 5th, 6th (no play) 8th & 9th 1964**

England won the toss. England 1st Innings 8 dec for 216 Australia 1st Innings 168 England 2nd Innings 9 dec for 193 (McKenzie 5/53) Australia 1st Innings 2 for 40 Match drawn.

**Second Test 1964 England v Australia: Lord's C.G. London June 18th (no play) 19th (no play) 20th, 22nd, 23rd 1964.**

England won the toss. Australia 1st Innings 176 (Trueman 5/48) England 1st Innings 246 (Edrich 120) Australia 2nd Innings 4 for 168 Match drawn.

**Third Test 1964 England v Australia: Headingley Leeds July 2nd, 3rd, 4th & 6th 1964**

England won the toss. England 1st Innings 268 (Hawke 5/75) Australia 1st Innings 389 (Burge 160) England 2nd Innings 229 (Barrington 85) Australia 2nd Innings 3 for 111 Australia won by 7 wickets.

**Fourth Test 1964 England v Australia: Old Trafford Manchester July 23rd, 24th, 25th, 27th & 28th 1964**

Australia won the toss. Australia 1st Innings 8 dec for 656 (Lawry 106 Simpson 311 Booth 98) England 1st Innings 611 (Dexter 174 Barrington 256McKenzie 7/153) Australia 2nd Innings 0 for 4 Match drawn.

**Fifth Test 1964 England v Australia: Kennington Oval London August 13th, 14th, 15th, 17th, 18th (no play) 1964**

England won the toss. England 1st Innings 182 (Hawke 6/47) Australia 1st Innings 379 (Lawry 94) England 2nd innings 4 for 381 (Boycott 113 Cowdrey n.o. 93) Match drawn.

**First Test 1965–66 Australia v England: Brisbane C.G. December 10th, 11th (no play) 13th, 14th & 15th 1965**

Australia won the toss. Australia 1st Innings 6 dec for 443 (Lawry 166 walters 155) England 1st Innings 280 (Philpott 5/90) England 2nd Innings 3 for 186 Match drawn.

**Second Test 1965–66 Australia v England: December 30th, 31st 1965 January 1st, 3rd & 4th 1966**

Australia won the toss. Australia 1st Innings 358 (Cowper 99) England 1st Innings 558 (Edrich 109 Cowdrey 104 McKenzie 5/134) Australia 2nd Innings 426 (Burge 120 Walters 115) England 2nd Innings 0 for 5

**Third Test 1965–66 Australia v England: S.C.G. January 7th, 8th, 10th & 11th 1966**

England won the toss. England 1st Innings 488 (Barber 185 Edrich 103 Hawke 7/105) Australia 1st Innings 221 (Brown 5/63) Australia 2nd Innings 174 England won by an innings and 93 runs.

**Fourth Test 1965–66 Australia v England: Adelaide Oval January 28th, 29th, 31st, February 1st 1966**

England won the toss. England 1st Innings 241 (McKenzie 6/48) Australia 1st Innings 516 (Simpson 225 Lawry 119 Jones 6/118) England 2nd Innings 266 (Barrington 102 Hawke 5/54) Australia won by an innings and 9 runs.

**Fifth Test 1965–66 Australia v England: M.C.G. February 11th, 12th, 14th, 15th (no play) 16th 1966**

England won the toss. England 1st Innings 9 dec for 485 (Barrington 115) Australia 1st Innings 8 dec for 543 (Lawry 108 Cowper 307) England 2nd Innings 3 for 69 Match drawn.

# Australia v England Test results no. 5

**England v Australia First Test 1968: Old Trafford Manchester June 6th, 7th, 8th, 10th & 11th 1968**

Australia won the toss. Australia 1st Innings 357 England 1st Innings 165 Australia 2nd Innings 220 (Pocock 6/79) England 2nd

Innings 253 Australia won by 159 runs.

**England v Australia Second Test 1968: Lord's C.G. June 20th, 21st, 22nd, 24th & 25th 1968**

England won the toss. England 1st Innings 7 dec for 351 Australia 1st Innings 9 dec for 78 (Brown 5/42) Australia 2nd Innings 4 for 127 Match drawn.

**England v Australia Third Test 1968: Edgbaston Birmingham July 11th (no play) 12th, 13th, 15th & 16th 1968**

England won the toss. England 1st Innings 409 (Cowdrey 104 Graveney 96) Australia 1st Innings 9 dec for 222 England 2nd Innings 3 dec for 142 Australia 1 for 68 Match drawn.

**England v Australia Fourth Test 1968: Headingley Leeds July 25th, 26th, 27th, 29th & 30th 1968**

Australia won the toss. Australia 1st Innings 315 England 1st Innings 302 (Connolly 5/72) Australia 2nd Innings 312 (Illingworth 6/87) England 2nd Innings 4 for 230 Match drawn.

**England v Australia Fifth Test 1968: Kennington Oval London August 22nd, 23rd, 24th, 26th & 27th 1968**

England won the toss. England 1st Innings 494 (Edrich 164 D'Oliveira 158) Australia 1st Innings 324 (Lawry 135) England 2nd Innings 181 Australia 2nd Innings 125 (Underwood 7/50) England won by 226 runs.

**Australia v England First Test 1970–71: Brisbane C.G. Nov. 27th, 28th, 29th, Dec. 1st & 2nd 1970**

Australia won the toss. Australia 1st Innings 433 (Stackpole 207 Snow 6/114) England 1st Innings 464 Australia 2nd Innings 214 (Shuttleworth 5/47) Australia 2nd Innings 1 for 39 Match drawn.

**Australia v England Second Test 1970–71: W.A.C.A. Perth Dec. 11th, 12th, 13th, 15th & 16th 1970**

Australia won the toss. England 1st Innings 397 (Luckhurst 131) Australia 1st Innings 440 (Redpath 171 G Chappell 108) England 2nd Innings 6 for 287 (Edrich 115) Australia 2nd Innings 3 for 100 Match drawn.

**Australia v England Third Test 1970–71: M.C.G. Dec. 31st 1970**

**Jan. 1st, 2nd, 4th & 5th 1971**

Match abandoned without a ball being bowled.

**Australia v England Fourth Test 1970–71: S.C.G. Jan. 9th, 10th, 11th, 13th & 14th 1971**

England won the toss. England 1st Innings 332 Australia 1st Innings 236 England 2nd Innings 5 for 319 (Boycott 142) Australia 2nd Innings 9 for 116 (Snow 7/40) England won by 299 runs.

**Australia v England Fifth Test 1970–71: M.C.G. Jan. 21st, 22nd, 23rd, 25th & 26th 1971**

Australia won the toss. Australia 1st Innings  9 dec for 493 (I Chappell 111 Marsh n.o. 92) England 1st Innings 392 (Luckhurst 109 D'Oliveira 117) Australia 2nd Innings 4 dec 169 England 2nd Innings 0 for 161 Match drawn.

**Australia v England Sixth Test 1970–71: Adelaide Oval Jan. 29th, 30th, Feb 1st, 2nd & 3rd 1971**

England won the toss. England 1st Innings 470 (Edrich 130 Lillee 5/84) Australia 1st Innings 235 England 2nd Innings 4 dec for 233 (Boycott n.o. 119) Australia 2nd Innings 3 for 328 (Stackpole 136 I Chappell 104) Match drawn.

**Australia v England 7th Test 1970–71: S.C.G. Feb. 12th, 13th, 14th, 16th & 17th 1971**

Australia won the toss. England 1st Innings 184 Australia 1st Innings 264 England 2nd Innings 302 Australia 2nd Innings 160 England won by 62 runs.

**England v Australia 1st Test 1972: Old Trafford Manchester June 8th, 9th, 10th, 12th & 13th 1972**

England won the toss. England 1st Innings 249 Australia 1st Innings 142 England 2nd Innings 234 (Lillee 6/66) Australia 2nd Innings 252 England won by 89 runs.

**England v Australia 2nd Test 1972: Lord's C.G. June 22nd, 23rd, 24th & 26th 1972**

England won the toss. England 1st Innings 272 (Massie 8/84) Australia 1st Innings 308 (G Chappell 131 Snow 5/57) England 2nd Innings 116 (Massie 8/53) Australia 2nd Innings 2 for 81 Australia won by 8 wickets.

**England v Australia 3rd Test 1972: Trent Bridge Nottingham July 13th, 14th, 15th, 17th & 18th 1972**

England won the toss. Australia 1st Innings 315 (Stackpole 114 Snow 5/92) England 1st innings 189 Australia 2nd Innings 4 dec for 324 (Edwards n.o. 170) England 2nd Innings 4 for 290 (Luckhurst 96) Match drawn.

**England v Australia 4th Test 1972: Headingley Leeds July 27th, 28th & 29th 1972**

Australia won the toss. Australia 1st Innings 146  England 1st Innings 263 (Mallett 5/114) Australia 2nd Innings 136 (Underwood 6/45) England 2nd Innings 1 for 21 England won by 9 wickets.

**England v Australia 5th Test 1972: Kennington Oval London August 10th, 11th, 12th, 14th, 15th & 16th 1972**

England won the toss. England 1st Innings 284 (Lillee 5/58) Australia 1st Innings 399 (I Chappell 118 G Chappell 113) England 2nd Innings 356 (Wood 90 Lillee 5/123) Australia 2nd Innings 5 for 242 Australia won by 5 wickets.

**Australia v England 1st Test 1974–75: Brisbane C.G. November 29th, 30th Dec. 1st, 3rd & 4th 1974**

Australia won the toss. Australia 1st Innings 309 (I Chappell 90) England 1st Innings 265 (Greig 110) Australia 2nd Innings 5 dec for 288 England 2nd Innings (Thomson 6/46) Australia won by 166 runs.

**Australia v England 2nd Test 1974–75: W.A.C.A. Perth Dec. 13th, 14th, 15th and 17th 1974**

Australia won the toss. England 1st Innings 208 Australia 1st Innings 481 (Edwards 115 Walters 103) England 2nd Innings 293 (Thomson 5/93) Australia 2nd Innings 1 for 23 Australia won by  9 wickets.

**Australia v England 3rd Test 1974–75:  M.C.G. Dec. 26th, 27th, 28th, 30th & 31st 1974**

Australia won the toss. England 1st Innings 242 Australia 1st Innings 241 (Willis 5/61) England 2nd Innings 244 (Amiss 90) Australia 2nd Innings 8 for 238  Match drawn.

## Australia v England 4th Test 1974–75: S.C.G. Jan. 4th, 5th, 6th, 8th & 9th 1975

Australia won the toss. Australia 1st Innings 405 (Arnold 5/ 86) England 1st Innings 295 Australia 2nd Innings 4 dec for 289 (Redpath 105 G Chappell 144) England 2nd Innings 228 Australia won by 171 runs.

## Australia v England 5th Test 1974–75: Adelaide Oval Jan. 25th (no play) 26th, 27th, 29th & 30th 1975

England won the toss. Australia 1st Innings 304 (Underwood 7/113) England 1st Innings 172 Australia 2nd Innings 5 dec for 272 England 2nd Innings 241 (Knott n.o. 106) Australia won by 163 runs.

## Australia v England 6th Test 1974–75: M.C.G. Feb. 8th, 9th, 10th, 12th & 13th 1975

Australia won the toss. Australia 1st Innings 152 (Lever 6/38) England 1st Innings 529 (Denness 188 Fletcher 146 Walker 8/143) Australia 2nd Innings 3/3 (G Chappell 102) England won by an innings and 4runs.

## England v Australia 1st Test 1975: Edgbaston Birmingham July 10th, 11th, 12th & 14th 1975

England won the toss. Australia 1st Innings 359 England 1st Innings 101 (Lillee 5/15 Walker 5/48) England 2nd Innings 173 (Thomson 5/38) Australia won by an innings and 85 runs.

## England v Australia 2nd Test 1975: Lord's C.G. July 31st, August 1st, 2nd, 4th & 5th 1975

England won the toss. England 1st Innings 315 (Greig 96) Australia 1st Innings 268 (Edwards 99) England 2nd Innings 7 dec for 436 (Edrich 175) Australia 2nd Innings 3 for 329 Match drawn.

## England v Australia 3rd Test 1975: Headingley Leeds August 14th, 15th, 16th, 18th, 19th (no play) 1975

England won the toss. England 1st Innings 288 (Gilmour 6/85) Australia 1st Innings 135 (Edmonds 5/28) England 2nd Innings 291 (Steele 92) Australia 2nd Innings 3 for 220 (McCosker n.o. 95) Match drawn.

**England v Australia 4th Test 1975: Kennington Oval London Aug. 28yh, 29th, 30th, Sep. 1st, 2nd & 3rd 1975**

Australia won the toss. Australia 1st Innings 9 dec for 532 (McCosker 127 I Chappell 192) England 1st Innings 191 England 2nd Innings 538 (Edrich 96 Woolmer 149) Australia 2nd Innings 2 for 40 Match drawn.

# Australia v England Test results no. 6

**Australia v England Only Test 1976–77: M.C.G. March 12th, 13th, 14th, 16th & 17th 1975**

England won the toss. Australia 1st Innings 138 England 1st Innings 95 (Lillee 6/26) Australia 2nd Innings 9 dec for 419 (Marsh n.o. 110) England 2nd Innings 417 (Randall 174 Lillee 5/139) Australia won by 45 runs.

**First Test 1977 England v Australia: Lord's C.G. June 16th, 17th, 18th, 20th & 21st 1977**

England won the toss. England 1st Innings 216 Australia 1st Innings 296(Sarjeant 81 Willis 7/78) England 2nd Innings 305 (Woolmer 120) Australia 2nd Innings 6 for 114 Match drawn.

**Second Test 1977 England v Australia: Old Trafford Manchester July 7th, 8th, 9th, 11th & 12th 1977**

Australia won the toss. Australia 1st Innings 297 (Walters 88) England 1st Innings 437 (Woolmer 137) Australia 2nd Innings 218 (G Chappell 112 Underwood 6/66) England 2nd Innings 1 for 82 England won by 9 wickets.

**Third Test 1977 England v Australia: Trent Bridge Nottingham July 28th, 29th 30th August 1st & 2nd 1977**

Australia won the toss. Australia 1st Innings 243 (Botham 5/74) England 1st Innings 364 (Boycott 107 Knott 135) Australia 2nd Innings 309 (McCosker 107 Willis 5/88) England 2nd Innings 3 for 189 England won by 7 wickets.

**Fourth Test 1977 England v Australia: Headingley Leeds August 11th, 12th, 13th & 15th 1977**

England won the toss. England 1st Innings 436 (Boycott 191)

Australia 1st Innings 103 (Botham 5/21) Australia 2nd Innings 248 England won by an innings and 85 runs.

**Fifth Test 1977 England v Australia: Kennington Oval London August 25th (no play) 26th, 27th, 29th & 30th 1977**

Australia won the toss. England 1st Innings 214 (Malone 5/63) Australia 1st Innings 385 (Hookes 85 Willis 5/102) England 2nd Innings 2 for 57 Match drawn.

**First Test 1978–79 Australia v England: Brisbane C.G. December 1st, 2nd, 3rd, 5th & 6th 1978**

Australia won the toss. Australia 1st Innings 116 England 1st Innings 286 (Hogg 6/74) Australia 2nd Innings 339 (Yallop 102 Hughes 129) England 2nd Innings 3 for 170 England won by 7 wickets.

**Second Test 1978–79 Australia v England: W.A.C.A. Perth December 15th, 16th, 17th, 19th & 20th 1978**

Australia won the toss. England 1st Innings 309 (Gower 102 Hogg 5/65) Australia 1st Innings 190 (Toohey n.o. 81 Willis 5/44) England 2nd Innings 208 (Hogg 5/57) Australia 2nd Innings 161 England won by 166 runs.

**Third Test 1978–79 Australia v England: M.C.G. December 29th, 30th, 1978 January !st, 2nd & 3rd 1979**

Australia won the toss. Australia 1st Innings 258 (Wood 100) England 1st Innings 143 (Hogg 5/30) Australia 2nd Innings 167 England 2nd Innings 179 (Hogg 5/36) Australia won by 103 runs.

**Fourth Test 1978–79 Australia v England: S.C.G. January 6th, 7th, 8th, 10th & 11th 1979**

England won the toss. England 1st Innings 152 (Hurst 5/28) Australia 1st Innings 294 (Darling 91) England 2nd Innings 346 (Randall 150 Higgs 5/148) Australia 2nd Innings 111 England won by 93 runs.

**Fifth Test 1978–79 Australia v England: Adelaide Oval January 27th, 28th, 29th, 31st February 1st 1979**

Australia won the toss. England 1st Innings 169 Australia 1st Innings 164 England 2nd Innings 360 (Taylor 97) Australia 2nd

Innings 160 England won by 205 runs.

**Sixth Test 1978–79 Australia v England: S.C.G. February 10th, 11th, 12th, 14th 1979**

Australia won the toss. Australia 1st Innings 198 (Yallop 121) England 1st Innings 308 Australia 2nd Innings 143 (Miller 5/44) England 2nd Innings 1 for 35 England won by 9 wickets.

**First Test 1979–80 Australia v England:  W.A.C.A. Perth December 14th, 15th, 16th, 18th & 19th 1979**

England won the toss. Australia 1st Innings 244 (Hughes 99 Botham 6/78) England 1st Innings 228 Australia 2nd Innings 337 (Border 115 Botham 5/98) England 2nd Innings 215 (Boycott n.o. 99 Dymock 6/34) Australia won by 138 runs.

**Second Test 1979–80 Australia v England:  S.C.G. January 4th, 5th, 6th & 8th 1980**

Australia won the toss. England 1st Innings 123 Australia 1sty Innings 145 England 2nd Innings 237 (Gower n.o. 98) Australia 2nd Innings 4 for 219 (G Chappell n.o. 98) Australia won by 6 wickets.

**Thjrd Test 1979–80 Australia v England: M.C.G. February 1st, 2nd, 3rd, 5th & 6th 1980**

England won the toss. England 1st Innings 306 (Boycott 99 Lillee 6/60) Australia 1st Inning 477 (G Chappell 114) England 2nd Innings 273 (Botham n.o. 119 Lillee 5/780 Australia 2nd Innings 2 for 103 Australia won by 8 wickets.

**Only Test 1980 England v Australia: Lord's C.G August 28th, 29th, 30th, September 1st & 2nd 1980**

Australia won the toss. Australia 1st Innings 5 dec for 385 (Wood 112 Hughes 117 England 1st Innings 205 (Pascoe 5/59) Australia 2nd Innings 4 dec for 189 (Hughes 84) England 2nd Innings 3 for 244 (Boycott n.o. 128) Match drawn.

**First Test 1981 England v Australia:  Trent Bridge Nottingham June 18th, 19th, 20th, 21st 1981**

Australia won the toss. England 1st Innings 185 Australia 1st Innings 179 (Border 63 ) England 2nd Innings 125 (Lillee 5/46 Alderman 5/62) Australia 2nd Innings 6 for 132 Australia won by 4 wickets.

## Second Test 1981 England v Australia: Lord's C.G. July 2nd, 3rd, 4th, 6th & 7th 1981

Australia won the toss. England 1st Innings 311 (Willey 82 Lawson 7/81) Australia 1st Innings 345 England 2nd Innings 8 dec for 265 (Gower 89) Australia 2nd Innings 4 for 90 Match drawn.

## Third Test 1981 England v Australia:  Headingley Leeds July 16th, 17th, 18th, 20th, 21st 1981

Australia won the toss. Australia 1st Innings 9 dec for 401 (Dyson 102 Hughes 89 Botham 6/95) England 1st Innings 174 England 2nd Innings 356 (Botham n.o. 149 Alderman 6/135) Australia 2nd Innings 111 (Willis 8/43) England won by 18 runs.

## Fourth Test 1981 England v Australia: Edgbaston Birmingham July 30th, 31st August 1st & 2nd 1981

England won the toss. England 1st Innings 189 (Alderman 5/42) Australia 1st Innings 258 England 2nd Innings 219 (Bright 5/68) Australia 2nd Innings 121 (Botham 5/11) England won by 29 runs.

## Fifth Test 1981 England v Australia: Old Trafford Manchester August 13th, 14th, 15th, 16th & 17th 1981

England won the toss. England 1st Innings 231 Australia 1st Innings 130 England 2nd Innings 404 (Botham 118 Alderman 5/109) Australia 2nd Innings 402 (Yallop 114 Border n.o. 123 England won by 103 runs.

## Sixth Test 1981 England v Australia: Kennington Oval London August 27th, 28th, 29th, 31st Sept. 1st 1981.

England won the toss. Australia 1st Innings 352 (Border n.o. 106 Botham 6/125) England 1st Innings 314 (Boycott 137 Lillee 7/89) Australia 2nd Innings 9 dec for 344 (Wellham 103) England 2nd Innings 7 for 261 Match drawn.

## First Test 1982–83 Australia v England: W.A.C.A. Perth November 12th, 13th, 14th, 16th & 17th 1982

Australia won the toss. England 1st Innings 411 (Tavare 89 Yardley 5/107) Australia 1st Innings 9 dec for 424 (G Chappell 117 ) England 2nd Innings 358 (Randall 115  Lawson 5/108) Australia 2nd Innings

2 for 73 Match drawn.

**Second Test 1982–83 Australia v England: Brisbane C.G. November 26th, 27th, 28th, 30th December 1st 1982**

Australia won the toss. England 1st Innings 219 (Lawson 6/47) Australia 1st Innings 341 (Wessels 182 Willis 5/66) England 2nd Innings 309

Australia 3 for 190 Australia won by 7 wickets.

**Third Test 1982–83 Australia v England: Adelaide Oval December 10th, 11th, 12th, 14th & 15th 1982**

England won the toss. Australia 1st Innings 438 (G Chappell 115) England 1st Innings 216 (Lawson 5/56) England 2nd Innings 304 (Gower 114 Lawson 5/66) Australia 2nd Innings 2 for 83 Australia won by 8 wickets.

**Fourth Test 1982–83 Australia v England: M.C.G. December 26th, 27th, 28th, 29th, 30th 1982**

Australia won the toss. England 1st Innings 284 (Tavare 89 ) Australia 1st Innings 287 England 2nd Innings 294 Australia 2nd Innings 288 (Cowans 6/77) England won by 3 runs.

**Fifth Test 1982–83 Australia v England: S.C.G. January 2nd, 3rd, 4th, 6th and 7th 1983**

Australia won the toss. Australia 1st Innings 314 (Border 89) England 1st Innings 237 (Thomson 5/50) Australia 2nd Innings 382 (Hughes 137) England 2nd Innings 7 for 314 Match drawn.

**First Test 1985 England v Australia: Headingley Leeds June 13th, 14th, 15th, 17th & 18th 1985**

Australia won the toss. Australia 1st Innings 331 (Hilditch 119) England 1st Innings 533 (Robinson 175) Australia 2nd Innings 324 (Phillips 91 Emburey 5/82) England 2nd Innings 5 for 123 England won by 5 wickets.

**Second Test 1985 England v Australia: Lord's C.G. June 27th, 28th, 29th, July 1st & 2nd 1985**

Australia won the toss. England 1st Innings 290 (Gower 86 McDermott 6/70) Australia 1st Innings 425 (Border 196 Botham 5/109) England 2nd Innings 281 (Holland 5/68) Australia 2nd

Innings 6 for 127 Australia won by 4 wickets.

## Third Test 1985 England v Australia: Trent Bridge Nottingham July 11th, 12th, 13th, 15th, 16th 1985

England won the toss. England 1st Innings 456 (Gower 166 Lawson 5/103) Australia 1st Innings 539 (Wood 172 Ritchie 146 ) England 2nd Innings 2 for 196 Match drawn.

## Fourth Test 1985 England v Australia: Old Trafford Manchester August 1st, 2nd, 3rd, 5th & 6th 1985

England won the toss.Australia 1st Innings 257 England 1st Innings 9 dec for 482 (Gatting 160 McDermott 8/141) Australia 2nd Innings 5 for 340 (Border n.o. 146) Match drawn.

## Fifth Test 1985 England v Australia: Edgbaston Birmingham August 15th, 16th, 17th, 19th & 20th 1985

England won the toss. Australia 1st Innings 335(Wessels 83 Ellison 6/77) England 1st Innings 5 dec for 595 (Robinson 148  Gower 215 Gatting n.o. 100) Australia 2nd Innings 142 England won by an innings and 118 runs.

## Sixth Test 1985 England v Australia: Kennington Oval London August 29th, 30th, 31st September 2nd 1985

England won the toss. England 1st Innings 464 (Gooch 196 Gower 157) Australia 1st Innings 241 Australia 2nd Innings 129 (Ellison 5/46) England won by an innings and 94 runs.

## First Test 1986–87 Australia v England: Brisbane C.G. November 14th, 15th, 16th, 18th & 19th 1986

Australia won the toss. England 1st Innings 456 (Botham 138) Australia 1st Innings 248 (Dilley 5/68) Australia 2nd Innings 282 (Marsh 110 Emburey 5/80) England 2nd Innings 3 for 77 England won by 7 wickets.

## Second Test 1986–87 Australia v England: W.A.C.A. Perth November 28th, 29th, 30th December 2nd & 3rd 1986

England won the toss. England 1st Innings 8 dec for 592 (Broad 162 Athey 96 Gower 136 Richards 133 Australia 401 (Border 125) England 2nd Innings 8 dec for 199( Waugh 5/69) Australia 2nd Innings 4 for 197 Match drawn.

**Third Test 1986–87 Australia v England: Adelaide Oval December 12th, 13th, 14th, 15th, 16th 1986**

Australia won the toss. Australia 1st Innings 5 dec 514 (Boon 103 Jones 93 ) England 1st Innings 455 (Broad 116 Gatting 100) Australia 2nd Innings 3 for 201 (Border n.o. 100) England 2nd Innings 2 for 39 Match drawn.

**Fourth Test 1986–87 Australia v England: M.C.G. December 26th, 27th, 28th 1986**

England won the toss. Australia 1st Innings 141 (Small 5/48 Botham 5/41) England 1st Innings 349 (Broad 112) Australia 2nd Innings 194 England won by an innings and 14 runs.

**Fifth Test 1986–87 Australia v England: S.C.G. January 10th, 11th, 12th, 14th & 15th 1987**

Australia won the toss. Australia 1st Innings 343 (Jones n.o. 184 Small 5/75) England 1st Innings 275 (Taylor 6/78) Australia 2nd Innings 251 (Emburey 7/78) England 2nd Innings 264 (Gatting 96 Sleep 5/72) Australia won by 55 runs.

**First Test 1989 England v Australia: Headingley Leeds June 8th, 9th, 10th, 12th & 13th 1989**

England won the toss. Australia 1st Innings 7 dec for 601 (Taylor 136 S Waugh n.o. 177 England 1st Innings 430 (Lamb 125 Alderman 5/107) Australia 2nd Innings 3 dec for 230 England 2nd Innings 191 (Alderman5/44)

Australia won by 210 runs.

**Second Test !989 England v Australia: Lord's C.G. June 22nd, 23rd, 24th, 26th & 27th 1989**

England won the toss. England 1st Innings 286 Australia 1st Innings 528 (Boon 94 S Waugh n.o. 152 England 2nd Innings 359 (Gower 106 Alderman 6/128) Australia 2nd Innings 4 for 119 Australia won by 6 wickets.

**Third Test 1989 England v Australia: Edgbaston Birmingham July 6th, 7th, 8th, 10th & 11th 1989**

Australia won the toss. Australia 1st Innings 424 (Jones 157) England 1st Innings 242 Australia 2nd Innings 2 for 158 Match drawn.

## Fourth Test 1989 England v Australia: Old Trafford Manchester July 27th, 28th, 29th, 31st, August 1st 1989

England won the toss. England 1st Innings (Smith 143 Lawson 6/72) Australia 1st Innings 447 England 2nd Innings 264 Russell n.o. 128) Australia 2nd Innings 1 for 81 Australia won by 9 wickets.

## Fifth Test 1989 England v Australia: Trent Bridge Nottingham August 10th, 11th, 12th, 14th 1989

Australia won the toss. Australia 1st Innings 6 dec 602 (Marsh 138 Taylor 219) England 1st Innings 255 (Smith 101 Alderman 5/69) England 2nd Innings 9 for 167 Australia won by an innings and 180 runs.

## Sixth Test 1989 England v Australia: Kennington Oval London August 24th, 25th, 26th, 28th, 29th 1989

Australia won the toss. Australia 1st Innings 468 (Jones 122) England 1st Innings 285 (Alderman 5/66) Australia 2nd Innings 4 dec for 219  England 5 for 143 Match drawn.

## First Test 1990–91 Australia v England: Brisbane C.G. November 23rd, 24th & 25th 1990

Australia won the toss. England 1st Innings 194 Australia 1st Innings 152  England 2nd Innings 114 (Alderman 6/47) Australia 2nd Innings 0 for 157 Australia won by 10 wickets.

## Second Test 1990–91 Australia v England: M.C.G. December 26th,27th, 28th, 29th & 30th 1990

England won the toss. England 1st Innings 352 (Gower 100 Reid 6/97) Australia 1st Innings 306 (Fraser 6/82) England 2nd Innings 150 (Reid 7/51) Australia 2nd Innings 2 for 197 (Boon n.o. 94) Australia won by 8 wickets.

## Third Test 1990–91 Australia v England: S.C.G. January 4th, 5th, 6th, 7th & 8th 1991

Australia won the toss. Australia 1st Innings 518 (Boon 97 Matthews 128) England 1st Innings 8 dec for 469 (Atherton 105 Gower 123 Stewart 91) Australia 2nd Innings 205 (Tufnell 5/61) England 2nd Innings 4 for 113 Match drawn.

**Fourth Test 1990–91 Australia v England: Adelaide Oval January 25th, 26th, 27th, 28th & 29th 1991**

Australia won the toss. Australia 1st Innings 386 (M Waugh 138) England 1st Innings 229 (Gooch 87 McDermott 5/97) Australia 2nd Innings 6 dec for 314 (Boon 121 Border n.o. 83) England 2nd Innings 5 for 335 (Gooch 117 Atherton 87) Match drawn.

**Fifth Test 1990–91 Australia v England: W.A.C.A. Perth February 1st, 2nd, 3rd & 5th 1991**

England won the toss. England 1st Innings 244 (Lamb 91 McDermott 8/97) Australia 1st Innings 307 England 2nd Innings 182 Australia 2nd Innings 1 for 120 Australia won by 9 wickets.

**First Test 1993 England v Australia: Old Trafford Manchester June 3rd, 4th, 5th, 6th & 7th 1993**

England won the toss. Australia 1st Innings 289 (Taylor 124 Such 6/67) England 1st Innings 210 Australia 2nd Innings 5 dec for 432 (Boon 93 Healy n.o. 102) England 2nd Innings 332 (Gooch 133) Australia won by 179 runs.

**Second Test 1993 England v Australia: Lord's C.G. June 17th, 18th, 19th, 20th & 21st 1993**

Australia won the toss. Australia 1st Innings 4 dec for 632 (Taylor 111 Slater 152 Boon n.o. 164 M Waugh 99 ) England 1st Innings 205 (Atherton 80 ) England 2nd Innings 365 (Atherton 99 ) Australia won by an innings and 62 runs.

**Third Test 1993 England v Australia: Trent Bridge Nottingham July 1st, 2nd, 3rd, 5th & 6th 1993**

England won the toss. England 1st Innings 321 (Smith 86 Hughes 5/92) Australia 1st Innings 373 (Boon 101) England 2nd Innings 6 dec for 422 (Gooch 120 Thorpe n.o. 114) Australia 2nd Innings 6 for 202 Match drawn.

**Fourth Test 1993 England v Australia: Headingley Leeds July 22nd, 23r, 24th, 25th & 26th 1993**

Australia won the toss. Australia 1st Innings 4 dec for 653 (Boon 107 Border n.o.200 S Waugh 157) England 1st Innings 200 (Reiffel 5/65) England 2nd Innings 305 Australia won by an innings and 148 runs.

## Fifth test 1993 England v Australia: Edgbaston Birmingham August 5th, 6th, 7th 8th & 9th 1993

England won the toss. England 1st Innings 276 (Reiffel 6/71) Australia 1st Innings 408 (M Waugh 137) England 2nd Innings 251 (May 5/89 Warne 5/82) Australia 2nd Innings 2 for 120 Australia won by 8 wickets.

## Sixth Test 1993 England v Australia: Kennington Oval London August 19th, 20th, 21st, 22nd, 23rd 1993

England won the toss. England 1st Innings 380 Australia 1st Innings 303 (Healy n.o. 83 Fraser 5/87) England 2nd Innings 313 Australia 2nd Innings 229 England won by 161 runs.

## First Test 1994–95 Australia v England: Brisbane C.G. November 25th, 26th, 27th 28th & 29th 1994

Australia won the toss. Australia 1st Innings 426 (Slater 176 M Waugh 140) England 1st Innings 167 (McDermott 6/53) Australia 2nd Innings 8 dec for 248 England 2nd Innings 323 (Hick 80 Warne 8/71) Australia won by 184 runs.

## Second Test 1994–95 Australia v England: M.C.G. December 24th, 26th, 27th, 28th, 29th 1994

England won the toss. Australia 1st Innings 279 (S Waugh n.o. 94) England 1st Innings 212 (Warne 6/64) Australia 2nd Innings 7 dec for 320 (Boon 131) England 2nd Innings 92 (McDermott 5/42) Australia won by 295 runs.

## Third Test 1994 95 Australia v England: S.C.G. January 1st, 2nd, 3rd, 4th & 5th 1994

England won the toss. England 1st Innings 309 (Atherton 88 McDermott 5/101) Australia 1st Innings 116 (Gough 6/49) England 2nd Innings 2 dec for 255 (Hick n.o. 98) Australia 2nd Innings 7 for 344 (Slater 103 Taylor 113 Fraser 5/73) Match drawn.

## Fourth Test 1994–95 Australia v England: Adelaide Oval January 26th, 27th, 28th, 29th & 30th 1995

England won the toss. England 1st Innings 353 (Gatting 117) Australia 1st Innings 419 (Taylor 90 Blewett n.o. 102) England 2nd

Innings 328 (Defreitas 88 M Waugh 5/40) Australia 2nd Innings 156 England won by 106 runs.

## Fifth Test 1994–95 Australia v England: W.A.C.A. Perth February 3rd, 4th, 5th, 6th & 7th 1995

Australia won the toss. Australia 1st Innings 402 (Slater 124 S Waugh n.o. 99) England 1st Innings 295 (Thorpe 123) Australia 2nd Innings 8 dec for 345 (Blewett 115) England 2nd Innings 123 (McDermott 6/38) Australia won by 329 runs.

## First Test 1997 England v Australia:  Edgbaston Birmingham June 5th, 6th, 7th, 8th 1997

Australia won the toss. Australia 1st Innings 118 (Caddick 5/50) England 1st Innings 9 dec for 478 (Hussain 207 Thorpe 138) Australia 2nd Innings 477 (Taylor 129 Blewett 125) England 2nd Innings 1 for 119 England won by 9 wickets.

## Second Test 1997 England v Australia: Lord's C.G. June 19th (no play) 20th, 21st, 22nd & 23rd 1997

Australia won the toss. England 1st Innings 77 (McGrath 8/38) Australia 1st Innings 213 (Elliott 112) England 2nd Innings 4 dec for 266 (Butcher 87) Match drawn.

## Third Test 1997 England v Australia: Old Trafford Manchester July 3rd, 4th, 5th, 6th & 7th 1997

Australia won the toss. Australia 1st Innings 235 (S Waugh 108) England 1st Innings 162 (Warne 6/48) Australia 2nd Innings 395 (S Waugh 116) England 2nd Innings 200 (Crawley 83) Australia won by 268 runs.

## Fourth Test 1997 England v Australia: Headingley Leeds July 24th, 25th, 26th, 27th & 28th 1997

Australia won the toss. England 1st Innings 172 (Gillespie 7/37) Australia 1st Innings 501 (Elliott 199 Ponting 127 Gough 5/149) England 2nd Innings 268 (Hussain 105 Reiffel 5/49) Australia won by an innings and 61 runs.

## Fifth Test 1997 England v Australia: Trent Bridge Nottingham August 7th, 8th, 9th & 10th 1997

Australia won the toss. Australia 1st Innings 427 England 1st

Innings 313 (Stewart 87) Australia 2nd Innings 336 England 2nd Innings 186 (Thorpe n.o. 82) Australia won by 264 runs.

## Sixth Test 1997 England v Australia: Kennington Oval August 21st, 22nd & 23rd 1997

England won the toss. England 1st Innings 180 (McGrath 7/76) Australia 1st Innings 220 (Tufnell 7/66) England 2nd Innings 163 (Kasprowicz 7/36) Australia 2nd Innings 104 (Caddick 5/42) England won by 19 runs.

## First Test 1998–99 Australia v England: Brisbane C.G. November 20th, 21st, 22nd, 23rd & 24th 1998

Australia won the toss. Australia 1st Innings 485 (S Waugh 112 Healy 134 Mullaly 5/105) England 1st Innings 375 (Butcher 116 McGrath 6/85) Australia 2nd Innings 3 dec for 237 (Slater 113) England 6 for 179. Match drawn.

## Second Test 1998–99 Australia v England: W.A.C.A. Perth November 28th, 29th & 30th 1998

Australia won the toss. England 1st Innings 112 (Fleming 5/46) Australia 1st Innings 240 England 2nd Innings 191 (Gillespie 5/88) Australia 2nd Innings 3 for 64 Australia won by 7 wickets.

## Third Test 1998–99 Australia v England: Adelaide oval December 11th, 12th, 13th, 14th & 15th 1998

Australia won the toss. Australia 1st Innings 391 (Langer n.o. 179) England 1st Innings 227 (Hussain n.o. 89) England 2nd Innings 237 Australia won by 205 runs.

## Fourth Test 1998–99 Australia v England: M.C.G. December 26th, 27th, 28th & 29th 1998

Australia won the toss. England 1st Innings 270 (Stewart 107) Australia 1st Innings 340 (S Waugh n.o. 122 Gough 5/96) England 2nd Innings 244 Australia 2nd Innings 162 (Headley 6/60) England won by 12 runs.

## Fifth Test 1998–99 Australia v England: S.C.G. January 2nd, 3rd, 4th & 5th 1999

Australia won the toss. Australia 1st Innings 322 (M Waugh 121 S Waugh 96) England 1st Innings 220 (MacGill 5/57) Australia 2nd

Innings 184 (Slater 123 Such 5/81) England 2nd Innings 188 (MacGill 7/50) Australia won by 98 runs.

**First Test 2001 England v Australia: Edgbaston Birmingham July 5th, 6th, 7th & 8th 2001**

Australia won the toss. England 1st Innings 294 (Warne 5/71) Australia 1st Innings 576 (S Waugh 105 Martyn 105 Gilchrist 152) England 2nd Innings 164 (Trescothick 76) Australia won by an innings and 118 runs.

**Second Test 2001 England v Australia: Lord's C.G. July 19th, 20th, 21st & 22nd 2001**

Australia won the toss. England 1st Innings 187 (McGrath 5/54) Australia 1st Innings 401 (M Waugh 108 Gilchrist 90 Caddick 5/101) England 2nd Innings 227 (Butcher 83 Gillespie 5/53) Australia 2nd Innings 2 for 14 Australia won by 8 wickets.

**Third Test 2001 England v Australia: Trent Bridge Nottingham August 2nd, 3rd & 4th 2001**

England won the toss. England 1st Innings 185 (McGrath 5/49) Australia 1st Innings 190 (Tudor 5/44) England 2nd Innings 162 (Warne 6/33) Australia 2nd Innings 3 for 158 Australia won by 7 wickets.

**Fourth Test 2001 England v Australia: Headingley Leeds August 16th, 17th, 18th 19th & 20th 2001**

Australia won the toss. Australia 1st Innings 447 (Ponting 144 Martyn 118 Gough 5/103) England 1st Innings 309 (Stewart n.o. 76 McGrath 7/76 Australia 2nd Innings 4 dec for 176 England 2nd Innings 4 for 315 (Butcher n.o. 173) England won by 6 wickets.

**Fifth Test 2001 England v Australia: Kennington Oval August 23rd, 24th, 25th, 26th & 27th 2001**

Australia won the toss. Australia 1st Innings 641 (Langer ret hurt 102 M Waugh 120 S Waugh n.o. 157) England 1st Innings 432 (Ramprekash 133 (Warne 7/165) England 2nd Innings 184 (McGrath 5/43) Australia won by an innings and 25 runs.

**First Test 2002–03 Australia v England: Brisbane C.G. November 7th, 8th, 9th, 10th 2002**

England won the toss. Australia 1st Innings 492 (Hayden 197 Ponting 123) England 1st Innings 325 Australia 2nd Innings 5 dec for 296 (Hayden 103) England 2nd Innings 79 Australia won by 384 runs.

**Second Test 2002–03 Australia v England: Adelaide Oval November 21st, 22nd, 23rd & 24th 2002**

England won the toss. England 1st Innings 342 (Vaughan 177) Australoia 1st Innings 552 (Ponting 154 Martyn 95) England 2nd Innings 159 Australia won by an innings and 51 runs.

**Third Test 2002–03 Australia v England: W.A.C.A. November 29th, 30th December 1st 2002**

England won the toss. England 1st Innings 185 Australia 1st Innings 456 (White 5/127) England 2nd Innings 223 Australia won by an innings and 48 runs.

**Fourth Test 2002–03 Australia v England: M.C.G. December 26th, 27th, 28th, 29th & 30th 2002**

Australia won the toss. Australia 1st Innings 6 dec for 551 (Langer 250 Hayden 102) England 1st Innings 270 (White n.o. 85) England 2nd Innings 387 (Vaughan 145 MacGill 5/152) Australia 2nd Innings 5 for 107 Australia won by 5 wickets.

**Fifth Test 2002–03 Australia v England:  S.C.G. January 2nd, 3rd, 4th, 5th & 6th 2003**

England won the toss. England 1st Innings 362 (Butcher 124) australia 1st Innings 363 (S Waugh 102 Gilchrist 133) England 2nd Innings 452 (Vaughan 183) Australia 2nd Innings 226 (Caddick 7/94) England won by 225 runs.

**First Test 2005 England v Australia: Lord's  C.G. July 21st, 22nd, 23rd & 24th 2005**

Australia won the toss. Australia 1st Innings 190 (Harmison 5/43) England 1st Innings 155 (McGrath 5/53) Australia 2nd Innings 384 (Clarke 91) England 2nd Innings 180 Australia won by 239 runs.

**Second Test 2005 England v Australia: Edgbaston Birmingham August 4th, 5th, 6th & 7th 2005**

Australia won the toss. England 1st Innings 407 (Trescothick 90) Australia 1st Innings 308 (Langer 82) England 2nd Innings 182

(Warne 6/46) Australia 2nd Innings 279 England won by 2 runs.

## Third Test 2005 England v Australia: Old Trafford Manchester August 11th, 12th, 13th, 14th & 15th 2005

England won the toss. England 1st Innings 444 (Vaughan 166) Australia 1st Innings 302 (Warne 90 Jones 6/53) England 2nd Innings 6 dec for 280 (Strauss 106 McGrath 5/115) Australia 2nd Innings 9 for 371 Match drawn.

## Fourth Test 2005 England v Australia: Trent Bridge August 25th, 26th, 27th & 28th 2005

England won the toss. England 1st Innings 477 (Flintoff 102) Australia 1st Innings 218 (Jones 5/44) Australia 2nd Innings 387 England 2nd Innings 7 for 129 England won by 3 wickets.

## Fifth Test 2005 England v Australia: Kennington Oval September 8th, 9th, 10th, 11th & 12th 2005

England won the toss. England 1st Innings 373 (Strauss 129 Warne 6/122) Australia 1st Innings 367 (Langer 105 Hayden 138 Flintoff 5/78) England 2nd Innings 335 (Pietersen 158 Warne 6/124) Australia 2nd Innings 0 for 4 Match drawn.

# ABOUT THE AUTHOR

Ian Ferguson has been closely involved in cricket as a player, captain, coach, umpire and writer for nearly 50 years, and during his teaching career he represented several clubs in country and suburban areas of Victoria.

In 1986 Ken Piesse and Ian Ferguson wrote *Bradman and the Bush*, a book which received a literary award from the Australian Cricket Society. Since then Ian has become the author or co-author of six sporting books, and he has also contributed many articles to national magazines and regional newspapers.

Ian is married with four children and lives in Pakenham, a West Gippsland town on the outskirts of Melbourne.

Order your copy of:

# Wearing the Baggy Green

by Ian Ferguson                                           Qty
ISBN 1920785 93 0   RRP                    AU$39.95   .....

Postage within Aust.      AU$8.00   .....

----------

TOTAL★                    $_________

★ All prices include GST

Name: _________________________________________

Address: _______________________________________

_______________________________________

_______________________________________

Phone: ________________________________________

Email Address: _________________________________


**Method of Payment:**

❏ Money Order ❏ Cheque ❏ Amex ❏ MasterCard ❏ Visa

Cardholders Name: _____________________________

Credit Card Number: ___________________________

Signature:_________________________ Expiry Date: ___________

Allow 21 days for delivery.


**Payment to:**
Better Bookshop (ABN 14 067 257 390)
PO Box 12544
A'Beckett Street, Melbourne, 8006
Victoria, Australia
Fax: +61 3 9671 4730
Email: betterbookshop@brolgapublishing.com.au